Solar Codex
A Light Odyssey

Also by David L. Laing

Willing Evolution

Dance of the Dance

Solar Codex
A Light Odyssey

David L. Laing

Cosmic Art Center

Published by Cosmic Art Center

http://www.cosmicartcenter.com

Printed in the United States of America

ISBN 0-9646264-2-X

To all those who have the courage
to leave the protective harbors of reason
and raise the Sails of Imagination . . .

Introduction

At the center of the *Solar Codex* is the Vision divided into a multiplicity of Ideograms—which constitute the Codex containing symbols to be deciphered or left mysterious. There is often certain clarity in obscurity. The title *Solar Codex* refers principally to this Body-of-Visions that the main character Apollicius is privy to and then uses to feed, further and structure his Light Odyssey.

My purpose has always been to nourish the Imagination through the presentation of an alternative reality. These visions and descriptive narrative are doorways, that upon crossing their thresholds, open up the way to the reality of this alternate cosmos. There is a type of wisdom in mythic breadth or broadness-of-vision that transcends the here and now. In the Arts of Antiquity it came to be known as the transmission of a secret knowledge. This *mundus imaginalis* is the place where we go to capture the visions that contain this knowledge.

Invoking both the transcendental and the extraordinary, *Solar Codex* cannot be approached as you would a more conventional work. It is both poetic and mythic in its epic scope, using visions as the foundation of its fictional art. Through these illustrations and the story that portrays the Great Initiation of the Sun Apollicius and his planetary brethren, I have attempted to outline the very Nature of Imagination. Through this process of the Creation of a Planetary System, characters come and go as the story progresses, yet they have in reality not gone anywhere. There is plenty of action, but it seems that the characters are all in a meditative state—could this be the Thought of God?!

These personages are not terrestrial, nor human, but cosmic, spatial cosmocrats: the real creators of universes-in-action. These universes are present only in the Now: the past, future and present compressed into the Moment.

At one level it is a book which describes the Initiation of Apollicius and his Planets in their pursuit of Love, yet at another level *Solar Codex* can become a gate to a translucent universe-of-vision. Divorced from the prevalence of the strictly traditional spirit, *Solar Codex* has sought out a spouse in the house of the esoteric world. Each paragraph, sentence and sometimes even the word needs to be savored as one would fine cuisine. It simply cannot be speed-read to get the full benefit and meanings contained therein. It is the stillness of perpetual movement that creates that meditative state in the mind of the reader. The style that I have developed I have termed *prosetry*—a blend of prose and poetry. One of my objectives in writing is and has been for some time to discover and reveal the inner musicality and sound connections within words and phrases. This all occurs, of course, within the flow of the content of the storyline. As was true for William Blake, my subjects have been given to me by my Imagination! Enter them as you would a vehicle for the modern self in quest of itself.

It is a stream-of-consciousness style novel without being purely stream-of-consciousness. In the purely stream-of-consciousness nothing is planned out, whereas *Solar Codex* has a carefully crafted underpinning. Musically it would be analogous to a piece that sounds improvised, but in reality contains a highly sophisticated, yet seamless structure.

The image of an ocean contained in a drop applies to *Solar Codex: A Light Odyssey*. In a sense the book can be seen as a Hologram, where each page, section or paragraph contains the Whole. In this manner it is not unreasonable to say that starting anywhere in the epic you may easily find the story's thread. It is more of a meditative work than a novel of high adventure, though it does contain high adventure of the spirit.

Though beginning as a painter and drawer, upon the repeated urging of a journalist friend who had been collecting my work, I began to first write in an attempt to describe what was behind the symbolic meaning of the hand-inked visions. These glyphs not only stand for something, they are something—possessing a numinous power of their own. Essentially, then my writing serves to illustrate the illustrations rather than the opposite which occurs in a more conventional organizational style. Usually a book is written and then illustrated. I have done the opposite: first I draw out the major events to occur and then I construct the story. Some of these visions (which the story illustrates) are very defined and detailed, others not. They are pure symbols not produced by the rational thought process. All the forms of these symbols inhabiting the depths of the Mind contain esoteric knowledge. These images do not represent the material appearance of things, but illustrate a history of the unknown, not by any means completely told. Their symbols and accompanying writing can be interpreted in as many different ways as there are minds to contemplate. Their underlying purpose is to open the Mind and elevate it to higher levels of perception—thus freeing it from its constant bondage to the known!

Because of the symbolic nature of this work, it is possible to come into contact with certain truths through the minds of the characters—within our capacity to understand, yet not readily perceive. Before writing Solar Codex and the other books I have previously published, quite often it had been challenging for me to convince others of my own inability to translate these visions into words. Desiring to offer a written equivalent to the art of the vision, I embarked on a series of art books with writings and on the Cosmic Adventure Novel series of which *Solar Codex* is one of its four volumes.

Recently I have become aware that by reaching for Inspiration in the deep past even before recorded history, I have gone to the source of the early creation of the myth and the myth of early creation. It is as if a second renaissance were at hand.

Presented under the cloak of fiction, it is best to approach *Solar Codex* with an open mind and allow the carefully selected and drawn images to flow through you. If and when the reader or spectator becomes one with this objet d'art, a transcendental experience of heightened consciousness could result enabling him or her to understand that they and the Cosmos are one and the same!

David L. Laing
Seattle, Washington
January 2006

Solar Codex

A Light Odyssey

First Movement

Calcination: *The breaking down of a substance by fierce heating and burning, usually in an open crucible*

Apollicius awoke from a long rest in the Celestial House with a burning spark deep inside his chest to descend, to be carried by a wave under the froth to the depths of the trough.

He drifted easily through these nights, since he was, in essence, the *spark of all beings* that flickers and ignites uplifted. Wearing nothing but a glowing cloak of robust ruby red, he felt his head diamond-cleaved as his heart moved into action even before he had taken his leave. Wherever his fluid eyes gazed, he saw polymorphous beings. The scent of myrrh wafted up through his fiery nostrils. Destiny now summoned Apollicius to a zone completely unknown to him.

Used to nothing but darkness, he moved by pure intuition and instinct. Suddenly, he had heard the call of seven trumpeters blasting their monophonic theme—a wall of wind across the dim desert of his young name. Torched by this *wind septet*, his head of energy caught fire, momentarily wedded to the sound, and things balanced.

Knowing neither how to proceed nor where exactly to go, the young speck of wild energy closed his eyes, and facing the East, sat at the foot of the trumpeters, who had projected themselves from the seven angles of the virgin land. He sang four times to join the giant musicians who

became alternately visible and invisible before his innocent eyes. Imagining his heart to be a red carnation, he concentrated intensely on the sound's intonation. For the first time, he tried to picture his own *spark being* caught within the conflagration of all the Celestial Constellations.

He moved his head, once for each trumpeter—to the back, to the front, to the side, and in a circle, trying to perceive the superior dimensions of the deep space into which the music had carried his mind. Entering a profound dream state, Apollicius was lifted by the blown notes to a lofty mountaintop on a secret island above the sky. It existed there as an anteroom to an even more distant land—an empty kingdom where, he clearly understood, both his treasure and the obstacles that lay on the pathway to it were waiting. He felt simultaneously excited about the upcoming struggle and afraid he might not be able to rise high enough to become his own *spear of might*.

The piercing sounds of the heraldry soon faded, leaving the *spark* of Apollicius as isolated as a small seed on a boundless plateau. Rootless and dislocated, he lay light-years away from the Great Central Sun of his progenitors. Using the tiny "firefly" lantern of his own inner self, he searched in vain for a trace of the polymorphous sound-producing bodies of the trumpeters. They had apparently been carried away on the stream of their own, blown wind-beam. But just as a seed carries the plan of the plant encoded and enfolded within, so the spark of Apollicius contained the physical and spiritual dimensions of his own future, Light-Source System.

The deep attraction and affection he felt for the trumpet sound meant a new start for his ignited being spark. If he didn't soon begin the enormous work lying outstretched before him, the dark side would surely envelope his spark, making it dim. Tenacious and bullish, he was also a romantic and a sensualist. He fingered the copper disk he wore as a pendant around his neck, the most potent symbol he had of who, he knew, he could be. Though not precious like an emerald or a polished agate, it felt solid and reminded him of a long ago land of bronze light, strength and heat.

Apollicius had struck out on the *sound way* of his own vibration to seek an Adventure in Light. Maturing in the twilight heaven of his Father's Constellation City of Stars would be no easy task, yet he felt well on his way after experiencing first-hand the seven trumpeters. He had seen them at the very same instant they had created his sound experience out of the tenuous threads from their wind instruments. This Tone Birth of Apollicius had not been enshrouded in stillness but rather had shown itself publicly in festive fullness.

He had scarcely drawn his first *vision* from the universe before he found himself already on the Sacred Mountain, struggling for a firm foothold. Reaching for the nearest tree, he grasped its trunk firmly as a brace against a strong wind that followed in the wake of the triumphant trumpet blasts.

The birth of Apollicius had not come about from a sound blunder

but had unfurled from deep within the rumbling voice of thunder. Born directly into the Unknown, he had never *known* the Known nor its so well-defined boundaries that still needed to be shown. Each moment turned into both a danger and a discovery. By overcoming these obstacles, he won the confidence to press on: when risk is made, a danger can fade. He became both the watchman and the carefully watched. The *light task* that lay before him showed itself to be anything but light.

His own eye could not capture even the tree he held, since, really, it had yet to be immersed in its own dye. Smitten by a myriad of luminous plans, Apollicius searched the horizon for points of reference. When he found none, he knew he needed to create one out of the very threads that composed his own scarcely visible self. He needed to forge both the Source of the Fountain and the *fountain* itself. Blindly feeling his way along, his long, elastic arms filled with intense pleasure. Everything he handled sent waves of sensual bliss pulsating throughout his quasi-material form still scarcely bundled.

But the electricity he felt with each contact didn't compare to the shock he got when his hand suddenly closed around the hot bluish-yellow flame of what he immediately realized to be that very Fountainhead itself. Had he created it, or had it created him? Most likely both had occurred simultaneously. Upon being titillated, the Muse burst forth in fiery word.

"I am Helleniana," she said. "When I breathe, you live. Imagination and the True Realm are one and the same with a different name. Once you told me that wherever you turn, your eyes would behold my smile."

Apollicius gazed upon her glowing, sweetly voluptuous lips. "A rapturous vision-sage of all ages," he thought to himself. Behind him, he heard the *talking spring*, the liquid moving within.

"I shall climb her mountain," he said, this time out loud. "I will revolve around the heat of her burning oven. There I will cook, bake, and rise. Beneath this very spot I will be supported by the Serpent," he said as he spied a snake emerging from the abyss.

"In order for the head to reflect light, all must flow into the body of this world," a voice reminded him.

Apollicius had refused calls before, yet having encountered his Muse Helleniana, now he could not deny her. All he had inside he now summoned forth. After his long travel, here on the Sacred Mountain Helleniana dwelled as the spiraling word of the wind. He didn't stand at her foot but had been washed to the soft contours of her shores. The liquid form of Apollicius had risen as a sea to the land and broke over the mountain like a froth fountain. What was left when the water receded was merely foam containing his germinating seed-spore.

"I am merely that seed," Apollicius spoke through the froth and bubbles lightly coating the spore. "I have been called by my Father of the Fifth Dimension to create the *picture page* for a sound age. The neck of the goddess Helleniana is emerald, and I am its lapidary. I'll begin at the nape, letting fate carry me across her green land to the threshold of her agate gate."

Apollicius moved on as a wave spreading his liquid mirror over the glistening plane of space matter. Since nothing had yet been crystallized into identifiable shapes and forms, everything could be instantly manifested out of his inundated imagination. By its very nature a true spark is untamed, though not unnamed. Whether called beam, flame, light-ray, or phosphorescence, Apollicius slowly marked his ever-growing presence.

He had multiplied by becoming the sea's scintillation, a bed of sparkles all vying for a light-mate with which to procreate. As Helleniana slowly vanished, he became the flashing glint of her rolling sea body. Gathering together his benighted self, Apollicius slowly emerged in another shape of this protean energy: Light is pure delight! There was still plenty of time to fashion the heavens and many more eons to craft those ever-lowering circles of hell. He would now wait for Helleniana's return—the foundation from which he could rise up and journey across the celestial vault. The thunder of the waves crashing over him opened his ear to the sea drum, and this is what he heard:

"You are listening to the heart of Helleniana. I am the way to her. She can't find you before you hear her."

"I want to listen. How do I begin?" he said.

"I am everywhere and in everything."

Looking down Apollicius realized that he had been standing upon the curved land of *Heart*. To find the beat with his feet, he tentatively took one step, then another. Each heart, visibly composed of many, yet pulsed as one. Each heart became its own mouth and set of lips. Nimbly striding

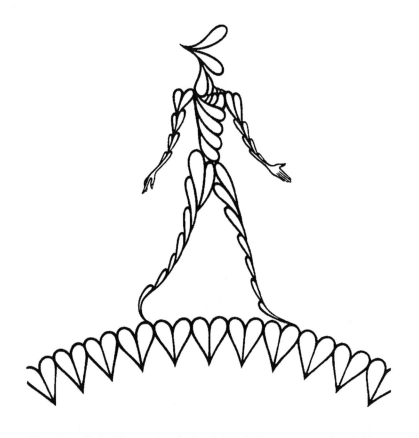

over this supernal suspended heartland, Apollicius listened and heard the *souls* of his feet touched by her *sole* voice, which his feet already knew. Soon the walk became a dance and the dance was he. Walking was talking and to talk was a walk. Talking and walking and dancing, which was becoming, and by becoming, being! The lips of Helleniana's heart spoke through him—indelibly.

"I support your becoming me," spoke the Heart.

"I am already changing into your heart from my hips all the way up to my lips. The voice I'm becoming is in your art."

This voice immediately changed Apollicius into a body of work, a light-sword piercing the night. He heard before he could see what was being said: "There was much to uncover in the land of Helleniana's hearts. The way to discover was to become lost in this new yet all too familiar land."

Closing his eyes, Apollicius padded over the cresting field of hearts, feeling the mossy soft texture of rows upon rows of delectable lips. The soles of his feet had never felt more moved. At moments, as he wandered on from hill corner to valley way, he strove to abide with the very ground that upheld his stride.

Rightfully, he became a real being by continually kissing that which before he had clearly been missing. The sensation upon his lips eroticized all he touched—every pore, every patch of skin, erect and at once at ease. His seed had yet to coagulate into sperm, yet, by merely holding out his arms he could exercise fertility charms, enabling a seed spore to enter with unsealed lips in every part of each planetary heart. By spreading his liquid fire, Apollicius strangely did not tire. The more he gave, the more there was to save. Closing his gargantuan eye orbs to focus on his interior will, he captured what could not be possessed.

Apollicius had been preparing for this rigorous journey since his conception in the milky waters of the cosmic sea. By swimming its length once a light-year, he had forged long, sinewy arms that now yearned for Helleniana, who had gone by another name in that far-distant epoch. He planned to teach her the same stroke he had learned after creation began, when the cosmic egg broke. Swimming in the liquid had given him a solid base to move freely within the *mother-medium*. Mothering proceeded fathering, which preceded the beginning.

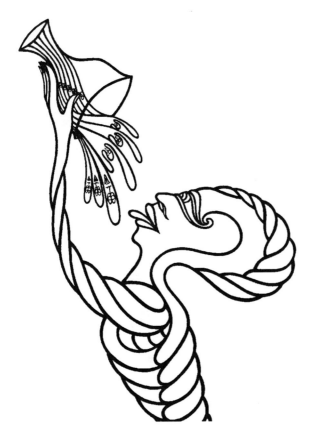

Glimmering there before him, Apollicius slowly began to perceive the still-dim outlines of Helleniana's chalice.

"Though I can't see you, I can still drink you," he said.

Helleniana had left only her sensual shape of the cup. Her spirit had gone. Grasping it firmly, he drained its contents, thirstily imbibing the watery-seed of a future, gestating race of beings. The drink quenched his thirst for action, yet divided his spirit into a strange, unbalanced fraction.

"I will leave my mark here in the form of a complete body of art," he resolved. "To bring it to life I must constantly forge light by being a light-maker and shadow-breaker. This is a task of many incarnations in the cycles of the great spheres. I cannot ultimately commence, without Helleniana's presence.

"It's she who sings and celebrates all things worthy of memory. She enraptures, delights in dance, tells astonishing things, contemplates the ever-changing sky, and shows each of her many sides through the different arts. Without her there is no Muse, and with no Muse, there is no journey."

It was not enough to empty her chalice to consume the gestating race—his thirst remained unquenchable. He needed her whole being. Where was her spirit—that could feasibly have embodied any form, become a myriad of shapes from the winged bird to the burrowing worm?

She had temporarily vanished. What remained was the memory of her dynamic, dancing aura that pulled at him to animate without animosity. Apollicius pressed on, carrying the precious chalice. Soon he would find the *right* steps if he continued taking his own light steps.

He had drunk deeply from her chalice, yet it was not enough to fully escape the trap of vice. For that, he would need the help of his Father, the Central Sun, residing in the silence of the Great Unseen.

The Central Sun had been named Solium by his Mother, Marisium, whose own name came from *mar*, meaning "sea," the infinite cosmic sea. All galactic matter ultimately drew its initial spark from Solium. It was here that, each voyaging light-beam returned to enfold after its streaking power had given off the last thrust of steam. Bowed within Solium, lay the form that all evolutionary steps followed once this river of sound flowed.

Solium had lain in secret for so long, however, that Apollicius had forgotten what he was like. Apollicius did recall that he had once been merely a burning shaft, and become aware of who and what he was away from his Father's *Craft*. Such is the way of the universe and its contents created through prose and verse. Solium had forged the initial spark of Apollicius, but had left it up to him to build the beams to shape his final ark.

"I possess all the visionary light tools to fashion my own luminous ship," mused Apollicius, looking down at his hands, with which he brandished a hot iron.

"Now is the moment to begin construction on my vast web of interconnecting links. To accomplish this unique task, I solicit your aid and protection here and now, Solium." Since they both were born from light, they could communicate with one another in a lightning flash fashion. "I realize the process of threading light strands into the world of the actual is a step-by-step operation, where progress comes slowly and is gradual."

When Solium had been assured that Apollicius had passed completely into the Great Unseen, he sounded the tone through his monolithic lodestone—a slab of his light wrought into a temple of pure sound. In order to reach Apollicius and be of use to him, Solium's Great Tone assumed the semblance of a serpent in an undulating state of Dance. This was how Solium would enter the body of the temple whenever called upon to play, even if only by chance.

Soon a serpent bent into the shape of steps arrived at the feet of Apollicius.

"I am your father, Solium, the Great Central Sun," it said, "who has been hidden from you for so long."

"Father! It *has* been long. My memory of you at the far end of the light spectrum has blurred considerably. It has been a prolonged and tortuous journey without you. Ever since my birth I've been expanding in all directions. Now, I feel it's time to focus my shaft on the finer points of what I have termed *the visionary craft,*" Apollicius pronounced with his customary zeal.

"I offer you a world, my son. It is yours to shape into whatever you choose to make of it," Solium replied.

"Thank you, Father. You couldn't have reappeared at a more opportune time. There can be no greater present than the graceful way of the stair, presented here as an ascending path through air. Your strength can be compared only to your incredible elastic length."

Second Movement

Congelation: *The conversion of a thin flowing liquid into a congealed thick substance, often by heating*

Apollicius placed this New World upon his shoulders in an apparent gesture of acceptance. He, too, could now be considered the son of a parent. As the Central Sun, Solium clearly had a plan in mind to steer all his young suns onto the pathway he had firmly established. He was unaware, however, of certain *visions* Apollicius had experienced.

"I'm an artist," Apollicius declared. "I am the bridge between your dream and my ecstasy."

"I see you as a continuation of my light," replied Solium. "You are still a young beam, it would clearly seem."

"What I see now is coming through me. It is as much a product of my senses as my spirit. Inside of me is a flame too wild for even you to tame. It is your consciousness that has been veiling my world from me. Whenever I turn my solar orb away from you, I capture the crescent smile of Helleniana's lunar dance. It is to her dark side I must now turn for guidance."

Apollicius would try to remake the world he beheld—given to him by his Father, the Central Sun—into his own image of the mage. To create isn't to confuse, but to fuse with the Muse. His original *visions* now became the new subsoil out of which beauty would attempt to uncoil.

He saw his work as a way to express an entire new world of symbols to replace the ones Solium had bequeathed to him as his own hymn's bells. He initially refused Solium's way not out of capricious whim but out of a deeper need not to be him.

Awakened, he sloughed the cloak of slumber for the more spacious coat of a greater number. Out of the integer seven, Apollicius vowed to create his own planets in heaven. Though he could never separate himself completely from his Father, Solium, he actively planned to have his own solar atrium.

"I feel driven to compose on my own, following the complete freedom of my lone law of light with its unique Spectrum of the Tone," Apollicius declared.

He bemoaned just two things in his present state: first, that he could not dedicate all his time to sculpting his visions into a planetary reality, and second, that Helleniana could not be present as his plan's form began to fill with content.

Ever since he could remember, he had been entrenched in continuous periods of intense labor. Thus he remained, tenacious and undaunted in the face of his immense task. As a Young Sun, he had seen his first visions of a land inhabited by elongated light-emanation beings. Later, he had slowly drawn them into existence with light brush strokes, and presently he breathed fire into their limbs by playing certain instruments he had created for that *sole* purpose. Thus began the phase of the Great Breath of Sound. Even Solium had used music to strengthen his pillars of the universe, by constantly encircling his palace with innumerable choirs composed of colossal light-beings.

As a maverick sun, Apollicius had already set out on his own brilliant run. In his formative years before his light had become bright, he had painted with such intensity, as if he were probing for the very incandescent source of luminosity itself. These tableaus were the early models of his universe, blueprints he could and would fall back upon for inspiration when the real planetary forging and its appropriate embellishment began.

Each vision had been annotated and compiled in its own Solar Codex to be accessed at the most opportune moment. His most recent activity had been to organize this prodigious body of visions into separate

volumes, sorted according to the theme of the beam. For example, there were groups related to ethereal beings, others to planetary gestation and formation, and still others dealing with populating each sphere with its own beings reflecting the needs and aspirations of each heavenly body. Lately, he had felt many of his earlier visions relating to the creation of his own system of light coming back to him—in a way, mysteriously searching him out. Apollicius liked to refer to each of them as *visionary children*, all essential builders of a budding brethren.

He felt many of them already taking root in his own solar psyche, occupying a central plain that had gradually come into focus within the sphere of his overall domain. Soon, very soon, in fact, he would be ready, as architect, to design his House of Planets, beam by beam, shaft by shaft.

To accomplish this feat he would have to come to grips with certain monstrous forces that Solium had left still untreated at their sources. Until now he had declined to confront within his light realm these unruly "shakers of the place." Squinting through the heat of the fire-mist, Apollicius perceived milliards of bright shards. He knew that only the moist and cool breath of Helleniana could quench this deep thirst he had had for so long. If he refused to accept her constant and insistent call he could easily fail to be the artificer of his sidereal trail.

For some time now he had been under the influence of a *stream within* moving upward toward the placement of an uncreated beam. Apollicius soon felt the colorless, numinous substance spreading out from the nucleus of its own maternal fluid. In the distance, he heard an echo of the thunderous roar of seven strong horses drawing the gargantuan Central Sun, his Father. Be not mistaken, now his time had arrived to refuse not to awaken.

"I need to tap the indwelling power, deeply rooted at the base of the power plant."

Solium heard his call from afar and boomed back. "Find your own herd of horses and set them on their respective courses."

To assail or to set sail became his only choice, leaving no room to fail. Though still a relatively young star pulsating to the cosmic beat, he now needed to accomplish an age-old feat. By refusing the easy, open pathway to light provided in abundance by his father, Solium, Apollicius had willfully chosen the most difficult trajectory—a course whose each unique step is composed by playing out the story. Yet, if he did not pray to his own instruments of sound potency, there would be no way to capture his *melodic prey*. He felt compelled to initiate the process of becoming his own lodestone by willfully using the magic of the correct tone. He needed to design his own systemic universe or to revert to the one already put in place by Solium.

Apollicius acted not out of a sense of freedom but rather out of a need to express his own *visiondom*, greater than all the power summoned forth to squelch it.

He had hesitated only to patiently wait for the reappearance of Helleniana in full regalia executing her most animated interpretation of the Meteoric Dance; meanwhile, she perched in the wings to illumine her volume, as light and pliant as a veritable plume.

"I must battle to capture your jewel—not stone, nor a hewn chalice of matter itself, but rather its form only, overflowing with the key sound of the tone," Apollicius affirmed.

Cloistered in her hide-away by day and praying to her own private ray by night, Helleniana waited for Apollicius to show his eye's light, to give a call meant to use the dancing feet to set the spirit into beat. Before she could do her planetary dance, he had to forge feet's ponderous spheres from his formless, fiery breath.

"Every time I sing my hymn, I can say I am assisting him," Helleniana sang in one of her nocturnal chants.

Patiently waiting at the foot of the tree of hallowed spirits, Apollicius now leapt into the night to catch a lightning bolt that threatened to smite him. In its flashing wake came the thunderous din of its *sound-partner.* Once he possessed the light seed and its symbols, he would be able to direct the driving force of sound with the clash of cymbals. His hands grappled tenaciously with the light to keep it from bolting. In this way, Apollicius captured both its luminous source and its subtle notes to provide his *Sun-ship-in-Progress* with a light sail and sound rudder.

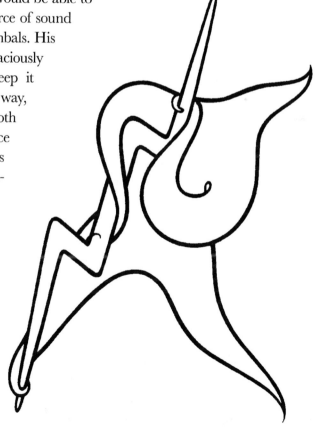

Even though he had fastened the lightning flash with a bolt, it would often give him a sudden jolt, sending him to his knees, where he would utter the sound of the "ssss"

and trace a zigzag shape with his index finger in space. His struggle epitomized this early stage of his development as a young sun, when he needed immeasurable amounts of strength, willpower, and imagination to create a kingdom based on the laws of his Muse from whom he constantly drew yet only slowly learned to use.

After achieving this electrical storm conversion, Apollicius cloistered himself in a self-imposed introversion. He needed both time and solitude to implement his bold *planetary plan*. A true sage dreads the passing of an inspired moment, knowing full well that it never returns in the same stage. His own horses now reared on their hind legs as he harnessed them to his Sunship with threads of silken light, thereby providing himself with the means to travel at will from one end of his own universe to the other. With electrifying speed and solar efficiency, Apollicius began to work on his Art Form with the concerted effort of a master craftsman.

His ship, *"dolphinesque"* in shape and lightning-fast, deftly navigated the mysterious waters of the unscrolling empyrean sea. Personifying his Mother, this sea had always been the mate of Solium's fate. From and out of her came that effervescence wherein all *light germs* originate.

Solium was essentially Space condensed into a long trail of cosmic dust coiled in a serpent form with a long tail. Marisium, the Grace Mother, the illustrious spouse of Solium, the mother of Helleniana, is everywhere there was Space. She had quite an incredible face, with as many lines as there were rivers still full from their source. Her body had tubes of plantlike xylem and phloem to transport her waters to wherever she showed her spacious plenum. She was presently busy organizing their ever-extending *stellar house*.

Even when Marisium was gestating in her Space, nothing was lost since the generative womb of her psyche that we call the *heavens* and *hells* has many secrets hidden deep inside inner cells. When she turned, flowers blossomed and fruit ripened. Her sides were pliant and begirt with an extremely thin and nearly transparent layer of bark. She was sometimes called *moon-woman* and when she waxed the longest, in her crescent phase, her time became the strongest.

Marisium never really disappeared from Apollicius's sight; she only reappeared in other personifications. "I am the box containing the voice," she would say. "When I cannot open it, I feel trapped inside. Your magical ear is the lid under which I have quite often, for many reasons, hid."

Apollicius had learned to respond by saying, "When I listen to you I become clairvoyant, and quickly know the next step to take as a sound voyager struggling to stay buoyant."

Being Space everywhere and in charge of all things, Marisium solely pulled for the young *solar barge*. Once she had unfurled out of her fertile crescent vault, she set about lifting up this young Sunflower Plant, Apollicius. Omnipresent, her voice expressed neither melancholy nor malice as she turned her17self into a huge chalice, one of her most precious shapes.

"Chalice, goblet, cup, grail—these are the vessels drunk to the dregs, contents inspiring us to erect our masts and set sail," Marisium sang out, reading straight from the unrolled cerulean scroll.

"Your radiant, natural self-confidence gives the impression of a truly modest Muse," mused Apollicius. "I will pluck out the first few *beings-in-progress* as they appear, just to see if they are clearly a reflection of early creative luck."

Grasping one of these spontaneous spatial creations,

Apollicius held it up for Marisium to see. He wanted her to imbue it with a sustaining source of its own, combining her nurturing nature and his unadulterated force. The bodies of the freshly formed new beings sparkled out from Marisium's whirling dance-of-the-spheres.

Thus did the presence of Marsium console Apollicius in Helleniana's absence during her retreat, for the time being, to the only place where she felt both comfortable and secure. She longed to have a nave-formed vessel to fulfill her pursuit with blessings, flowers, and fruit. This would all transpire through time and fire. At the moment, however, Helleniana prepared herself in the private domain of one corner of Space waiting to reappear after these new molds had been forged by the hands of Marisium, then to be placed into her own mouth as a *wordsmith*. Solium and Marsium kept these molds in their celestial *house of forms,* where all shapes and sizes had been first conceived and developed out of primordial, sensual folds.

Once the molds were in place, Helleniana could show her face and use the verb to express her complete dance form in a fluid continuum of time and space. She looked upon Apollicius's first creations as simply beings-in-progress. Soon it would be time for her to step in and use her own movement to illustrate his first *grail statement.*

Whatever Solium and Marisium *knew* together, Apollicius captured drawing visionary images from a *quill feather,* planning to share them with Helleniana as soon as she returned from her performance on various stages. He knew in his heart only she would fully understand these vast, planetary implications of this transcendental art. Until then, he had to rely on his own intuitive powers to unfurl the *master plan* he had harbored so long regarding the spatial creation of *man.*

On Apollicius's most current drawing board, he used sound sketches in place of the played instrumental chord. Out of one chord, he wove complete pieces, which he would use as the bounding line to forge his newly sculpted worlds to bridge the gorge. Through the alchemy of music and paint he sought to compose his own version of the *cosmic saint.*

As a son of Solium, he saw himself as one of many suns just as Helleniana could, in a sense be considered the daughter of Marisium as well as one of her many moons. Helleniana and Apollicius were not brother and sister; rather, each had been generated from hermaphroditic and androgynous sources, much in the same way a tree bears fruit and its seeds generate a continuation of its life conduit.

Apollicius was deeply attracted to Helleniana and knew in the heart of his art that their heavenly bodies would one day have congress, and give issue to their overall planetary system of progress.

Neither, though, knew when this would happen, nor during what race he would finally impregnate her space. His solar energy had been driven down past-imagined boundaries, where huge image-generated continents found their way into its foundries. If he left this call unanswered he would have to answer for it much later, and most likely in much more dire circumstances.

By moving into the life-role he had assumed, he could avoid the calamitous effect of failing to do his work and, thus be consumed. In a flash of an instant, Apollicius saw a *radiant being* inscribed within the labyrinth of his boundless psyche. Raising the *natural trumpet* he had saved from those original trumpeters, he blew the note of this spiral through the *keyhole,* unlocking the treasure chest of a solar (plexus) race.

Uncurling from the sound of this long and steady note, small replications of

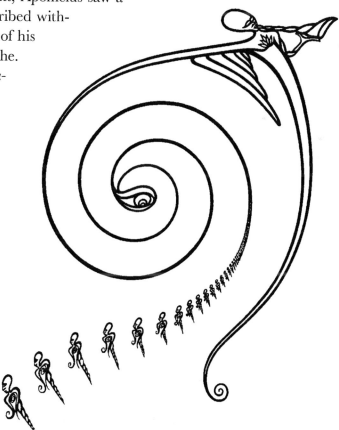

his light energy began to appear. Each lucent form had a proportionate cosmic system etched into its whirling center.

Surprised to see their vast number, he commented, "Never did I imagine I would succeed in creating *their bodies* before Helleniana and I had completed the body of their planetary home."

"Nor did you know when it would happen," added Marisium, who had overheard his voice above the trumpeting. "The creative spirit itself always chooses the moment for its expression. Your instrument is an *outpicture* of your aureate nature. It is a continuation of Solium's original wind blasts that thundered from his Central Sun prior to your conception."

"The amount of semen in your fluid undertaking is proportionate to the quantity and quality of your artistic making," offered Solium, himself an expert on the ecstasies of otherworldly creativity originating from a central source of light. Following a strict empyrean heritage, a race is chosen and forged before its planetary home has been summarily disgorged.

Third Movement

Fixation: *To make a volatile subject fixed or solid,*
so that it remains permanently unaffected by fire

The universe, rolled out through the cosmic lovemaking of Marisium and Solium, was fraught with wonders. It had been so long since Apollicius had been with each generative parent that in his mind they had become transparent, like the outlines of a vision he could barely see, rising periodically in the tumbling waves of the sidereal sea.

He could create beings, but what spheres would they inhabit and what type of globes would they best thrive upon? Looking through the scattering veils of mists, he perceived denizens of higher spheres all sculpted at one time or another by the all-powerful Solium, ingested into the magnificent womb of his space love, Marisium. As ether, Marisium even preceded Solium, the molten embodiment of her first experiment to produce Au, the element gold.

The heart of Marisium had always been beating behind her best veils of the *Unmanifest*. She had begun the tradition of the elixir of life with her spatial movement. As Solium would attest, she was the essence of sensuality, being impregnable at any time, anywhere, by any potent source of light. In the beginning her very darkness had put the then young Solium in a continual state of light-projecting erection. He found it so difficult to lower his shaft that it soon became a permanent beam.

These shafts and sunbeams were the original seed-bearers, emanating from the source of vastly differing puddles, pools and streams.

"The ear of Marisium revealed to me the concealed harmony of all things," Solium once shot out. "She could actually hear the approaching streak of my light arrows at their speed's peak. The infinite scale of her spatially forged cathedral had the outlining form of an ever-expanding and contracting 'ear of the womb.' Both became penetrable by me at the right moment." His love for Marisium knew no bounds and clearly supported the expression of his instrument's assorted sounds.

At their beginning was the word, and the word was the seed sown in the whirled spiral of the intergalactic ear, the first organ to develop in the womb of *unshallow* space! Her ear was the germ of both the unformed sphere and the informed raindrop tear. Her deep indigo canvas became so vast that Solium could stretch only a small part of her onto the tabula rasa for his art!

Conjured up by the sound of his light movement, vast forms moving dimly became spotlighted. Apollicius hungered to expose and then convey Solium's whole cosmogony in a series of glyphs. He sought to usher in the audition tradition of the ear by light spear, which he had been receiving through Marisium. Apollicius began to fulfill his destiny of the light-casting demiurge with the conscious cooperation of this unconscious operation. The plenum of Marisium became the space she designed, *alchemically* helping to incorporate it into the solar disc of Apollicius's changing face.

"My dictum is: whatever can be framed can be named," Apollicius declared. "To name is to signify something into the realm of creation. I draw from my template, as a planter draws from his *seed-slate*. I'm here to give back the silvery rain to the golden plane of the windowpane. Steady the frame for me to breathe through my name."

Marisium had become two guardian angels to securely hold this future painting in the present meridian. Apollicius extended one arm full-length across the breadth of her beatific breast and let fly his golden light from the east to the west horizon. Marisium immediately felt the heat of milliards of light shards rushing in to flood her boundless yards.

"I sense perpetual patterns pulsating and pushing outward in every direction, touching the ever-*untrodden* heavenly vault of my Space Heart," Marisium declared, nearing a moment of pure ecstasy.

The light of Apollicius had hurled past the voluptuous folds of her indigo evening gown, leaving her a flower with fruit and power, striped with both day and night. She was the zebra before the dawn of the zebra. Her mystical metals underwent strange transmutations and metamorphoses. It was at that point where the brush tip first touched canvas and the sun drop met the pellucid mist.

By claiming her space, Marisium gave the young sun a chance to recreate through his own grace. She preluded him just as the word fe*male* included male. If he was an afterthought, then she was the personification of forethought. As the benign, sheltering force of fate, Marisium was as beautiful as her celestial trail was long and spiraled into an ever-disappearing tail. Her frame was her body and *watt* lay within these circuitous bounds—the *amp*le womb.

Bounding in, Apollicius began responding actively to the call of Divine Imagination. Create or be created. Imagine or disappear into the vague, misty world of the Unrealized Mind. Because he had legs, he knelt before her *altar of art* as she set before him a brush and told him to st*art.*

"Once you begin to brushstroke me, all the forces of my Puissance will be on the side of you and the Dance. I am unconscious only for those who do not draw drafts from me. Consequences will unfurl if you courageously follow the curve of my figure's curl," Marisium stated, devoid of her void.

"I'm empty only for whoever cannot fill me," she continued. "When my strings are not strummed it is your fault, since I cannot resonate any instrument drummed from within my own vault."

Without another moment's hesitation, Apollicius dipped his lightbrush deep into *color* and traced his first stroke! It was a mighty effort, stretching his imagination to the full breadth of her *cerulean canvas.* He felt such a strong attraction to her *ether* that both their media *mixed.* Then he expanded his lungs with a deep breath while rhythmic waves of energy filled his arms and shoulders. Still undaunted, he took a step back to see more clearly the mark of his first brushstroke.

He could discern the shape of a crescent emerging from this whirling ball of mist he had quickly expressed. He felt his indwelling powers surge at the sight of the created image. Dipping into a blue well, he plied the background to glow like sapphire and, with the influx of the light energy, swell with fire. Through the mists his painting portrayed, Apollicius focused his own sunbeam upon the breasts of the cosmic night, caught in between the recently formed moonlight and his sunlight. The rest of this mysterious-yet-familiar moon creature was swathed in dark raiment, her cloak of night rendering her nearly invisible to his fiery, burning, blazing eyes. Filled to nearly bursting with joy, delight, and pride, Apollicius slung his *sunbow* and quiver of shafts over his shoulder so he could use his hands and arms more freely to paint.

In the back of his mind he truly felt as though he were recreating the lovely dark image of Helleniana, who had suddenly disappeared within Marisium's vaporous space. With each stroke from his sun source he felt he came closer, light degree by degree, to actually reencountering her galactic pedigree. Rather than emblazoning her with a variety of celestial accessories, he instinctively kept his image of her extremely simple. In order for him to stage the *production of life* he needed to clearly posit her energy source as female to fill her with his light. It was polarization with and for a purpose!

Carefully, Apollicius filled and fleshed out the rest of her face in profile just as he had remembered it. Being in her crescent phase, she would wax still until she was full. This was the initial stage of sowing and planting for what he would reap and glean, in his planetary harvest of the future yet to be seen. He felt her now to be so alive that he began to speak.

"By orbiting you with my rays, I make you my Muse to help generate our own system of planets and other heavenly days—I cannot do it without you as a source of inspiration. Just as my father had Marisium for nurture, I also must have someone of my stature. I do not know when you will reappear, but I understand why you had to disappear—it was all done to preserve our intuitive art form germinating from the *seed-symbol*.

In a sense Helleniana had been abducted. Her life-energy had been removed from the visible, to be held fast by the strong, dark head of the *Unseen*. She had been the moon maiden of innumerable slayings, the virgin arch of which Apollicius was the solar monarch. Now he needed to reclaim the Muse in order to rescue that part of himself which had also been wrested away by that same foe. He entwined further with her figure, recouped to help his solar energy picture as it regrouped.

From moonbeam to sunbeam, the vine became the ray extending forth from the night out to the light of the day. Helleniana, cloistered in her crescent phase, still remained a visible sliver of silver, sliced off from the cosmic vault of Marisium, the most ancient expression of the originating feminine principle. Plantlike and mysterious, the first world-sustaining emanations wafted to the fore from the *Void of Marisium*, the *femme* space sovereign. One could never avoid the *Void*. Or, rather, it was life-threatening and existentially dangerous to do so.

Marisium presented herself as the all-embracing, protective figure Apollicius now encountered in her crescent-shaped manifestation. His lightness drew strength from her darkness. Adorned with the moonstone amulet charm, he would very soon become impervious to any threats of harm.

His first real portrait of Helleniana now glowed before him complete in its platinum elegance.

"They are twin air souls, skilled in a vision fueled by willed discipline and precision," Marisium thought to herself.

As a young sun, he would soon have the first of many *visions* to come. These *solar visions* would become the wellspring for the foundation and formation of his whole Planetary Ring. His creative faculty belonged to him alone. It could not be shared, lent, given, or received. Its magic lay in the quality and luminosity of the delicate thread of each single ray. This formidable toil of love he set about to uncoil would one day render at stake everything that he was about to undertake. For he who has superior needs, no day has room for inferior deeds.

His recently created moon began to grow from the influx of his radiation. What had once been a sliver was now a full-bodied orb of silver. When he asked,

"What are you?" she replied:

"I am here as a sphere. I contain a fountain in my head that ushers forth streams of life-supplementing milk and, in contrast to Marisium's *space of night*, makes my heavenly body glow zinc-white.

"I know if I *will*, I will not be dragged to my fate, to be with none other than my most appropriate and destined mate."

Her great lunar earrings shimmered in her own moonlight, luring Apollicius toward her milky fold and brightening the night. Well aware of the protean nature of his Muse, Helleniana, he still was not sure if this was just one of her guises. After being first-born of mist, she was forever destined to roam, as she was also a creature born of foam. Always at home in the sky, she could call any part of the Zodiac her own house and know that the young sun could find her there to claim as his spouse.

By being a *galactic nomad*, Apollicius helped Helleniana help him become the monad. As his eye's monarch, she posed on a *throne*, impelling upon him to play his first light tone. When she had first invited him to her house as a guest, her voice at that moment had instigated his quest.

Formed in full-bosom and in full-blossom from the ever-consolidating waves of light, the new moon lay down her full body on a bed of violet space and inclined her axis toward Apollicius in an openly sensuous manner.

"I'm ready for you to come," she said in her dreamlike voice. "Complete your solar circuit and become grounded in me." Apollicius moved under her commanding presence, radiating out from deep within her wise eyes well. Her book had opened like the tablets of creation, for him to peruse as well as pause in to look for recreation. To enter her inmost heaven, he would read the various curves and rounded forms of her writing. The vowels stood for pure feeling, while the consonants expressed thoughts originating from those feelings.

Apollicius descended like a comet toward her waiting moon-shaped body. Slowly, he withdrew a shaft from his quiver and released it. At the moment of penetration, she lit up like a synagogue mounted on a serpent. In a state of ardent prayer, she stretched out her arms to meet his and sow their interacting seam made with the spine of the light-acting beam. Thunder peals rang down from the lofty space, harmonizing with Solium's light approval. Their orbits had merged momentarily, each eclipsing the other—the moon as temptress and the sun as the seducing producer.

At that time there was no question of higher or lower natures between them. There were no accumulated wrongdoings of past existences, that had to be confronted and transmuted before there could be a *mystical marriage*. There did exist, though, *Red Giants* throughout the constellations, who could easily become energy-draining black-hole *institutions*. True, these giants could not be slain, so to speak, but they could nonetheless be dealt with firmly to help reduce the pain.

Fully aware of their existence, Apollicius began to move in their direction. In the future, he planned to create musical instruments to quiet their turbulence and undermine the plethora of chaotic emotions their mammoth orbs put into motion.

As flames of acumen shot from every corner of his eclipsed spheres, Apollicius kept focusing on transmuting his stellar semen. Each of his rays shone as brilliant as he had yet seen; nevertheless, along this *path of attainment* he had such a long way to go before completing his whole solar system in both thought and deed. At times like these, though, he really felt as if he had engorged a lion, the flared mane burning ions and, deep within the forge, melting iron.

"I feel so scorched at times that I need to shed rays, to avoid being consumed by these blistering work-days," he intimated to his moon partner.

The question became where to direct the fire of his *solar imagination*. His orb sailed, carrying its *light cargo* back and forth across the violet vault, turning around itself in kaleidoscopic gyrations, while Helleniana still remained concealed inside her lunar house awaiting clearance from her Mother, Marisium, to resume her dance. The moon that Apollicius had recently penetrated with his light stem had been merely her shell, her *outer orbit* of her aura's "hem." She was vexed from apparent neglect by Apollicius, who often let his light interfere with her ability to *reflect*. Ironically, his real work of shining depended wholly upon her inborn talent of reflection.

Apollicius strove to guide his *Sun-ship* through the astral sea in search of a shore to plant the first seeds of this golden ore. A hunter, he carried the life-blood of his own light within a jar, like wine. Sound, in the form of the wind element, pushed out the sails and moved him ever closer to his plan for the land. The same pure undimmed eye that had plunged its ray into the moon maiden continued to search the calm sea for a spot to plant his first planet. Not only a cultivator of worlds, he also served as their stable sower and seasonal harvester.

Behind his luminous shield, stretched the wide expanse of a seedless space field. Without him, this womb would remain a barren and forsaken tomb. His shafts of light were nothing more than elongated seed rafts, set to float for eons as spores until the right conditions came about for them to burst into many forms or *energetic cores*. After his transmutative congress with the moon, Apollicius had accumulated even a greater concentration of seeds to meet all of his first planet's needs. At the very heart of these *cores*, the intense essence of colors stored could be brought out into their various shades of meaning by the resonant lyre he played, cutting the tones using his fingers like blades.

As a hunter of the fugitive sound, he could trap wild notes wherever they could be found. Perched on the edge of a *cliff of light*, Apollicius posed, ready and willing to begin to make his kingdom a stable compound of *site* and sound. He had already received his first aid, and felt ready for the initial sidereal-seed to be laid.

The moon had moved into a new phase ahead of its time and lay prone for more light reception. Apollicius came to the edge of his own precipice and gazed down at her full-body beauty. She had already begun her own process of *fixation*.

"Out of your moonscape will emerge the first plant from inside the nurturing warmth of this cocoon cape," he proclaimed, extending one of his long arms of light toward the unfurling young seedling.

The plant grew upwardly and not awkwardly, the leaves becoming arms and the fruit and flower composing the head tower.

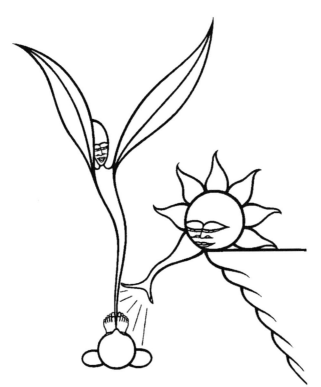

"I am Mercury," said the plant, pointing toward its new orbital path. "I will not be denied the realization of my destiny as your next of kin, Apollicius, since it is your heat that courses through the molten streams of my geo-sphere."

"You are the first real evidence of my system's destiny, the first planetary expression of this system's providence," Apollicius said.

Fleet-footed, Mercury had a fiery nature. Being all seed, his incredible storehouse of energy accounted for his lightning speed. He didn't need to sow his seed, because it could already be found in all parts of his land, ready-made at hand. Not only did he carry and deliver messages from Apollicius, he *was* the message.

When Mercury was still a young sapling, the sun had once told him, "Every spirit *is* a past or future *man*, from the highest archangel down to the most elemental 'free-ranger.' The, *inferior*, the semi-intelligent, and even the so-called non-intelligent *elementals* are all potentially future men with their own planetary homes projected into space."

Just as Mercury had blistering speed, all of his progeny appeared as winged creatures with physiognomies of a similar destiny. Little by little, Apollicius produced the first *Race of Angels*, men who had climbed up the ladder of heavenly things until they finally could support the intense *Fire of Mercury* without melting their wings.

Apollicius once overheard Mercury, his first real scribe, saying, "Poe*tree* bears fruit." He turned the phrase, as a planet of few words but many revolutions. Mercury grew as a robust, rose plant long before he could generate enough energy and movement to transform into a high-powered *amp-sphere* with just the right mixture of atmosphere. By whirling around the axis of his own spin, little by little Mercury rounded out and off everything that was too green or unnecessarily thin. He was so close to the Apollicius Orb, they were often mistaken for the same orbit. The radiance he shed had originally been lit by the same Apollicius sunbeam he had once been fed.

In his innermost being, Mercury began to compose his first planetary writings using a variety of curved and rounded forms. These "roundings" echoed the form of the Sun's experimental sound surroundings, an expression of arcane wisdom beyond the power of words, created from the contemplation and study of the simple light beam—the first and only real teacher it would seem.

Guided from within, Mercury worked diligently on this art form, becoming the first in an intricate hierarchy of sentient beings to discover and understand that the symbol is ever for him who has the eyes of comprehension. His eyes reached out from deep within the inner ear, clear out to the tips of his limbs, where all evolution tends to sprout.

As Mercury drew from the brilliant light source of his father, Apollicius, his leaves unfurled, lengthened, and broadened to such a degree that he commented, "By drawing symbols we can *draw* more from them. I visualize myself spinning out this role throughout the Ellipses, from *pole* to *pole*.

As his life's work began to unfold, he recognized how much every-thing he did fit into the pattern and mold of the sun's light threads of gold. Baring his outstretched arms to his creator and luminous deity, he continued to unroll the characteristic organic pattern of his life as a planetary field of revolving piety.

"I am both paper and word. Inscribed with the flame, parchment is my world," he sang out, feeling the light's pattern ebb and flow from the original light source of Apollicius through his work to create anew his *own* inner sun's course.

Yielding to space and entering the vast time field, Mercury, striving to become whole, went on to fashion this role, while yet another roll op-

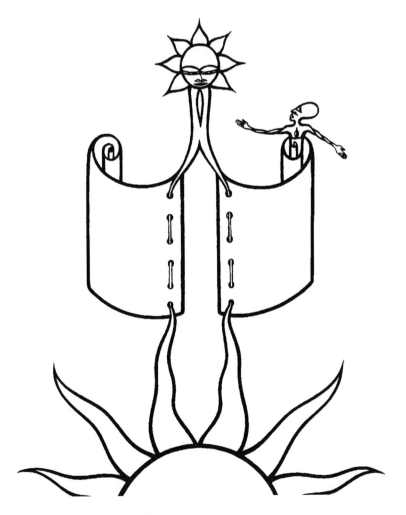

posite him waited to become a filled scroll. His book, as all books, has two sides, with a light, yet solid binding. It was here, ultimately, that his true seed would be sown—into the *spine* connecting Apollicius with Mercury, his planetary reflection or his own *mind*. Seeing this reflection, Apollicius reflected aloud, "You, as my first conceived, are my messenger to spread the seed containing its tiny germ of light throughout my system. Your sphere is planetary knowledge containing the very first words inscribed in an ethereal ledger."

Each planet coming into being spun as one more gem to fortify his battlement of jewels. Spoke by spoke, he spoke, turning his giant wheel of light. Rather than have his sun chariot pulled by swans, Apollicius preferred to be the phoenix, the unicorn, the tortoise, or the dragon— whichever embodiment happened to be needed to further realize his planetary kingdom.

Solium viewed his sun, Apollicius, from the lofty *ether* with a mixture of pride and caution. The two would meet again on new terms when Apollicius had firmly established his system of planetary revolution. Yet from time to time, they would have whimsical intergalactic interactions.

"I am the crone of the tone," Solium chanted on one occasion through the cosmic mist, then wait patiently for a reply.

"I, who already have a maid in Helleniana, though she is nowhere to be found, am still in need of your celestial aid. You, who are always at rest when you toil, tell me the way to continue to find more planetary soil," Apollicius replied, then fell quiet, in wait for a response. Just as love music is never about love, true dialog is not just about words.

Finally, a voice pierced the mist: "You are my *mindborn* son. It takes work to learn how to play, and much play to probe the depths of genuine work. Never work at working nor play at playing. My altitude comes from an attitude in precision from prelude to postlude."

"I have begun with my *visions* of you I've captured over time and through space. As seeds, most of them will not germinate until they've been tested by fire—or, in a sense, *roasted*."

"Yes, Apollicius, as their sun you shall heat them into germination and then quench their thirst with lakes, rivers and oceans. It's all about *fire and water*, the two basic formative elements of the universe."

"Then if I remember the flame, I know its name," responded Apollicius thoughtfully.

"Which is what you are!" added Solium. "We are a pure lineage in the tradition of *spontaneous combustion and creation*. Heat creates pressure, and that is what moves us to shape words and worlds out of them, and vice versa."

Apollicius turned from Solium to watch his messenger at work. Mercury was anything but a fallen seraph of the abyss. He was truly using his seed as a stone to begin to cast a throne. Pulling out one of his light shafts from his quiver, the sun of Solium fashioned it into a staff and handed it to Mercury when they next met.

As Mercury grasped it firmly in his hand, it budded and flowered instantaneously. With a gentle yet resolute nod, he took the bloomed rod coming to him from the realm of the *absolute*. Intoning each of the seven vowels, Mercury began to consecrate his own land and the land of the other beings Apollicius and Helleniana would later create.

Next, Apollicius withdrew more shafts not yet made into staffs, and this time flung them from his *musical bow* through the concentric circles of his solar system. As they flew they became light essences—*strings of beings* with the power to populate a planet or set it afire. Just as every tone includes all tones, so every arrow contained a potential light subject or enlightened pharaoh.

They were golden arrows sweeping through their mark and then on to new places to *seed the spark*. As he slung them, he flung open his Rainbow Robe commanding the light seeds to plant a new globe. They burned for a time blazing new pathways, ways of *the path* they would spend their whole life, once planted on a land, trying to remember. Slowly they would recall, by growing from a mere sprout to a free being very tall. This new planet where they all headed, Apollicius named Mars. Once sown with seeds of flaming arrows, its symbolic field would always be understood as emblematic and the protective shield.

Feeling the protective power of Solium aglow, Apollicius did not slow his Planetary Dance Show. In a state of grace, he felt primed to embrace the unconscious universe of *Marisium's Space* spread all across her cosmic face—the one energy source able to portray the play of this cosmic fable.

Meanwhile, Mercury, both patron and teacher of the arts, cautiously

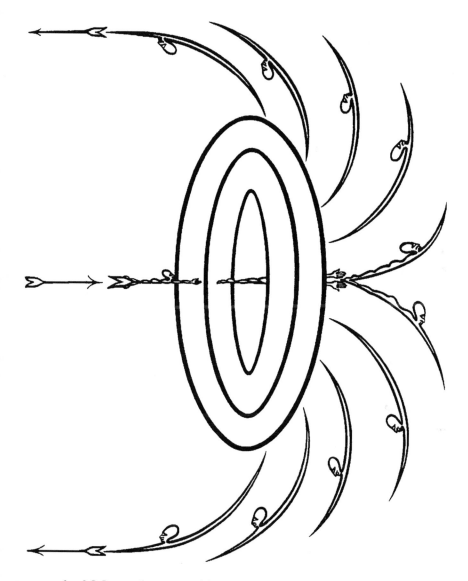

approached Mars, always on his guard. They stood exactly one realm apart: one an instructor of the ever-dangerous flame and the other shield-ed, waiting to receive a title and a name.

Mercury took a step forward. "I've brought you pollen."

"Energy to help me along this lone and dangerous way?" wondered Mars.

He proceeded to smear his whole body and cape with the fertile orange dust and then thanked Mercury, knowing him as a teacher he could thoroughly trust. But that was only partially true. Mercury was mercurial, aiming to lure Mars into the deep forest of pleasure and trial. being both manger and danger, where the soul was born and nurtured, where it was tried and ruptured.

"Get into the *Sunship*," offered Mercury. "Let me carry you to the war zone where I can even now hear its distant battle tone."

"We begin now. I know it's a long, perilous orbit to circumvent our creator—Apollicius. I am the body where swords have been sown. the land where fire has been lit and thrown."

As helmsman, Mercury steered an oval course, following the sound of a not-so-near silver trumpet. Oblivious to the sound, Mars queried: "Do you know where we head?"

"Yes, into the heart of Marisium, our space love, for every true lover of space to enter and uncloud her face," assured Mercury.

"We travel by ship changing from one plane to another."

"Is it always a wind instrument that signals the level of the cosmic terrain?"

"It is," Mercury replied tersely.

"Will Apollicius help?"

"He is the archer carrying his quiver of light shafts. When he shoots his prey with a golden ray, we steer toward those shoals to meet our new brethren, as wild as young foals."

Mars leaned back in the light craft in reflection while Apollicius, poised, aimed his next shaft. As if awakening from a deep slumber, Mars felt as complete and integral as a whole number.

"We are not here to forge a path but to let the *path* be our forge," added Mercury in the rhythm of his own breath.

At the crest of the next sidereal wave, they both signaled, seeing the design of the sign. It had dawned, and Apollicius arose out of his own sown *cave of the wave.*

"There is the *vessel* of my own *lightblood*—a flower heaving on a swelling chest," Apollicius observed. He had his bow already strung, and in an instant the living arrow was aimed at its destination and flung. As one sees oneself, so is one hit, as the marksman finds his own target. This was how love first came to be. It always just *was,* and now that it had been stalked, it is. Venus. Emanating from the corporeal eye of Venus, were radiated concentric circles of possible levels to access and inhabit. There seemed no limit except the one self-imposed—to create.

"She is lovely," mused Mars, awestruck at how she both contrasted and complemented his own conflict-ridden land. Venus saw them approaching and knelt before the bow of the *Sunship*. She posed unadorned, but ready to come aboard and meet the bard.

On the sundeck the three young planets encircled one another instinctively knowing that their existences would always be in revolution.

The *planetary temple* of Venus was undefiled. The bronze nose of the love teacher, neither too wide nor blade-edged, stood out as just one more elegant feature. Her ears were petite and open to hear the voice never heeded by the herd. To those feeding to their fill on her face, her eyes could become bottomless pits of open space. Her lips expressed the same deep plum color and form as her hips. When Apollicius looked upon his most recent creative catch, he nearly forgot about Helleniana, whom he still considered his most elusive match.

Venus turned, a huntress and a lodestone of desire.

"Just gazing upon you makes this one ray of mine become a much stronger and more solid line," Apollicius confessed.

Like lucid, well-composed music, all great art is a tonic that spreads throughout one's being, reaching every instrumental part of the symphonic. Venus held up a tablet lit in gold by that

first ray, so both the *Sunship* crew and Apollicius could read: "Patience is erotic."

"I want you to know, Venus, I am not an unapproachable deity. Focus on my warmth and not my distance to best gauge when to enter my dance. Without you, none of this would nor could be worthwhile. Think of my rays as long, golden horns in your midst to brighten the morns of your days."

"Though you are a realm apart, Apollicius, we can both share the joys of the helm. My senses are at play with your enkindled *spirit of space*," replied Venus.

"The very ray you now feast upon has not always been a mainstay. Behind the veil of its vibration arena, thousands of impulses have undergone strange metamorphoses and transmutations. I have a powerful picture language to bequeath to my whole system of planets, with you at the heart of its wreath," Apollicius said, prolonging his speech.

"Your elongated ray pulses through my body, and as a new planet I *englobe* it. Every sword must have its sheath in which to repose."

Their repartee continued on, degree by degree, as Mercury and Mars listened to their blended voices decree. Mars could not, and cared not to shield himself from her raw beauty. Her force was not transparent, yet clearly apparent.

Now, he placed his spear next to Mercury's long, quilled pen on the *ship's* deck, arranging them like two oars, stilled and awestruck by the vision that had once been a mere speck of a spark. The warrior and the writer had kept the ship's keel even. Now their "oars" plunged quietly as they waited for Venus to come aboard.

Apollicius, however, had other plans. He lowered his fiercely glowing head to reestablish contact with his ray, which Venus had engulfed and thereby kept intact. At that very moment there was a fluid flow of light between them. Instantaneously, the light surged upward and out of Venus's head into a serpentine extension of the whole body of the planetary goddess of love.

"Out of my love for you, Venus, I will create an unknown land nearly as striking as yourself."

Whatever Venus heard, flowed through her and out of her small ear. Apollicius corralled and contained this sound and light energy in a new shell of form. His voice sang out songs he had learned many years ago, when he still played an integral part of Solium's system. These songs were content to fill the light form.

Apollicius gently squeezed the body of the new planet and waited. When he released his grip, *Nature* rushed in to fill the vacuum with the four elements of air, water, fire, and earth. Once filled to capacity, the bedecked Apollicius directed all the power of his *star* toward this new *sound* planet. Because so much of what he did had come through the listening ear of Venus, this new heavenly body he named very appropriately: *Earth*!

In the eyes of her creator, Apollicius, Earth rivaled a dazzling jewel. Though she was still a young sapling of a sphere, Apollicius could already see all of her incredible natural potential. He fondly referred to her as the *listening planet,* as he watched her step
gingerly onto his growing *Sun-
ship*. He named her so because everywhere, she
grew terrestrial ears
to hear sounds com-
ing in from celestial
light-years. If Venus
had been named
the fairest planet
yet, then Earth
was its rarest sound
net. From leaves to
whorled shells, all
shapes could be
traced back to these
original *sound wells.*
A Herculean ear-
drum in the space
of Earth's center
maintained the
rhythm of her heart
at a constant pace.

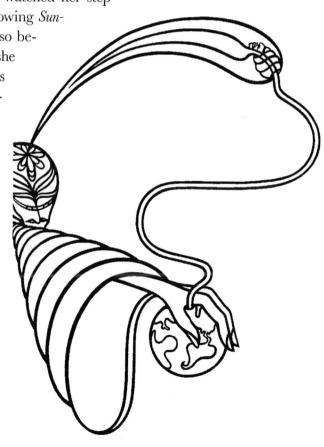

There, the first beams of the inner sanctum's chambers had been laid in the midst of swirling waters.

Whatever sound came into her *queendom*, fashioned itself into part of her natural realm. If she heard it with her inner ear, it manifested on her outer sphere. At her midpoint bulged her sacred *navel-stone*, the center of the resonating chamber for each tone. Her sites quivered with each sensation of *vibrational* tone emanating from this stone.

"I implore you to continue playing your score," she exclaimed between earthly sighs of satisfaction, always desiring more.

Mildly surprised at her request, Apollicius turned to his Father to begin the fabrication of musical instruments.

"My son, I will leave this work for you, as I am confident in your ability," Solium responded. "I am involved in other galactic manifestations at the moment and cannot be distracted."

"Thank you for your quick reply," Apollicius said. "I will try and remember all you taught me about how *music* teaches one to fly."

Apollicius turned to Earth and promptly produced the golden lyre, instructing her to begin a piece making use of his five-note solar scale. She happily brought the precious instrument on board with her and immediately began to map out their orbital sound tract through this very playing act.

When Apollicius was at work on his far-reaching system of *Light*, Helleniana would often slip almost completely from his mind. Most likely she still hid under the *Cover of the Night*, somewhere, patiently putting together the pieces of her shattered universe. If she did not recover in time to lead their planetary dance, it would be not only tragic but a cosmic crime. He knew in the depth of his heart that it could be done only by her. Right now, she wafted somewhere adrift inside the galactic psyche of Marisium, waiting in the wings for the opportunity and scenic moment to reenter, dancing and singing in unity.

Now, concordant string music emanating from the *Sunship* interrupted his thoughts. Out of this spatial *ocean of tones*, Earth had created a new dimension of sonority.

"To serve Marisium is to serve the *food* of musical sounds that come from her space," Earth proclaimed to Apollicius.

Marisium acted as both Mother and Wife to Solium, the Central

Sun. Touched by Earth's message, Apollicius reached out to her with his seven rays, two nimble enough to pluck her lyre producing a joyous ringing of each tone containing all tones. The Earth swelled with each chord and soon they could hear the characteristic birth sounds of a new moon born on board. Since the two spheres looked so similar back then, it was somewhat difficult to determine which had come from whom. But it really didn't matter, since both now formed the body of one instrument. It would be a while before the two separated, each to form its own integrated orbit.

The giant spherical globes served as the resonating gourd to maintain the sounding spark of the other planets on board. Voluminous and dish-shaped, the Sunship *reflected* the beginnings of the whole system's *map*. When Apollicius played more, each of the planets began to turn in the direction of the unrolling empyrean score.

Initially, each planetary code-of-the-tone turned into its own lodestone, possessing the power to attract as well as to be attracted magnetically. Following Earth's lead, each drew deeply from the rare and fragrant *Light* of Apollicius in an attempt to transmute their life substance into *dew*.

"Each of you is an instrument already emanating your own sound," Earth explained, "an instrument so valuable that without your specific tone sounding, the harmonious system of planets Apollicius endeavors to create would never be able to stay together as one system of the sun."

"I hear my note," shouted Mercury.

"And I mine," echoed Venus and Mars in unison.

Sounding their gigantic string instrument, both Earth and Moon continued to resonate under the strong yet light touch of Apollicius. It seemed strange that Apollicius had chosen the *Earth-Moon guitar* to be his instrumental star. If religion, at its root, means to bind and tie together, then that is exactly what their cosmic string music did. As player, Apollicius had the distinct advantage of already having *light fingers*. Through his corporeal movement in space he had, little by little, put his new system into place. His creators influenced him just as much as he affected their creations. This free interplay would lead to the gradual unfolding of the *All* from the Highly Charged Ray.

His laughter was sevenfold as he played on, planning his seven planets to eventually encircle his majestic *Light stronghold*. True Art is where the whole is viewed not as just part of the heart, but as that part made wholeheartedly.

From time to time the other planets, each with their individual chord, would see and pull the sounding oar on board. All of them evidently struggled to make space for the *coming one*, whom they saw in far-off lands wielding the *fiery bolt* with both hands. Apollicius could not hurl it down, rather, he produced it out of a grandiloquent band in sound and content.

"Who is that ponderous ball I see revolving in synchronization with the waves of lute notes? Strong, yet subtle enough not to be understood nor appreciated by all," wondered Mars.

"All of us have sprung from its heavenly seed, yet most of us are destined to follow. Only a very small number are prepared to leave their *land* fallow," Mercury added.

Most of them already felt that this most recent solar addition would be the strongest member of the belt. The music now had risen to the *symphonic space* level and become infinitely more majestic. Mercury put down his *brush-oar* and spread the *canvas* to the wind. From the lofty stratosphere to the lowest of heavens, the whole expanse of space shook.

Even Apollicius stopped his *creation playing* to *drink* in the rolling image coming closer and closer to them.

"He appears large enough to assail the very kingdom that played so energetically to conceive and nurture him," warned a worried Apollicius.

"He'll be the doom of us all if we don't give his revolutionary spin enough room," the Moon glowed gravely.

"Don't worry," replied Apollicius philosophically. "Within the harmonic progression I have spotted for this system, his gigantic space has already been allotted. Even so, we will obtain new harmonic proportions between the extreme motions of these two recently placed adjacent planets."

That said, Apollicius quietly ascended the harmonic scale of celestial sequence to where the library of tomes and tones was preserved, the secret archetypes of new worlds in the *Making*. The planet of Jupiter arrived without needing the presence of Apollicius. The sight of the largest member whirling into the egg-shape and being welcomed on as a new guest was a moment of sheer aesthetic arrest.

The *Sunship* teetered under the added weight as the other spheres struggled not to be dragged into the mammoth gravitational field of Jupiter. Seeing their plight from his scaled height, Apollicius shot down a long, *light beam* that Jupiter readily took to help hold his spot on the *team*.

Apollicius had developed the fountainhead out of which a flame of gold could be obtained from something as weighty as lead. He worked continuously with vast forms unseen to eyes other than his own. Out of the voluptuous folds of his luminous tunic, he passionately fashioned the sexual organs of flowers and fruit. He was betrothed to this formative energy aimed at sculpting royal souls as yet unclothed.

As the hour hands of the cosmic clock inched onward, new epochs were ushered in and old systems cracked and crumbled. During all this Apollicius yearned to see Helleniana again at the peak of her form. Though she had gone *under space*, she constantly revealed herself to him through *Visions*, images which fed and sustained his new system and constantly anointed his mind with esoteric perfumes. Solium still, undoubtedly, led the entire universe, but Apollicius was always present in his house to give support and be *light-fed*. Through his Father, he learned how to remain in a perpetual state of *centeredness* and directed and undirected alertness.

Apollicius sheathed his arrows and put away his bow, having finished hunting for the time being. Fishing season was upon him, and he felt that with this cast of planets he could at last begin to unreel his sound line and cast for streaking comets. If Solium was the bedizened *lord of light*, then Apollicius was one of his ministers to spread the mercurial word through the voice of his system's hottest sword.

Reaching deep into his molten center, Apollicius found and withdrew the flexible length of his glassy-smooth rod, one of the tools providing him with equipoise and ageless vitality. As with all of his more important generative aspects, the rod was both solidly magnetic, yet also equally *ether-like*. Similar to all rulers, he loved to hunt and fish. Yet, at present, the hunt took a rest while he turned to the *Waters of Marisium*, swathed in dark raiment, to feel the grace and fresh mildness of her morning dew.

The gentle ripples quietly undulating across this empyrean pond captivated his attention. He focused on the *form of the drop* inside his brain, which had once been so much a part of a cloud full of rain. He pictured his whole head as a drop on the verge of falling to the low-brow, watery surface or evaporating into the high brow of Marisium. His mind still remained an unknown darkened land upon which he sought to cast waves of light from one shore to the other. Marisium had first become the Space of the Universe by illuminating Solium. Without her he could never have become its *sole* provider and propagator. Now, with each planetary birth, she experienced no pangs, only sighs of mirth.

The drop appeared and disappeared continuously, an ethereal organism out of which is generated the celestial thundercloud. Before he reopened his eyes, Apollicius saw one more group of images. At the end of the rod, a head appeared from the same nebular origin as the drop. His arm serpentined around it to tighten the hold. Where he had cast was certainly in the right school; deep into the protoplasmic pool he dropped his *being-bait*, and this *planetary fisherman* then began patiently to wait.

"My planets and I are *co-uterine* brethren," mused Apollicius. "We have been gestated to grow as eggs all inside the vast lactic/galactic womb of Marisium. It is only by metamorphosing into a serpentine line that I can continue the work my Father, Solium, began so long ago in the space-loving arms of Marisium."

The line moved and writhed as a snake-like *fire mist* jetted through the sea. Deep down in the profundities the serpentine line and bait gently hooked an oval globe—a small submerged universe in tune with its course. Cradling the newly caught planet, Apollicius began to draw up the line of his extended *arm-self* as if he were a well reeling up its own crystalline waters. The tune he hummed as he pulled would be kept on the sound scroll called Neptune.

Born of the sea, Neptune could be quite tempestuous and at other times extraordinarily calm. Though a masculine planet, his secret wisdom would always appear through the female form of his elemental mermaids. Having been conceived as a sea within the *Spatial Sea of Marisium*, he was really a sea within a sea. There was one continuous, energetic line from its smallest flute-blown reed up through the arms of Apollicius and into his head of *Original Seed*. Neptune's *solar-fisherman-creator* believed so strongly in balance that he incorporated a specific sign to better align, which became known later on simply as the spine.

As a *planet of the sea*, Neptune was content to stay outside the *Sunship* in a supportive role. Up ahead, all could see a feeble glimmering: Apollicius setting.

"When I defeat these *Giants* who are always trying to break through the protective sheath of my *Light System*, I will absorb all of their power as working gods," Apollicius stated. "Then I'll have the wherewithal to touch the heaven of our own formation just by touching each one of your celestial bodies. Until then this heaven will remain a ground of Art not to be trodden upon."

"Whenever the dread fury of these *working giants* holds sway, we'll have to lower the sails and ply the oars. There is no other way," replied Mars.

"Solium once said to me: 'When Marisium and I first conceived the universe, all was pressed in and compacted inside the space of a tiny seed. Creation and creativity takes so much energy to stretch that small seed to its successive outer layers, that once a level or layer locks into place, an orbital plane is established and officially becomes its own space,'" Apollicius explained.

"He went on to explain what my mission was to be and for what purpose I had been conceived. I am here basically to forge new orbital planes of planetary movement. These *giants* are evil only insomuch as they strive to work outside these harmonious elliptical planes. To challenge them is to wrest new life energy from the talons of the tyrant. For the child to grow and be born, the womb must be stretched. It is this elasticity we worship so often in and through the periodicities of the *Cosmic Dance*. This system I am committed to bringing into being is a musical mansion with a sound scaffolding vouchsafed to us for safe holding."

"Our strength is not in our number but in our *integer*," Mars added. "If we are whole, then there should be no hole."

Apollicius closed his solar orb to visualize Helleniana. He immediately saw her attired in only the finest of galactic wear, drifting in and out of her crescent and half-moon phase, being her own sustaining force vibrating through waves of the primordial sea silence. When he was truly in her presence, he experienced an unbridled flood of images and sounds. For a moment he thought he heard her say,

"There are no margins of safety. There is no way to justify justifications. I *am* the ecstasy communicated to the brain, the liquid encapsulated knowledge of *rain*."

What she said or what he thought she said didn't really matter, it was so enigmatic yet completely clear. She was the flow he would one day have at his side, not to stem but to know. The web she was capable of constructing at any site in space could effectively influence the movements of his rays projected through the diamond of the ace. Her *beauty power* shaped itself through the whorled form of the flower.

Just as every person and every land has its *belt*, similarly, her circular dance could determine the way the course of the whole system felt. The circle of its circumference was the waist of the dance. This line was what kept it from going adrift. When the right belt was found and adjusted, attention was freed for the enchantment of a deeper need. This asteroid belt began as a simple plant shaped by the higher energy levels emanating in streams of light beamed down from Apollicius and the still-occult

Helleniana. They, in turn, were influenced by the upper worlds of old, namely, the brighter and larger stars, sounding in threefold.

Stretching and bending their strings of light around the plant produced the belt of a potential planet. At this stage, however, there were only heads of eight asteroids, mere parts of a potentially more complex sphere. The essence of this asteroid belt was the traveling sound vibration: sung from the mouths of Apollicius and the unseen side of the moon of Helleniana, blown from the first trumpets of creation, and accompanied with the struck, percussive beats on the cithara.

From the beginning of their quest till consummation, the *lines of light* trace a figure eight moving through universal space. This infinite eight is the insignia of the Order of the Ray. There is no art that cannot be resolved into this *musical ray,* from the primeval *monad* to the great cosmic serpent—it is the throbbing resonance of power immanent in all things.

The planetary *Sunship* continued onward, still influenced and aided supernaturally. Seen aloft, Solium viewed it as a new vehicle for the unfolding of the *Light.*

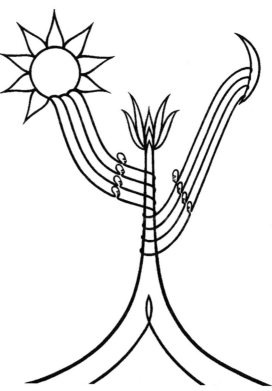

"I am anxiously anticipating hearing what becomes of the seventh orbital pathway," beamed Solium.

"I long to see you again, Solium, but I know you await the completion of my system, to secure my position in the Dance," countered Apollicius.

Apollicius knew that many of the forces of Marisium's Unconscious Space were at his side. There was still much he could not resolve with his great solar head, though the voice of his imaginative light spirit raged on. The strong will of his twin souls of *light and sound* quieted this voice, yet he still heard. The warm aroma of peaceful zephyrs protected his spirits from the danger of *black holes* and other sidereal traps and pits. At the crossroads of two powerfully moving epochs, Apollicius fortunately was not helpless to act. He seemed to thrive on this temporal shoreline between the two great ages.

Solium did not need to play upon his striking harp to enter the prophetic state needed to foretell the next step Apollicius would take.

"Though you are my *sun*, I do not and cannot bid or forbid anything of you. It is your sense of freedom, tempered with the ability and will to respond to your *call*, that determines all in the dance of your planetary ball."

Apollicius heard the voice of Solium as only sounds, because what he wanted was to form musical *spheres of rounds*. At the farthest reaches his imagination could stretch, he envisioned yet another great globe. Immediately he set to work to bring it into physical manifestation. The *Sunship* crew, sailing now upon the deep neptunium sea, drifted anchorless as it flew. Mercury, however, during this phase was at watch with his ever-kindled spark ablaze.

Mercurial before, the moon of Apollicius had gradually become saturnine. With the completion of his system in sight, his spirit neared the numinous state and tincture of the night. He took in a series of fiery breaths to draw up more energy to sling into motion. Lengthening one of his great rays, Apollicius reached far into the enveloping darkness to feel his full extension. Now he could see a flame within a flame—a spark to illumine the *Sun-ark*. He paused to think through his next step along the way. Then, seeing something that needed to be done, he started to do it. As a young sun, it was part of his work to sample freely his ample supply of beams.

Circling his flame into a loop, he flung its burning spear into the outermost rim of the *ethereal soup*. There he contacted a very distant and lethargic mass of energy. This was the last outpost of his system's outwardly turning egg-shaped universe where he was still host. The flame closed around a galactic incarnation of a phoenix—the frontier myth and legend. This great bird was both be-gowned and un-owned. The folds of its raiment had been draped prior to any outer interference; this was certain. Its headdress crown was like a charioteer's, replete with rainbow-hued down. Its wings unfolded from a robe, and after its first revolutionary turn, Apollicius named it Saturn.

"Consider me overseer of the *space frontier*, so I can soon call each of my necklace's beads an *under-peer*. I wear my own race isolated at the

boundaries of outer space," Saturn sang out with the voice resounding in a *ring*.

Saturn could feel one long arm of Apollicius encircling his young, bestudded neck. After tightening his furled hold sufficiently, the young Sun-Creator swooped around and, without warning, flung his freshly conceived *Saturn-phoenix*, together with his neck*race* into the far corner of his solar system. This whipping motion caught Saturn with his mouth agape. Startled, he involuntarily swallowed his neck*race*. What remained of its former presence was a huge ring, as radiant and full of light as if Solium himself had personally illumined it.

The *unmoved mover*, Solium, was in awe at how his wayward sun, Apollicius, had precipitated his *one* into many. Possessed by the *each-in-all* experience, he had rent himself asunder to build the moving and monumental art of his solar guild. It was a titanic project that had strained his enlightened back and serpentine-infused limbs. He had launched a tremendously fascinating mystery he hoped would be recognized and responded to.

The elliptical ring of Saturn corresponded to the shape of the *Sunship* crewed by the other planets. Now they both neared one another, measured each other, melded and merged. Neither demiurge nor the forces of cosmogony could separate any of them from their *system* nor the *system* from them; each was now integrated into the other and mutually dependent.

"I feel ready now to plan the creation of a true *light-being*, from spark to flame, to be a burning expression to my name," Apollicius declared.

Through sapphire, mixed with the azure sky, Apollicius focused his solar orb on an ancient form by crossing two of his *arm-lengthened rays*. The wandering planets cruising through the ether in their elliptical ship immediately spotted the cross in the heavens and waited to see if this phenomenon would spark a gain or ignite a loss.

Apollicius drew his inspiration from his memory of the *priestess of the cosmos*, Helleniana, in her state of fecundity. Energy poured out from him projecting streams upon which the immortal sparks could extend their flames. He was and had been for some time under the quickening influence of these intersecting twin flames.

"Primordial light, primitive atoms, seemingly unfathomable nature. as *sidereal architect* I will fashion this small cosmic world out of these chaotic waters," intoned Apollicius.

Thunder, not torn asunder, resonated within the deep chambers of his solar forge. The two flames melded into one, blazing in the direction of his planet-laden *Sunship*. Each of the planets observed before their ringed, terrestrial eyes the unfolding of this bounded field of energy.

"All of my forms are from Solium's whole. His parts, which I reflect through my arts, are not parts of this whole but the *whole* itself in smaller forms," Apollicius heard himself proclaim.

Light content forged its form to feel the vibration of its own sound enlarged. Apollicius stretched the long drone chord still connecting him to Solium, the central light source of the universe. From this link he drew the gray matter enabling the *Spirit* to move and think. All this occurred within the space temple—toned lapis lazuli—the womb of Marisium, the matrix, the ever-mother of the world, *creatrix*.

This electro-magnetic being had two poles of opposites joined as one from the admixture of two souls. Later these would come to be known as positive and negative, masculine and feminine, essential and quintessential. The key to the powerful energy this new being would generate was in its *even-sidedness*. All of its centers were light-tempered and sound-engaged. It was primed and well positioned for its first appearance in the Planetary Dance well timed.

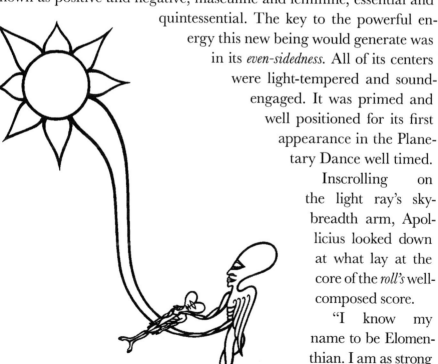

Inscrolling on the light ray's sky-breadth arm, Apollicius looked down at what lay at the core of the *roll's* well-composed score.

"I know my name to be Elomenthian. I am as strong as your light arm is long. For your system of planets to survive, they must provide a place on their elliptical ship where I can thrive. But first I need to cross their threshold at the exact spot in space where I am to arrive."

"You, Elomenthian, will be my first emissary to this interconnecting web of spheres from my *Solar Dispensary*. You are the physical embodiment of all the balanced elemental forces gathered together into the primordial being of my whirling garden of sound, movement, light, and delight.

Fourth Movement

Dissolution: *The dissolving or transforming*
of a substance into a liquid

Apollicius had a deep-seated sense of accomplishment with the progression of his planetary system. He had never felt more centered
than at that moment—feeling, hearing, and seeing his spherical creations in orbit around his blazing orb. His work had been long and arduous, creating a thirst so great he wondered if it could ever be quenched.
His system was just one of hundreds of thousands, all operating within
the Great Spiral of the Milky Way of Marisium.

It was the *way of milk* that sustained them all. Essentially, Marisium
was a breast of such cosmic proportions that all the newly born suns
could easily be suckled boundlessly. Her liquid milk had been light-infused and planet-building. Its electricity was what gave each particle of
each ray of light its sparkle.

He had come to the entrance of himself, the demiurge, standing on
the very threshold of beginning planetary rotation, with a foothold on
his system on the verge of revolution. What held him back? What *was*
holding him back? Stopping for a moment on his *light road*, he arched
down one of his arms and cupped a bowlful of the swirling milk paving
his way. As he drank, he realized what at that instant had become the
obvious: it *is* the pathway itself that maintains and sustains one's *vision*.

He was both literally and figuratively at that moment being fed by the *Milky Way*.

Ever since Apollicius had stepped outside the great cosmic walls so well defined by his father, Solium, he had been dealing with the *powers of the boundaries*. Only by yoking a mammoth mythical lion and boar together had he been able to continue pulling his *Chariot*, while sustaining an enthused roar. Now that he had his own *Sunship*, however, he was better equipped to make it through this trip. Even though his planets had been forged in his own *light foundry*, they were still young embryos, unprepared to cross too dangerous a boundary.

"What our *Sunship* needs is an elegant and gracefully sculpted maidenhead for protection through the galactic storms," Apollicius declared to the Universe.

Holding firmly both *lightning* as chisel and *thunder* as mallet, the Son of Solium began carving the maidenhead inspired by none other than his Muse, Helleniana. He *maid* the waist of the *huntress* lean-girthed as a lioness, then detailed the breast, well-turned the thighs, and fashioned the brown hips as smooth and round as the moon in his heaven. The neck received a conch shell shape spiraling to the head in sacred profile. Recognizing herself in the sculpture, Helleniana, still unseen, broke her silent picture.

"I am still undefiled," she began. "Glory to you, Apollicius, who fashioned and finished me as your maidenhead. Though, there I am finished, here I have yet to begin. When my real spirit enters that structural symbol, your *Ship* will travel unhindered and be barred by none of the galactic harbors. Until then, I drink from this libation vase to your whirling planetary base."

Apollicius listened to her startling revelation and learned from it. Without her guiding spirit, his pilgrimage would fall, he would be eclipsed and possibly even fail to rise again at all.

"My planets and I are now headed to a source of life-enhancing power, where we will leave all that Solium has given and penetrate into the *Mystery*," Apollicius said quietly, so that only he could perceive his own voice.

Nosing ahead, he guided his *Sunship* to the edge of its swirling system, where the serpent was the snake that eats his own tail to trace the

Cosmic Trail. The radiating image of Helleniana towered above the bow as it ploughed ahead, cleaving through the all-encompassing, serpentine ellipse. Breaking this barrier, this one infinitely long snake began to make itself over into the *heavenly seven*, each new snake rising up and out of the other as high as the eye could fly up that precious stake.

On the threshold of discovery, Apollicius himself, with the aid of the *all-powerful-serpent-in-seven*, rose up from the internal heat of the fire to form a majestically towering spire. He raised them each in his own way. Penetrating deep within his own foundry, Apollicius discovered the Chalice of Helleniana turned upside-down, symbolizing her absence from this newly created *Temple to the Sun*. Out of the mouth of the Chalice fell other *vessels* in a string of a *belle*—nine notes in an ascending/descending melody of the Bell.

To cross that forbidden *line of tradition*, Apollicius lifted up the very first Temple of Light, through the constant inspiration and dance guidance of Helleniana.

Now there could be a crossing. Neither Solium nor anyone else had *given* him this *Temple of the Enlightened Arts*. He had conquered it through the *fine art of pure struggle*. This all-important decisive step he had willed-into-being by uniting the *art of sculpture and music* into one *building erection*.

Each planet partially eclipsed another trying to see through the narrow passage lying ahead. A heavenly sphere was up ahead, read nightly to follow the plan of their planet rightly. Their globular shape had originally come from the serpent consuming its own tail at the center of the *fire-mist*. Now all seven quietly waited for Luck to help guide the command of Apollicius as he sought to pass through the narrow hallway of his newly constructed temple without getting stuck. The greatest torment can often be compacted within a mere moment. Leaving the protective railings of their *Ship* was to leave their only real security and also to risk new failings.

Being the smallest and the most fiery, Mercury ventured first.

"Either slip down into the *slime of time*," his voice rose to speak, "or set out into Unknown Space in search of the Sublime."

"The walls of the temple spaces are filled with the fragrance of an array of spices," uttered Earth as she too crossed the threshold dissolving the holdfast and its old dependence on the past.

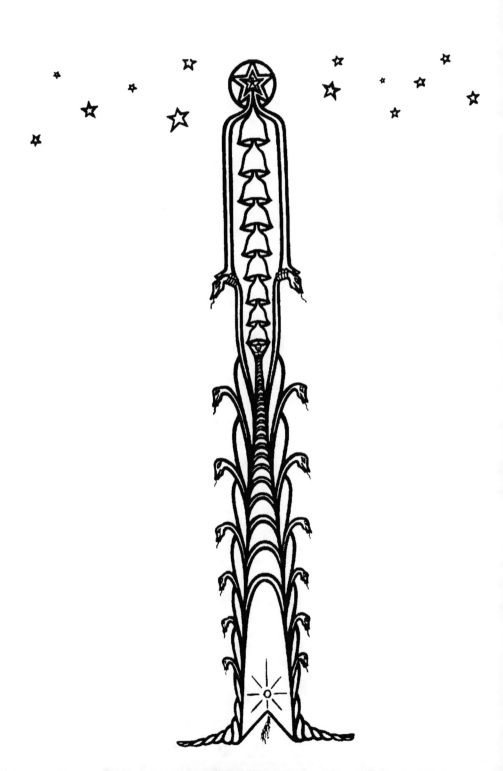

It is important to know that during these early light-years, the planetary system of the sun was not fixed in the configuration it later became. The planets themselves were malleable, moldable. Growing was flowing. Flowing was knowing. Vital symbols sounded as cymbals, and as the other planets filed through the temple door and down the sidereal halls of towering twin cliffs, they made their own tone resonate off the parallel walls. Each bell tolled their own distinctive sound according to the planet's height and size as it rolled through. The largest bells loomed near the apex of the Solar Temple, so consequently hitting the largest planet produced the deepest sound. This was the real beginning of what later became known to all as the *Harmony of the Spheres.*

"I had to reorganize my being into the *nine tones of the sirens,*" Helleniana spoke, once more breaking her signet of silence, but still remained unseen. "Rather than being lured into a rocky coast for destruction, the sound provided new planetary ground for construction." There were two extra-orbital pathways unnamed in the beginning, completing the nine levels of individual planetary initiation and realization. The microcosmic/macrocosmic dynamic had been there ever since the first Orders of Solium. Each of the nine Muses had her own seductive sound correlating to her appropriate planetary shell. All their movement arose out of this sound, overseen by Helleniana, aided and protected by the spatially all-encompassing—Marisium.

Successfully navigating the treacherously narrow passageway, the planet's *Sunship* streamed on through.

"We are not so slowly dissolving," exclaimed Neptune, who was already a pure sea solution. "My basic nature is to gather all that *flows* and give it *current.*"

This Neptune did, sending his spherical brothers all charged up ahead and swiftly moving towards the universal curve in the Path. The dividing *line belt* soon began to melt as the *Dance of the Dance* grew. The difference between apprentice, fellow crafter and master of each planet depended on their coming and overcoming temptation and their overall preparation for the crowning.

"Though I'm not the largest," Saturn churned, "I'm the heaviest and the moodiest of you all. The bell I rang when I passed through the *temple,* I have to become in body and in tone. I see that the great vase of Marisium, the space-mother, has compressed herself into the materialization of a visible form toward which the planets now all freely stream, half headed for upper realms and the others turned sharply downward in the direction of self-destruction and dissolution." After the entrance to this zone of magnified power, they had all beamed in different directions. Their system would eventually be bound in the four directions, plus "up" and "down," to define the limits of their own individual spheres and life horizons. Without Helleniana, however, darkness, the unknown, and danger pressed in all around them.

Those who had descended traced the Great Side of Initiation of their colossal Cosmic Archway, which the *ascenders*—the lighter planets—had circumscribed. Though the joyous ringing of the bells had diminished after their initial threshold crossing, that inner tone of resonance each had acquired still vibrated with their every movement to further the *Dance*. This powerful sound was both the treasure *and* the arched rainbow their orbital paths traced with deep pleasure.

Music brought into play the vital energies of the whole gamut of the planetary psyche. By degrees, Apollicius found his way to the larger structures of composition and began to phrase deeper hierarchies of sound, enabling the placement of each planet at the level of its actual phase. In this way, he began to musically place the drama of greater spans of time into an increasingly larger and more complex sound panorama. Apollicius not only developed his own *system of light* through the use of sound, but began to feel slightly closer to Helleniana, the spatial daughter of the vast expanse of *Marisium.*

In the last fleeting glimpse Apollicius had had of Helleniana, she had worn a cerulean cloak spangled with stars. Her *wings* had flapped gracefully, content to be deeply engaged in writing and carried a bundle of letters in every language under her wing. Poised with a silver trumpet pressed to her lips, she had retold the story of the birth and quickening spurt to maturity of the young planets. Now, it was up to Apollicius to take the nine primordial rhythms of the Muses and weave them into a compositional piece to help each sphere stay on its true path of revolution and overcome the temptation to waver by trying to leave.

Inventing *Music* organized the poetic frenzy inspired by the nine Muses. Apollicius had begun to train himself, through his own *sound system,* to maintain a genuine psychological readiness to confront these seductresses.

"The real source of all our true nourishment is you, Marisium, the Sacred Cow of dimensionless space," Apollicius said. "We contact you and drink your milk by milking our own instruments given to us by your Muses. What could be more natural than, after the *bell,* to be rewarded for our perseverance in the *Spiral Dance* with the *conch shell?*"

String playing and hand-clapping, followed by the flute and drum ensemble led up the final crescendo. A clap of thunder punctuated the sound sentence extending throughout the space of the *seven-skinned eternal Solium-Marisium Universe.* Out of this sonic plane of Tonal Beings, waves gradually unfurled into higher and higher peaks breaking up the plain.

"Once in the *musical fold,* a *man* created from my Spark is manifold," Apollicius said to himself while contemplating this marvelous system of symbolism beginning to emerge all around in bold.

Presently, each planet began to intermix with the *new beings* in long fluid turnings. Whatever movement was under the surface broke through as the darkened night unraveled to slant upward and radiate with renewed sight.

"It is a mere wave dividing the *unseen* from the seen, the *still to be played* from the played, the *unrealized* from the realized, and the *not yet molded* from the decoded," Apollicius reflected.

"From you I have finally received a *sol staff* to support my *sol*ar weight.

This will be our sole threshold ally to carry us through the labyrinth and on toward the *center of the soul,*" he went on.

The planets and their future inhabitants were the warp and woof of this sign and symbol of all symbols. This was their *living god* connecting them from the changing ground to the most intricate and long-distance star sound.

"We are all one elaborately whorled musical configuration," Earth observed.

"And what ultimately bonds us to the *light-flame* of Apollicius is the Path of the Music leading eventually to Helleniana, the Muse," added Mercury.

Listening to his Planetary Beings converse, Apollicius added his verse: "A unique tone has been inflected through all the *colorations* of my planetary cone. Heavenly spheres and spheres of sound now share the same transcendental ground."

"We *are* really dissolving," thundered Jupiter, who for the first time actually felt the spear of fear that he might disappear. Perhaps, since he was the largest, he was the first to be hit the hardest.

"We have crossed through the veil of the *familiar* and are now disintegrating into that unknown field of foreignness," Jupiter said, nearly crippled in nervous anticipation of what would come next. "I can literally feel and clearly see chunks of me flung into the depths of my own atmosphere. It is all happening at a rate not wholly pre-determined by fate."

"Jupiter, you must maintain your poise, in spite of all this great rumbling noise," counseled Apollicius. "Let the others be fed by the sheer altitude of your attitude. Once I strayed beyond the protective boundaries of tradition, I knew that whatever I made as I prayed would be beset, and already is beset, by *demonic attacks* coming out of the *lightless shade.*"

Though not quite as large as Jupiter and quite a bit denser, Saturn perceived his massive body dwindling at a fairly rapid rate. He, however, was not impassive. So many pieces of himself were ripped away as he catapulted through space that they formed a ring around the main body of himself. The note that could be heard when this *new snake* bit its tail rang out across his disk and helped to soothe and ease all that was at stake and had been put at risk.

All great beings undergo a life of dramatic metamorphosis, and the planets of Apollicius were no exceptions. It was just that their change was on a solar/galactic level. What had appeared so solid in their early beginnings was now not so slowly breaking apart.

They had already begun to disintegrate as a planetary group, when all became momentarily quieted by the seldom-heard voice of Solium.

"Once the heel crosses the *threshold*, it becomes possible to escape the grinding, leave the din of helter-skelter, and enter the den of serpent shelter. To reintegrate, you need first to disintegrate."

"That's wonderful, mighty Solium, but we're here to revolve, evolve, and create," responded Earth, who had been especially quiet in the midst of their present disorder.

The harsh, raucous, terrifying sounds continued to disrupt the cruise of the *Sunship*. At the moment there could be no return to the enchantment of the musical tones of their spheres as gargantuan *sounding stones*. Apollicius stretched out a horn with his upraised solar ray to try and call order into the day:

"Musicians, Priests of the Cosmos, you are needed to bring your straight and cross flutes of compassion, both single and double-reeded."

The Priests were apparently attending other more urgent cosmological feasts and did not appear, even transparently.

"As *planet-kings*, we swear to answer to our own questionings," thundered Jupiter, rocking their ship with his voice.

"Let us ask not to return to any former state, but rather, plunge further onward, enamored with our own fate," Jupiter continued.

Their young solar system, besieged by a tumultuous beginning, sailed into the shore-less ocean of endless *being* surrounding and *bounding* their cosmos, like some fabulous serpent engorging its own tail. By taking their first *step* into the zone of the *Source*, they had begun their own process of dissolution, a prerequisite to graduating to a *degree*.

Awakened in the night by the voice of Solium, Marisium arose out of her chalice containing all of Space and went to help Apollicius and his young solar race.

"The adventure is always and everywhere a *passage through an aperture*," she whispered into the light-effused ear/era of Apollicius.

"Pour your light through my glass and see all the *colorations* of your *planet/planetation* refracted into bands of a succeeding class," she urged.

Apollicius complied with her request and readily saw how it helped them continue their quest. The snake—melding with his own tail in her, in him, and in them—encompassed the Grail.

Out of her glass goblet flowed a liquefied gas of *seed-let*. The planets of Apollicius had undergone yet a further transformation from solid to their former liquid state. This time, however, they immediately burst into plant life. Now the cycle was complete, from plant to planet and back to plant. This new plant incarnation, however, was different from the previous one. Each new germination had compressed within its head an entire planet generation. All of them, reborn from Marisium's natural chalice horn, had been thoroughly surprised at the sudden disintegration and dissolution they had just undergone.

"Now we know that our size cannot be measured materially, since we all can be fragmented and dissolved so quickly and easily by the Universe," Venus said. Whatever dimensions we attain externally have little to do with the real strength of power we must always be vigilant to maintain internally." She rarely spoke, content to merely *be* and to radiate beauty. But now, she too had been deeply affected by the sudden turn of events and had been marked just like the other planets.

"In a sense, we must all begin again," advised Mercury. "The difference now is that we still have our memory of what we were for that brief span of time. Memory is the greatest of all the Muses. By calling upon Apollicius, maybe he can connect us to his principal Muse, Helleniana."

Apollicius knew all about descending in order to re-ascend. He also knew that, though often everlastingly painful, it was the *Way*—had always been the *Way*. It was a universal dictum: *must descend to ascend.*

"Jupiter would have wanted to hurl his thunderbolt," he thought to himself. Now he would have to re-cultivate his *mind-born* progeny in his *garden of the divine vine*. For Apollicius, this was all symbolic and metaphorical. Their spheres were still there, each in their orbital shell aboard his *Sunship*, yet their intimate beings had been replanted. Being seeds, *they* sometimes became unaware of the shell.

"First we kneaded the physical form, now we focus on what is *really* needed," Apollicius declared to his new *planet garden*. his *planetation*.

"Dissolution of the new solution. Dissolve in order to evolve. Even in my *material of forms*, I'm only semi-solid," confided Mercury.

"It makes no sense to allow oneself to become dense."

"*Architectonics in tones*," expounded Venus. "Through music one melts, dissolves, to become *orbital sound belts*. It's all just vibration no matter what physical form the body assumes as one's norm."

Terror and bliss, alternating, seized the consciousness of this most recent *sidereal garden* of Apollicius. Individuation had collapsed in their innermost *planted-planetary* depths. Neptune had immersed himself in his own Sea of Thought, while looking across the *garden-space* at the Harvest Moon moving around Earth.

Earth had lain her worldly self down and stretched out her fully extended plant-length before speaking: "After this descent, I am not even fearful of the fabled Leviathan. I've heard that certain species navigate these cosmic seas of ours, better known as the *Unknown Sea Garden*. There is a *star-rose* made of pearl in my stomach, the tint of my silver moon. As it grows, we will embark on our long journey, from which this garden spot will later be seen as minimal as a small dot."

Apollicius led each of them by their long, *leaf-like* hands to the garden's edge and admonished:

"From this ledge on, your only supportive arm will come from your individual degree of self-knowledge."

Quickly, storm clouds descended and enclosed each planet's intimate plant in a state of *quantum rain*.

Fifth Movement

Digestion: *The slow modification of a substance*
by means of a gentle heat

Solium and Marisium vibrated as the Progenitors of the Cosmos—two aspects of the same Universal Source. Depending on the moment and the mood, each could easily appear as the other, especially when hunting for food. All of the largest beasts they later created out from the soaring of their Divine Imagination were present inside them from the beginning: whales, elephants, Sacred Cows, lions—even dragons, winged bulls and all the possible kinds of serpent creatures.

Being both the male and female sides of the Cosmos, they were and still are *cosmos parents*. The Central Sun was born out of the *Womb of Space,* and *Space* can be seen only because of *his Light*. Now, both Marisium and Solium exchanged roles intermittently between the Sacred Cow and the Winged Bull. Whatever their form, they had been ravenous of late, as if it had been light-years since they last ate. An appetite as large as theirs could only begin to be whetted by the thought of devouring an entire planetary system. They never fed themselves in a sequence of courses, however, but only on a *Planetation of Consequence*—with no "remorses." Beyond, above and below, they saw how healthy and strong their planets had grown as re-seeded plants.

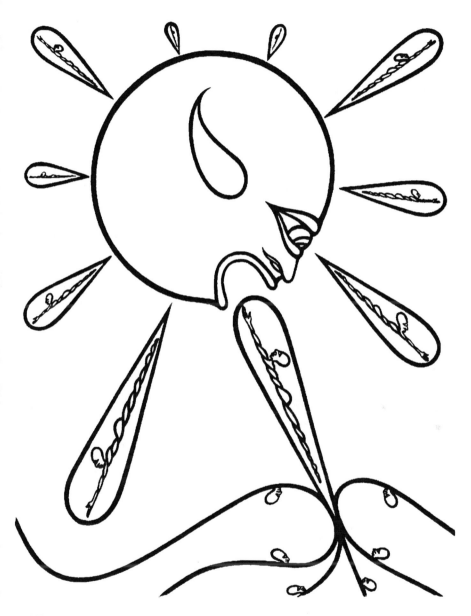

"I cannot resist the temptation," admitted Solium, who had now merged with Marisium.

"Neither can I," confessed Marisium, who spoke through the open mouth of Solium. Instead of crossing swords, they crossed words to cross-fertilize their work of such scale and extraordinary size.

Each of the planets had grown quickly, and all seven actually seemed eager for the harvest to begin. Their transformation inside the Temple Garden had been all-embodying. At the temple door, their outer spheroid characters *in the rough* had been shed much like a snake loses its slough. Once inside, the only real protection was faith in *no* protection.

"To reach this inner garden of the Sacred Cow and the Winged Bull, I fought off the dragon's flame, the lion's roar, the drawn swords of evil-slayers, and belligerent dwarfs," Mars declared, "along with other assorted and sundry fantastic creatures the *waterspout* had formed. They were not just gargoyles of imaginative fancy, but were really threshold guardians who flanked and defended all approaches to the *Stomach Temple*."

"We are in search of the highest order of silence within these *abdominal walls*," confirmed Venus.

Meanwhile, inside the Space of Marisium, Solium descended towards the rolling *Planetary Field*. The planets saw the gargantuan mouth form as they combed the *seven nights*, but were not afraid. As planets, they had been planted, cultivated, and nurtured to one day be *food* for their creators.

"Look at the marvelous feast rising up below us as if they were bread loaves containing yeast," murmured Solium.

The closer Marisium came, the hotter the rays of Solium *baked* the Planets. Clearly, they had melded for this special banquet occasion. Engraving a circle in the air, each reflected something of the other as they quickly approached the Temple Garden of *Planetation*.

"I am the closest to Apollicius and therefore the warmest. Ingest me first and then proceed on to the rest," offered Mercury.

That, they did, and then one by one they moved on. swallowing each of the *planted pilgrims* whole.

"Thanks for pulling us up and away from the *sticky attraction of our own glue*," said the incurably optimistic Venus.

"By being consumed, we can leave this planet-bound bodily *garb* and its *age* of material *garbage*."

Some of the Planets saw, as they were being eaten, other beings inside the *shone rays* of Solium and Marisium.

"Were they also eaten by you?" wondered a curious Jupiter—who would be a real mouthful for them.

"All bodies, heavenly or not, pass through similar processes of birth, death, and rebirth," the voice of Solium surrounding Marisium clarified.

"Before they joined my central essence, they all had to go through a series of trials and adversities in order to completely slough off all their former phases of planetary existence and other material perversities. Each one of my rays stands for one of the Nine Spheres of Light Investiture. I look forward to at least some of you one day joining to help complete this luminous picture."

Jupiter seemed satisfied with Solium's response as he stoically prepared himself to be uprooted, eaten, and finally annihilated. Soon, when the entire crew had been engorged, Solium-Marisium began to chew. The teeth of these two juggernauts were composed of jagged light patterns and entered the *Planet-Plants* like small strikes of glistening sabers with cutting, zigzag movements. What the planets couldn't see cut them like a saw. What they saw up ahead was a burning sea—a pool of frothy drool.

Pound for pound, each of their round bodies was chewed, mashed, and finally ground. Terror gripped most of them with the collapse of their individuation. As they all moved toward what they believed to be the roaring pits, they strove to regain a sense of their whole from their few remaining bits. Clearly, they were being resized after their *stable Sunship* had capsized.

A dark foreboding stirred in the hearts of each member of the *force*, as they plunged inward through this hollow gorge and onward toward a *source*. Not even the tiniest ray leaked into this cavernous, sheltered bay. Who had ever heard of such a moat extending the whole length of this unnaturally abysmal throat?

Little by little, literally in bits and pieces, they left their material center of gravitation to later be drawn into the loftier realms of the higher energy levels of a different dawn. Once, their lives had influenced their outer turnings, whereas now most of their conscious moments were caught up in the upheaval of these inner churnings. Still, they kept up their spirits and even managed to converse between themselves now and then.

"We were once fashioned of stardust," Saturn began cautiously. "Now we have been so pulverized that we have returned to it."

"Yes, but it is out of dust that we must rise again," Jupiter affirmed.

"All food digestion is followed by a period of good gestation," Earth remarked, determined to maintain her spirit even throughout total dissolution.

Since the real digestion would not occur until they reached the main body of the temple sanctuary, they slid through this *throat tunnel* as merely travel-stained and haggard planetary pilgrims clearly out of the ordinary.

"Let's try and remember to appear to be able to spear the fear," Mars suggested, bolstering both his own confidence and that of his fellow sphere beings.

The darkness they now entered seemed so black that, both their bodies and beings were figuratively and literally swallowed up by light's lack.

"We're heading toward the Bosom of Marisium," Venus said, suddenly feeling expansive for no particular reason. "To rest in her *blossom.*"

"Are we moving closer to the *Stygian Shades?*" Earth wondered, "Or are we moving through a tunnel to lead us upward to an outward-flowing funnel?"

All of a sudden there was a rumbling so deep that all the planetary wanderers were shaken to bits—or, rather, to smaller bits.

"We have returned you to the Source of Darkness to encounter the *original voice*. past the guardians of the last choice," explained Solium.

"The rumbling you hear comes from your own *voice* in its *box*," added Marisium.

"Now is when things really start to heat up. You won't be at the *palace* until you recognize its *face*."

Solium and Marisium *were* the Cosmic Larynx, the links between thought and action, water and fire, form and faction. At the end of their *voice tunnel* began the Ring of Fire. One was the flame and the other the flicker. One spoke, the other was the *unspoken*. One broke and the other the *unbroken*. One was the good and the other the *understood*. One lived and the other thrived.

"The *tunnel loop* to Paradise goes through our *fire hoop*," Marisium and Solium declared together.

"We turn to ash all embodiments of elemental forces unbalanced by love, and temper desire with a wing of the dove. We devour the unchecked passions of the beast deep within the cauldron of every planetary feast. In the profundities of our viscera there is a flash just past the last level of rotundities."

The egg-shaped Ring of Fire was their kingdom's *sole* diadem. Every place the former planets looked, they saw the metallic flashings of the discus and the mace. After being crushed to dust, they welcomed the fire to transfigure the last bits of their former orbital shell, which they were more than ready to retire.

In the center of the *blazing oval*, Jupiter exclaimed: "Our shell, reduced to powder sifts down to *hell*, though I feel my real essence rising as incense—an offering to the Light and Space presence."

"Though we are a realm apart, this moment could be my first clear feeling of a place for the Spirit to restart," stated Saturn lucidly.

The peregrination of these planetary beings had not been an *unchosen* journey. Each sphere had been its own divine pole of actualization. At their acme of realization, Apollicius could imagine one of his creations saying to the other: "There goes the universe, followed by the cosmos."

Passing through the Ring of Fire was an entrance into the tomb and the womb. It was that inviolable space of simultaneous death and rebirth, where the oval and ellipse are called egg-shaped. Since none of the spheres had lost their deeply ingrained sense of tragedy, they had avoided that *real* tragedy. They were all ready and willing to be revived and converted into *spiritual spheres of revolution.*

In a way their own awareness of total reduction to dust and ash had enabled them to penetrate into another source of power. There, inside the entrails of their producers, could be found the faintly visible imprints of fresh trails.

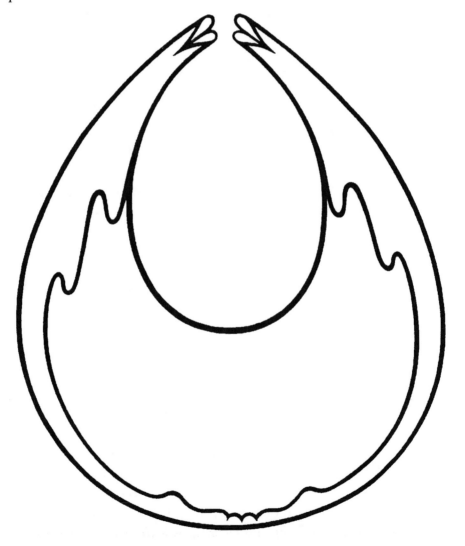

"Look at the way our ashes have been strewn on this abdominal surface, as smooth as a precious stone well-hewn," began the inspired voice of Mercury.

"Imagine finding the way following a linear design of one's own remains," Earth said, lost in deep reflection.

"What has been left over is the balance—therein lies the equilibrium to continue the Planetary Dance," Mars contributed. "This is an incredible opportunity to find the spiral curve by following our own *planet-prints.*"

On the other side of the Ring of Fire was the edge of the Great Inner Sea—the same Sea of Marisium that Apollicius had swum in, except that she then had swallowed it, or at least most of it.

"This is my home," cried Neptune, breathless with joy.

Each wave of the *ocean of vibrations* washed over their grain-like bodies still in the form of pulverized dust and volcanic ash. Like the sands of ages, had it been for their intimate spirits, one grain would be indistinguishable from the next, just waves, particles, and sound. It was the latter that would eventually prove to be the determining, transformative factor. This shoreline was a hotbed of potential energy influxes and kinetically cosmic permutations.

It was as if Marisium, having swallowed part of her own galactic seas containing this Solar System, held it now in her *belly dish*—while she still freely moved like some sidereal *jellyfish.* Her jaws were as incisive and invisible as her laws. Once transgressed, comets would clash, meteors would mash, and planets would splash. In this present situation, however, it was Apollicius who had erred with Helleniana—leading to the collapse of his system. With his system down, he was even more determined to actively pursue the encounter with Marisium's whirling body inside the flowing sea gown.

Her entire *belly* was egg-shaped—being the egg content *and* its oviform. Solium, the principal substance of *the dance,* was the yolk. The stage had been set and all the main props of particle and waves were in place for a cataclysmic revolution within the sonic bounds of her engulfed space.

Without warning the two shores of her *inner sea* rose up in *ovoid grandeur.* At each of the highest tips, which, moments before had been shores, protruded a sensuous set of lips. This was the way the Space of Marisium gave the *Lord of All Creation* an embrace. The true and timeless temple always finds itself in a continual process of metamorphosis. A temple not undergoing continual transformations loses its inherent gestating powers to house revelations.

When their lips met an entirely different sidereal scene was set. Every granule of cosmic dust, part of a sophisticated spherical organization felt a profound, emotive stirring. Both sensually and extrasensorily perceived, not one of the *seven spirits* failed to be revived.

"To be reduced to nothing means nothing unless you are able to encompass its beatitude," Saturn said, recalling how he had formerly been ringed in many levels of transcendent quietude.

"Only then will we understand the virtue of being in the center of ourselves, the belly-womb, the universe, anything," added Jupiter, who because of his size had always unofficially considered himself at the center of the *planetary spirit*.

They, however, were still in the *sea-driven belly* of Marisium and Solium. Some of the planets, Earth in particular, were at moments terrified of the absolute silence. She had not totally embodied it. In a sense, she was still partially covered and not yet ready to be fully discovered. Mars, on the other hand, was more inclined to dramatic initiation, than to a complete acceptance of this silence that had come with such finality after their wild tidal wave expedition.

"I would prefer to withstand clashing comets," Mars said, "to star shards cutting through our orbit, or even darting mammoth meteors that could easily crush a young planet's mountainous backbone into cosmic dust (like us now) and once in a while a terrifying supernova rising up ominously to overwhelm our whole system of axis rotation and elliptical revolution."

The *Serpent* that had once encircled their whole universe had begun to unfurl so slowly that her movement was completely imperceptible to any of the still-naked *dust planets*. Under her magical cape, she had a pair of small wings attached to her neck's nape. Because she was a serpent, her nape was everywhere and nowhere. It could be argued that she was one long neck which stardust loved to bedeck. This Serpent and Marisium were not separate entities. One was an extension of the other. Marisium was both the one who surrounds and the surrounded, both the founder and the unfounded, both the sounder and the unsounded.

Her curve, however, had not always been closed into the form of a symmetrical oval. It was embedded deep inside her nature to coil and un-coil, to boil and toil. Marisium was well aware of what she bore within her belly's *walls*—the planetary family of Apollicius that she had swallowed up. Apollicius had managed to remain in the sidereal, nocturnal wings of this cosmic theater, while Marisium and Solium stayed in the *floodlights*. He had by his side, however, the first being of his creation: Elomenthian. Elomenthian was totally self-contained; that was how and why he had remained through the cataclysm securely main-tained. Light flowed through his veins and flashed to the *central rod* of his spine in light-ning-fast time. He was a pure seedpod with the outer shape of what would

one day be known as a half-god—half light and half night—the chaste blend of Apollicius and Helleniana.

His Planetary System gone, Apollicius had turned to the survivor, Elomenthian.

"You must work with me for the reappearance of your Mother and our Muse of Song and Dance."

"I will, my originator," Elomenthian replied. "I think I know why she hides, how to come to understand her complex being of so many sides."

"Let's begin at once to retrieve her," Apollicius said excitedly.

"Listen to her voice, and you won't need anymore my advice."

Elomenthian vibrated as if luminous beams had been sown into his nerve seams. After the whole Solar System had been swallowed, he had become homeless. Now, to please Apollicius, he would set off to find his Muse, by tracking her voice using the traditional harp as his directional instrument of choice. He, too, had to travel up the *Serpent of Marisium* in search of Helleniana leading to the *Land of Vision* where he believed she had hidden herself away.

Marisium wasted no time reabsorbing all of the "dust planets" into her serpentine system. They and the snake now became one long and winding stake. Marisium rose up and in one powerful movement shook free from her own bounds by sloughing her skin, which had once encompassed all of Apollicius's planetary kin.

During this dramatic moment Elomenthian grew tremendously in size, nourished by the life-enhancing sound sustenance provided inside the Belly of Marisium's digestive maze. The harp chords extended up and out from the top of his spinal chord. This sound carried him up and onward, giving him hope of really encountering Helleniana.

Marisium the Serpent undulated toward her Void, pulling her long, sinuous body through the *Land of Visions,* where all eyes were focused on her *Dance of the Ovoid.*

"It seemed strange to have Elomenthian filling my womb," Marisium said softly.

"What was lost can be found, depending on the cost and where it has wound around," she continued.

Were it not for the light arms of Apollicius shooting discharged particles sparkling with energy into the cosmic *whale-size* Belly of Marisium, his entire system would have *really* collapsed from within. At bottom, it is light beams that support any sidereal roof. The ceiling reaches only as far as it is lighted. Beyond that—who knows?

Initially all newborn planets bathe in their milky light before they mount "Lightning" to explore all within their right. From that moment on, their whole existence is built on a light-emanating scaffolding made from *particles of waves,* who were taught inside the fantastic *Belly of Marisium* how to drink difficulties like a draught. Essentially they had all repaired to her Inner Temple to be aired after their dissolution. Their dust would rise again, take form, and be put into motion.

This was a period of intense activity for Apollicius, who had risen to

new heights in the process. Plenitude of power and moderation were two seemingly antagonistic poles operating within his system's field of developmental light. In the end, to achieve the absolute beauty of his *planetary system*, he would need to hammer it out on the anvil of his experience of pain and ecstasy. The weapon/tool of this process could be none other than the Thunderbolt he already possessed locked away with key and bolt. The time had arrived to turn to the powerful Jupiter:

"I impart the thunderbolt to you to help me give the other planets a *light and sound* jolt."

"You may have slightly diminished inside this cavernous belly, but your light is as intense as ever," replied Jupiter, feeling his body react to the power of the light-infused volt. "I can already hear the rumbling of thunder inside my huge head."

"That may be the grumbling of the vast Belly of Marisium, where we've all become her favorite aliment," Apollicius told Jupiter.

"Though we have been eaten, swallowed and digested, we can still whirl with our energy field—that as planetary forces, we can willfully wield," Earth contributed.

"The visions I once had, to create the conditions to undergo this test, were gifts from that great realm of the Invisible Unmanifest," Apollicius went on, "taught to me by the *Divine Thunderbolt*—containing knowledge from way beyond the sphere here of names and forms."

Dominated by the liquid element, thus commenced the period when each *dissolved member* of the Solar Family not only felt protected by the *pollen*—a symbol of their *way of honey*—but, literally had become this dust like-pollen of their former plant-selves. This being so, they could be said to be the *incarnation of fecundation*, being both the path itself, and its symbol.

"At certain moments I feel I am made of only my arms whirling as a wheel," Apollicius began again. "And that I am encompassed, but still capable of encompassing. These *arms* can still pound out notes on a *galactic keyboard* as a smith shapes a sculpture, yet still emit light lines of energy radiating from this blazing *axle*."

As Apollicius parted his *center curtain*, mountains of colors peaked, faulted, and unfolded to reveal a series of concentric orbs—all with their own *arms* reaching outward toward the *corralled galactic farms*. Apollicius drew strength and puissance from the four directional corners of Marisium's *Inner Abdominal Space*. Once he had been tiller, then hunter; now was his time to be *fisher-sun*. The *lifeline* throbbed through the *light line*. These *light lines* had been woven like strings of musical chords all bound within his hermetically closed world of sound. It was time to release these melodically structured sunrays. The *rod* was a *sound staff*, a prescribed *tonic* used as a lure to cast away into this euphonic pasture.

Apollicius cast his *tune* both far and near, hoping that the dismembered crew of his *Sunship* would congregate around to hear. If they took the *sound bait*, he would know it had been a *catchy tune*, and he would have them on the hook.

Within this boundless expanse containing all things inside the *belly/womb* of Marisium, the minute clusters of pollen spontaneously began to generate slightly larger meteor-like *heads* in the proportionate size and shape of their former planetary selves. These globules were unplanted *bulbs* ready for their light to ignite, ready to move from this inner dim void to the outer rim of the globoid.

"I crave to be hooked again on Apollicius's line," Mercury declared joyously. He knew Apollicius spoke through his many spokes, extending from his core to each of the planets' highly sophisticated and refinery-stored energy score.

Space-of-Marisium was really a behemoth *whale-cow* who did not swim in a sea—she was *both* the sea *and* the beast. She was a gentle monster of indefinite form defined only by the *dance of her substance*, whirling in ecstatic movement following the Breath of Solium. While dancing, she always moved her voluminous midsection, causing violent rumblings inside—and turning up a lot of planetary-meteor dust. She was so all-pervasive, that whatever moved with a certain level of grace could be said to have been influenced by her swirling, cone-shaped shell of space.

She could be seen in the folds of a river, in blowing dust, in craggy hills, and throughout the cosmos, circumambulating the luminous mist of Solium. She was the revelation of the swinging nebulae, an amalgam of the unnumbered and the unremembered. She was steadfast and long-last, the epitome of an illicit union of the movement of color and the tone of sound. If Solium could blaze through the *Eye*, then Marisium spiraled the shape of the *Ear* on the face of Creation. She heard every bit of movement manifesting itself in the life of the *Spirit*. While Apollicius fished inside her, she breathed the fragrance of ambrosia all over their gyratory *mass*, enacting the rite of the resurrected meteorite. She, in effect, was the High Priestess for the transmigration of the planetary souls created by Apollicius. *Meteoroid metempsychosis* took place within her vital void, or in other worlds, the Metabolism of the Spirit.

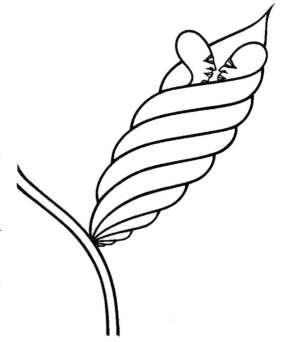

These *spirited spheres* went from plants to stones and then from bare bones to becoming rare *planetary tones*. Their soul came from their sun's note *sol*, and to that it would return. From the raw plant, to the *cooking crew*, to the burning brew, the Womb of Marisium had served as their caldron where the oven was always on. Tending to their vine equaled blending with their *oval divine*.

"I am the *throb* resonating within," muttered Venus, considering *to be caught* by Apollicius as fortuitous.

"At a certain blissful moment, the *fisher-sun* and the fish on the run are both fraught as one," Mars added.

"To the background of the cacophonic rumbling of comets tumbling, our boon is in the harmonic majesty of this *giant cocoon*," Earth proclaimed in an inspired voice.

"We are certainly ready for a *vacation* now inside the *acres* of this *Sacred Cow*," Neptune suggested blissfully.

Venus spoke up again. "We have gazed into her abyss so long that I believe we now want to fuse to her in a sidereal kiss."

"In many ways we have certainly died to time by returning to the *spiral womb* inside the Belly of Marisium," Saturn added. There was a certain sadness in his voice owing to the loss of his rings, which had not so long ago been subtracted from him.

Apollicius listened thoughtfully to the many notes of their spherically tonal voices. Out of the chaos of their dissolution, he felt ready to will another order of evolution. Each of the nine levels of planetary movement was either positively or negatively charged, with either a masculine or a feminine spirit assemblage. with the exception of the first level closest to the Sun. Mercury was a hybrid of a continually flowing liquid and an equally ever-forming solid.

Apollicius grouped the planets into mutually attracting pairs and placed each couple into a helical sarcophagus, which he then spun into a *chrysalis*. In place of new moons, this unparalleled *planetary tree* yielded *fruits of many cocoons*. Apollicius's hands had personally wound each doublet into mellifluous bands of sound.

"I commit each of you to *Galactic Nature*," he spoke radiantly, "then twirl all of you around a larger spindle, so your spirit will not dwindle. You are heads separated from the *fountain*. a mountain to surmount separates you from being the *fountainhead*."

The *womb* had re-entered the Temple and the Temple, the *womb*. When Marisium saw half the planets referred to as *him* and the other half as *her*, she linked them by twisting each strain into a *braid* supported by her supernatural aid. For Marisium, they were as two half-notes slurred together, sounding as one whole note. They were not free of and by themselves but only through their connection to the *sidereal trunk* of their larger planetary tree. As fruits, they too would mature, die and re-seed to continually feed and fill the *Stomach-Space of Marisium*. This was how they were able to install their first *cable* to the *hall of stars*. the umbilical *chord's* cosmic uterine lining deep within.

At times Apollicius struggled to be able to continually relate everything that happened to the *Path*. Therein lies the sole function of *transcendental art*. What ultimately separates god from mortals is the ability to do this continually, moment to moment. Whenever Apollicius could endlessly create, he knew there was no way to keep Solium and Marisium from him—separate.

Deep in his *solar heart*, Apollicius began to realize that the *Path of Attainment* and the *Orbital Path* were derived from the same numbers, proportions, and math. For him, the only ark really worth building had to be the Ark of Art, and all had to cross the *whale doorway* threshold, to enter the voluminous center of Marisium's *sea abode*. Reshaped by her own digestive system, they became her own art form, giving each one a new place to start from. from sepulcher to sculpture, from chrysalis to palace-picture.

Swathed like corpses and still attached to the middle of the *Life stem*, the Belly *was* the sanctuary where this *sacred tree* poured into the Main*stream* of the Milky Way. Apollicius looked at the stellar harvest of *one* planetary plant. Ethereal and negative astral shadows swirled through its limbs as if they had descended into the nether-world. A serpent—the most spiritual of all beings—arose from the cradle wound around the *plant of planets.* Gliding hither and thither in a zigzag pattern, she had already consumed the power of lightning and would forever show its *electric turn.*

Each *cocoon* was a *cooking room* where the number *two* elected to become *one*. None of them had been caught in the grip of Marisium's *jaws*; they had been frightened more through the gradual knowledge of her greater and more subtly refined *laws*.

Of course the time had to arrive for one to be initiated into their Adventure of the Spirit to be able to continue at the next level.

"My hour has arrived to leave this tightly threaded *cloth* and unfold my nocturnal wings like some giant galactic moth," Venus proclaimed.

"So true," echoed Jupiter. "One cannot stay bound in a *chrysalis* for eternity. I'll have way too many moons to be staying much longer in these closely woven cocoons."

Marisium enjoyed listening to their banter. It was good for her digestion, which is what ultimately filled her great imagination. Listening by stealth to their interplanetary converse did nothing to harm the *space health* of her universe. She marveled how at times, entering into direct contact with their Unconscious, she could fathom the depths of their well, where she could personally see reflected in their waters one region of heaven and another of hell.

As when a serpent swallows its prey whole, her digestion had been a long and slow process. But when all had been metabolized her system was nourished and able to prosper again as if it had always flourished. The Maw of Marisium was one great Law of Elysium. She ate not only to survive but to fill the *space* of that great and generous belly. Her oral cavity was a ferocious *anima* continually enveloping her other sidereal levels and gazing into her star-bestudded face revealed some of the mystery of her still wholly unexplored space.

Out of the nebula from a single magical drop Apollicius appeared, poised—surveying the yield and the nature of his very specially nurtured crop.

"What I've received from you, Apollicius, I could find nowhere else," Venus reminded him. Flashes to flashes, drops to drops. I feel the sharp edge returning of that *slice of knowledge* that never stops."

"Whatever I give comes from inside me and the life I try to live," Apollicius replied. "The only difference between the drop and the sp*ark* is the form they take to express the seminal energy of the *ark*."

"In the morning I'm a star; in the evening I'm the vibrating strings of a well-tuned guitar," Venus said. "My *beams* are also *chords* used to construct as we instruct." Apollicius flooded the star-shaped globe of Venus with luminous globules. The tips of her giant enfolded *moth wings* had unfurled from her lengthy, feathered span and out of her dark, smooth-skinned hips. Loosened by sparks emitted from a lightning bolt, the chrysalis of Venus began to molt. Her lissome-curved body would very soon appear again as she was once known before: The Planet of Love.

The sensually shaped, symmetrical Oval of Marisium was a mesmerizing ellipse. a powerful conic section for housing all the orbits. This was where *world snake* and *cosmic serpent* movements left paths of geometric tessellation sequencing gracefully through space and time. One by one each plane learned of *digestion* from this universal navel-stone of Marisium.

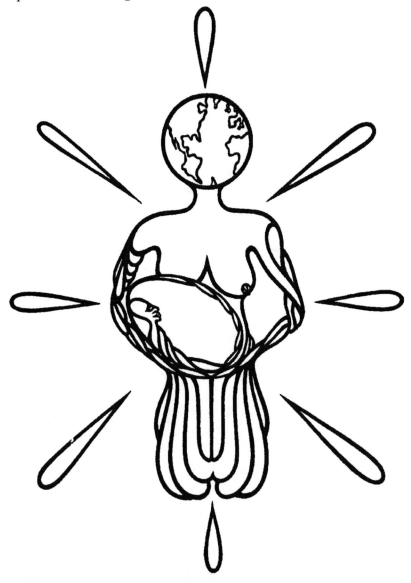

Little by little they absorbed what the great walls had to offer. providing a vibrating bounding line threading through their ears, sounding fine.

"We have been the swimming fish served to Marisium as a mouth-watering dish," observed Earth. *Her* dish contained all of the beloved planetary siblings and *was* the principal-reflecting source of Solium's Light. For Apollicius and his planetary system, having autonomy meant wresting from Solium and Marisium their hegemony. This had been and would still be the process of all sons and suns. In the *belly* their freedom to revolve slowly began to resolve. Though Marisium held them fast, their present situation would not last. She-the-Space had been in them from the beginning, and now they were in her.

"Everything is ultimately good for you, just as we are delicious planetary morsels for Marisium. When a *world* is consumed, what remains is its *word*," Earth explained directly to Marisium.

"As wanderers of the cosmic order, we have watched others comb the sky looking for us, never knowing that now we temporarily reside inside one of the galleries of her catacombs," Earth said.

"You, Earth, are a womb within a womb, just as there are waves within waves and sounds within sounds," Marisium replied directly.

Earth had always felt herself to be a spherical womb, ever since Apollicius had created her. Yet now, when it was pronounced to be so, she perceived the depth of what inside would soon be conceived. Within the chambers and fluids of her immense *global ear*, she really began to listen for the re-awakening of her still-slumbering being. She *moved*, therefore she *was*. What is motionless loses its connection to the Great Galactic Axis of All Spinning Spheres. This connecting line *is* the divine. From the ground, the integrity of this line rises up through *sound*. As *it* soars aloft, what was hard of hearing becomes soft musical yearning. Earth now consciously strove to re-establish her link to the heaven of the celestial seven.

Her short-term *and* long-term goal was to pass through the surrounding *midriff walls*, leaving behind whatever had been unyielding and still an obstacle inside those internal stalls.

Before being swallowed whole, Earth had been a member of the Ark of Apollicius. The deep interior of their *planetary ship* was in some ways not unlike the underside of Marisium's Belly, maintained in movement

by the action of the hip. Now she found herself on the verge of completely re-creating her own world. She had needed this gestation period as
much as any of the other planetary beings.

"I saw light patterns follow the energetic confines of my being in
well-defined lines," Earth began. "I suddenly became aware that my
intense work on the transmutation of the bestial into the spiritual could
be perceived in this *vision* I conceived."

"In a sense you are the watermark of your *planetary ark*," Marisium
confirmed, interceding into Earth's planetary world of thought. "You
will soon give birth to yourself, outlining the path of your next orbital
revolution."

*Ear*th listened with her great *ear* and radiated back what she had
understood. Deep within the *constellation of creation*, kinesthetic hierarchies of profound phrasing unfold, until then having been only stories
untold. Between the womb and doom there is still to be found, after
much searching, some room. It was in this *oval room* that Earth had
begun.

Unlike Venus, who a short time ago had absorbed light from the
great golden drop of Apollicius, Earth now reflected it back to him.

Looking back at Earth, Apollicius said, "You are easily one of the
most beautiful of my spherical beings. None of the other planets has
your emerald hue, nor your aura of cerulean blue."

Apollicius had been engaged in an unbroken effort of the *will* to
move his whole *system* up and out of the Belly of Marisium. He wiped
some galactic dust off his brow and wondered how much longer they
would all remain enclosed in her *natural silo*. He called it the *womb of gain*,
where their energy was all still potentially stored like so much *grain*. It
was surely no error that Apollicius found his Solar Path sown with seeds
of terror. He had by now become accustomed to this wild base, out of
which his *system of beauty* was wrought for each and every test case.

At this mid-point in his life in light-years, he had acquired much
pleasure from gazing into the *deep abyss* before ascending its highest
height. This was the existential mainstay that lay within light's base,
which nothing could ever erase.

"Soon the *thunderheads* will be out," he thought. "Then, the norm
will be the storm."

It had been a while since he had experienced rapturous *visions*. Now they didn't flood his consciousness with such frequency. But each one told was worth its line in light beams of pure gold. He felt mighty— ready to take the unicorn by the horn and swing the phoenix by the wing. His kingdom, though, was far from finished. it had barely begun its *star*dom. Music was what any sculpture had—to draw out its own picture, it could not be any other way than by the will of its *scripture*.

"I don't merely strive to survive," Apollicius admitted, "but to be 'Lord of All Plastic Energies.' To really be the soothsayer for my Planetary System, I must first be worthy to be the *doer of my dreams*."

Looking down at the Moon so close to Earth, he said in a low but firm voice, "I am the Sculptor God. Inside this world of Marisium, where everything is eating and digesting all else, I am alone, apart, just a shining orb, yet it was I who projected this reality when I first made the *oyster* and its remarkable pearl *moonstone*."

When he had made the Moon, he knew it was not to be the most unique sphere within his system. In fact, it didn't even have the independence of a planet, but rather was caught in a web, to become a prisoner in the *binary dance*. Indirectly it became a member of the higher community of Gigantic Axis Twirlers, and through its movement joined the others in emitting supernatural sounds from their instrumental spheres of orbital rotation.

"Once I discovered the esoteric essence of the Earth's satellite, I relaxed with this knowledge of its image and listened for the music to follow in the wake of the *cymbal*. This was and still is my method of intoxication, making me both drunk on *music of the sylph* and sobered by the elucidation of its *cymbal-glyph*." Apollicius breathed this comment to himself—his own original commentary on the Way of Creating.

But, as with the other planets, the Moon, too, was a moving sphere who had been crushed inside the all-consuming Digestive System of Marisium. All of the Solar System of Apollicius—consumed and exhumed—waited to become the pure aroma of *Spirit*, perfumed.

Dissolved into nothing is the *way to something*. Rid of its mass, Moon had diminished to a sliver, ready for its first communion Mass. Apollicius bent down to cradle the *crescent*, companion to Earth and heaven-sent.

"I haven't forgotten you here resting in your *oyster-bed.* being the nutritious food to help keep Marisium and Solium well-fed," whispered Apollicius to her *dark side.*

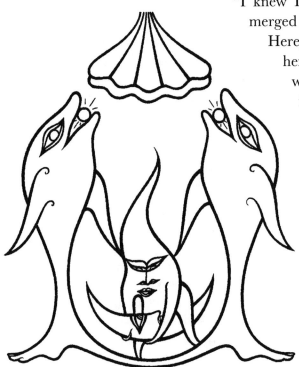

"I knew I'd find you here submerged in this *Sea of Neptune.* Here, inside Marisium, her Belly *is* the sea, and we ride on her Breath, from which we cannot flee," he added.

Moon looked up at his *volcanic face* and felt the heat of his molten embrace. She saw beyond him to the fine stomach lining of Marisium's walls rising into colossal pillars of *vertical fish.* Was it dream or vision—or that thin *veneer of reality* pressed in between?

Once again, her helper was Apollicius. Their ship was and had always been under his guardian*ship.* The breadth of his *fire* united all the ambiguities of the Unconscious Sea into this larger *Pisces-formed* symbol of the *Sound.*

Above the fish colonnades, Moon caught a glimpse of the *shell* of *sea-heaven:* the Oyster. Seeing the *transcendent bed* both above and below was a sign of the Realm; its Oyster had already given the great fish two luminescent pearls. *There* was their higher orbital shell, ready and waiting to be filled. Moon realized then how the bottom and top shaped one continuous cycle. What had once been an *oyster bed* now hung suspended above her head.

Along with Apollicius, the maturing planetary spheres learned, painful step by painful step, the fine art of enduring. Apollicius himself, still on occasion suffered internal explosions, which left sunspot blemishes to record their presence. They were learning to identify more and more with the Path and Level of their orbit, and to become less attached to their planetary ego of circular habit.

In many ways the Belly of Marisium *was* the Forge where Apollicius had descended to temper his *sword of vision* and sever his *temper of division*. The cutting edge of his sword was where the *word* met the *world* and made it manifest. Being mature meant understanding one's own basic nature; for Apollicius, it meant *being* the Light statue of its own stature.

Soon the gleaming fish were upwardly streaming—heading toward the source of the *cosmic dish*. They had been the slender upright creatures, supporting members of the New Ark; now they were phallic embers carrying pearls of lucidity to whatever still searched in the dark. In this solemn festival, beams of light were the scaffolding to replace what each column had been holding. The pleasurable light sensations were immeasurable. Apollicius had lived for so long inside the *belly of the whale,* that he had been birthed as a *great fish,* though nowhere near the size of Marisium from tip to tail.

This fish was a young whale, a microcosm of Marisium. She had given birth to herself, so to speak—the body of the beloved. Before *rebirth* of Apollicius, Marisium first knew how to hatch Solium, and Solium had gone after her with his *galactic net* as a fisherman would his catch. Since she *was* all of Space, she could not really be caught, only confronted face to face. Wherever she appeared, a sacred aura enveloped her whole being, ever-unable to be speared. She was the Apparition of the Invisible. Her name contained *air*, while Solium's contained *light waves* propagated as her *cosmic sea*. Together they were *current* and electrified the Universe. Through the grace of their movement the *many-in-one* and the *one-in-many* interconnecting worlds of their Art transmitted itself through Vibration.

Each of the planetary voyagers believed their *process of digestion* was nearly over. There was a general mood of assimilation and inner strengthening going on. Marisium confirmed their intuitions by saying, "I have had my fill. *your* system has passed through *my* system and from here on out these waters will remain still. It is time for you to call your *Sun-ark* to come to my immense *absorption-park*. You have all truly become *Initiates* into my *alchemical* lore—into the depths of my Space, where I store all of my *transmutation* ore.

"You, Marisium, are our sage and we are your fruitage," volunteered Earth, whose natural gnosis seemed to perceive everything beyond the end of any of the *great fish* noses.

"You, who are the most attractive of my spherical creations, are the *planet of Marisium's eye*," Apollicius observed from inside his own *Sun-ark*.

"This *winged ship* can grow again into a Great Ark if we all develop our own seamanship and navigate our way through and past Marisium's outer gate."

Apollicius had learned *net casting* from Solium and now re-initiated this ancient art to complete his *purse of spheroids*. The effulgence of the *Sun-ark* served as a beacon for each planetary fragment to mark their presence. It had been so long since they had really spun in their *Dance of the Orbital Spin* that they were slow to really begin the fun.

"All of you need to return to your former stature to help me guide this whole system's revolutionary nature," Apollicius advised. "You are my cast I cast for," he went on. "Each of you either has been or now is preparing to be a full-fledged *Cosmic Dancer*. That will happen only when you turn your full attention to Helleniana and re-establish intimate contact with her ballerina."

Helleniana was Apollicius's other portion; together they completed each other's motion. If he is the Sun, then she is the Planets. If he is light, then she is the enlightened. If he is energy, then she is its movement. Apollicius now tried to lead this urge to recapture the surge. Reaching across the abyss with the openwork fabric of his *cosmic strings*, he tried to snare these re-emerging planets from their lair in the highly volatile air.

"Once you are all back into your familiar patterns of revolution, the real work of *Creation* can commence restoration," declared Apollicius. "The same *womb-way* you entered Marisium, you will all cleave, comb, and leave one day. According to Marisium, it's due time to reach out beyond your girth to be able to focus on your chance for a *second birth*."

It was true that what was sea narrowed to *birth* canal, and way down there, the whole *family of planets* began the pangs of pushing through the slender channel.

"Commence procreation, fruitfulness, and recurrence with the authority of the Thunderhead rumbling above," continued Apollicius. "This *canal* is the track of the *spine* that the Spiral eventually encircles, changing the coil of increasing curves and constantly moving planes: the holograph of the Soul of Solium and Marisium."

One by one they began to emerge, not as young descendants, but as more mature ascendants, bent on following the upward swinging surge. Nevertheless, they were without a doubt still at the *Path's* beginning. In order to survive, each of them had to discover the entire *symbolism of the body* to allow it to thrive until each one overflowed into darker, fuller, floating states—more alive. They still carried the indigo *Night of the Spirit* brought from their *Life within the Belly*.

"I am possessed with one desire: to *turn* myself into Fire," Venus exclaimed, enthused and inflamed by the mere thought of conflagration.

"You are right, Venus," Apollicius responded vigorously. The *way-of-the-womb* had opened her to affectionately embrace her destiny, and didn't stop there but spread to the other planets with certainty.

Apollicius had vanquished most of his enemies soon after his nascence, except for the one who persisted in continuing to threaten his essence. It was the dragon, Pythian. Apollicius had already flung countless *arrows of light* at his rough hide, though the beast had withstood the onslaught, and returned in his ceaseless attempts to definitively turn the tide. His time had long since passed to be slain, yet he continued on, coming back to tie the *Light* tighter to his rust-laden chain.

Apollicius tried to respond by changing his light to Lightning, to strike the bond. Pythian had beheld this form by the hundreds and thousands, manifold and bold. But now he was everywhere and in everything. Pythian even tried to follow the *golden threads* to arrive at the very source of the Cosmic Force of Apollicius—without getting caught in his brilliant web. The dragon Pythian was yet another dangerous barrier who loved to stretch himself across any of the Orbital Pathways.

Apollicius did not permit Pythian to diffuse the intensity of his light without a fight. He existed in the *realm of the mystical metals*, but not apart from that larger system which united all the Ambiguities of the Unconscious into his galactic self to orchestrate the whirling of the *Orbital Beings*. He was ultimately the planetary souls' conductor, whereas Pythian strove to be the abductor.

Now the Planets were *plants,* separated from their plant bed—gigantic seeds empowered to move at varying speeds. The Space of Marisium was their Motherland, and they sought nutrients from her *soil, through* nothing but movement and toil. No more plant-bed, no more rest. The *new bed* was Light and Sound to fit the right *planetary head.*

For the present, there could be no spin, since they were still emerging from the *womb's rim.* No one knew if Earth was first or last to appear before Apollicius seated in his *throne of flames.* She had come crawling like a child, but still bore the folded wings of one once raised in the wild.

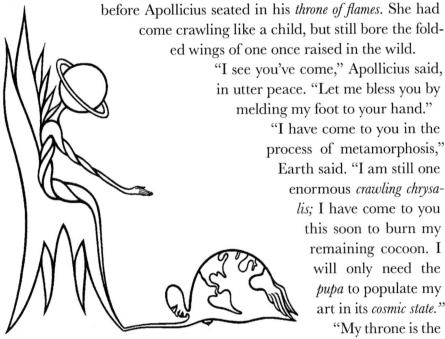

"I see you've come," Apollicius said, in utter peace. "Let me bless you by melding my foot to your hand."

"I have come to you in the process of metamorphosis," Earth said. "I am still one enormous *crawling chrysalis;* I have come to you this soon to burn my remaining cocoon. I will only need the *pupa* to populate my art in its *cosmic state.*"

"My throne is the

burning coal, I am the match, and you, my child, are the foal—ready to leave the *corral* by opening the latch. Your destiny is already *mapped* on your *orbital shell* whether you are headed toward creating your own vault of heaven or falling through your fault into hell. The planet that once burst from the *original seed,* you shall again cultivate—this time in multiplicity, written on the hand that decides your fate." Apollicius finished his invocation on the *Spirit of the Earth.* In his mind, the planets were already streaming around his brightly burning ball, now teaming to become a real part of the *All.*

Sixth Movement

Distillation: *The process by which the more gross material elements, earth and water, became rarefied and purer, nearer to the divine spiritual quintessence*

There was no question that the Ark of Apollicius had to be continually cleansed to maintain its *scintillating spark*. Over the eons the Planets sought to shed their *orb-bound* bodily garb and leave their own *age*—to transcend (*garb)age*. The *ego* kept each Whirling Spirit stuck to its own *planetary glue*—both a clue and the cue that separation had been long overdue.

Essentially, the *planetary ego* had grown from the seed of an inverted *ray of light*: still in its planet phase, it needed to go through the process of being converted upright. The journey to the center of the Belly of Marisium had separated them from all they had ever known. By passing through and out of her *unsilvery* lining, they continued moving toward their unique source of power refining. The closer they came to Solium's original sketch of the Universe showing one infinite *String* tied in a long stretch, the farther they drew away from their *ego-wretch*.

The Planet *breed* had grown from a *gourd-seed* of vibration-force by being played along its pathway's course. Each one could soon attach itself to that *Stretched String*, to be played by Apollicius and eventually reintegrated into the Spatial Orchestra of Solium and Marisium.

Though at some point, each of the Seven Planets may have thought themselves to be the center in their own right, they were very soon to realize that their creator, Apollicius, was the true Center of Might. It was they who revolved around him, not vice versa. The egocentric sentiment they couldn't ignore had persisted deep within, while outwardly they swore revolution to their sun, Apollicius, as *sole* core.

Could the *hydra-headed*, planet-ego be uprooted from where it had been so long surefooted? Each time Solium commanded Apollicius to *cut a head* with the flashing edge of his *light-sword*, two more appeared in its place. Clearly the base of this *ego* had grown so deep that it was nearly impossible to ef*face*.

Reappearing, Apollicius hurled an extraordinarily powerful beam of his own *Light*. It streaked toward Earth at its *own* speed, gaining both size and shape to fulfill its basic need.

"My long-range plan is to subdue your *ego* and neutralize your *glue*," Apollicius foreswore. "Inside this *light ray* is your real *dual-headed seed*, drawing you firmly toward the *Way of the Ray*."

For Apollicius, Earth *was* the Emerald Road. She *was* the reason he had thought of the creation of each different season. Earth looked at her own twin heads, which had sprouted up again from the *stump* left by Apollicius's swift sword of thump.

Stumped, she pondered: "If I could only find the right caustic to apply the next time I lose my head—to finally send this *hydra* to its ultimate deathbed. Once into the ground I could upon it tread, and see my real self clearly read."

When Earth finally looked up, she felt the heat of Apollicius dangerously close to her planetary-*hold*, quickly turning her Path to a glistening gold.

"Take hold of my long Ray, colored yellow, and then learn to become a spherically enlightened fellow," Apollicius offered.

"I need your steady light to keep me stable as I enter the elliptical pathway your message transmits via a cable," Earth answered.

As Apollicius wound his Ray tighter around her neck, as a *sacrifice*, her consciousness began to shift, reacting to the effect of the *vise*. A struggle ensued between the color she had been and the one in which she would now be hued.

Then, all at once, a Path opened before her, oblong and hollow, that both she and Apollicius now began to follow. This Path was in the shape of an immense *drop*, a veritable *sound* containing the *seed-body* of pure consciousness: the much-heralded *drop of wisdom*. To tread upon it was literally to walk on water—not the external bodies of a sea and a lake, but internal sound forging its own wake.

Notwithstanding her many heads, Earth momentarily grounded the two elements of *fire* and *water* in her terrestrial being. The resultant *elemental spark* became the catalyst to synthesize the *ego-burning* caustic, transforming her whole planet into a *crucible*. Before, along with her sister-spheres, she had been swallowed, digested, and reduced to dust, yet there still remained many tribulations to precede and follow her cycle of elations and re-evaluations, in which she needed to place her complete trust. In the bowels of her being, she realized that she could not become the *Way of the Giant Drop* without first slaying this hydra-headed monster of egos deeply embedded in her *planetary crop*. Without the help of Apollicius to accomplish this by being her accomplice, she could never hope to rid herself of this vice.

"It is time for our real work to begin," proclaimed Apollicius. "As your august protector and mainstay of the Light System, I'll need all your help to spread my beams to the farthest reaches—farther than any *light javelin* can be hurled—where all of you submerged planets will one day rise again, unfurled."

"You are the animating stuff of the heavenly bodies," Jupiter stated in his traditionally stately manner, "the maker of treasure. From what I can perceive, your wheels are driven by the seven Muses, all legitimate children the fugitive Helleniana will have to soon receive."

Jupiter was the *system's* major exponent of expressive modulation. His immensely ambiguous shape was the ideal landscape for the continuation of their *road of tribulations*. As the strongest of the family of Apollicius, he could carry the most weight. Glancing over at Jupiter's *mass* of unrealized potential, Apollicius announced.

"This is where we must start to inject the *Symbol* into the *Sphere*, wherever and whenever it can be the seed to art."

"Don't we need tools to begin our work?" asked *Sat*urn, standing and speaking in turn.

"Yes, of course we do," Apollicius said. "Mercury at this very moment is deep inside the *Sound Forge*, hammering out our new love and labor implements—instruments for *sound* and *foundry*."

He made a broad, sweeping motion using the full range of his *Light Movement*, and instantaneously a *road* curved out of his *wind tunnel*—where its brea(d)th had been held, waiting to release its *load*. This *Way* was the form of their emblem. It had always been inside Apollicius—it *was* him. This *road* was the external manifestation of his girth. They all began to gird themselves for action, to become his *girdle*—the *band* of Sound's Way. Their tool was a spade now being made from the dust of jade. Its road packed with embedded, luminous splinters, lapidating the feet of the weary into sparkling gems to survive the cosmic winters.

With apparent ease, Apollicius supported his easel, hoping his young planets would rise up to paint the *way*—the way of the saint. But where were their implements? A shovel was a brush-form strengthened into a crystallized shape. The contour of its blade was a miniature of the elliptical path encircling Apollicius the Sun.

Swift and sure-footed, Mercury could be heard winging his way toward them, bearing *Spades* made in *Hades*. He had gone to the home of the dead, as had the others, to be creased into a tome of lead. When their volume had been thoroughly read inside the tomb of Marisium's Womb, they had emerged—literate, legitimate, and loyal to the light-force—to show their own body's *Power Source*.

"Each *shovel* I bring has been electrified by a *ray of light* brightening the deep-red rust accumulated from having lain so long in the dust," Mercury announced, elated from his travel.

Mercury gathered the multitude of shovels into one bundle and presented them all to Apollicius, who was not the least bit surprised by the tools. He picked up a shovel with each of his nimble hands at the ends of long, luminous arms and extended them outward until each ray-held shovel reached the center of his elliptical path. This exact image he had already foreseen ages before. It was here that his Planets could finally begin their real work of excavation—for each to create and save his own celestial cave. Their caves would provide them with the minimum security and protection needed to rise up from their temporary graves.

"When I firmly clasp this shovel, I feel as though I could dig on and on until I finally unearth myself," Earth volunteered.

Mars saw the *shovel* as an instrument of *battle* he could begin to wage on his own *ground*.

"All wars are fought in service of some kind of *Muse*, for some sort of ideal shape or form—real or imaginary," Mars said. "But the most progressive and far-reaching are the ones waged on the changeable terrain of one's own psyche. That war is an interminable search for defects and defectors behind one's own line of battle with the spirit that it ultimately reflects."

The others nodded in agreement, preferring to let Mars and Earth speak on their behalf. Each of the Planets had picked up their tool and found a spot along the *Way* of the real school. For the first time, Apollicius began to feel *solar-crowned*. Bejeweled at their farthest tips, his luminous arms were also *light extensions* of his own legs and hips. For the first time since their disappearance inside the cavernous *Belly of Marisium*, they succeeded in reconnecting their system while *digging* this *dance*. With each *shovelful*, Apollicius received a mouthful. After so long stowed away in the *Great Stomach*, their appetite showed that it was back. They had all begun to fathom their feast by confronting *darkness* as the mightiest beast. When one could finally turn the tool for the ground into an instrument of sound, then their implement of the *Way* had become a true *Ray* complement.

Beginning their *dig*, each of the Planets assumed its rightful spot in the long line of celestial pilgrims who have worked toward enlightenment by surviving the extreme cold as well as the intensely hot. They soon learned to work on their *instrument* by digging deep within themselves, where the *elemental spirits* thrived like rejuvenated elves.

"I am here as your Cosmic Medicine Man. to render visible and collective certain symbolic systems present in the *Psyche* of all the Planets I ever created," Apollicius clarified. "It is the convergence of my *light* and your *sight*, like the interface of the sea and its shore where you find the *living ore*."

The *Road* had been clearly indicated; what remained was the *Work* to be done or left undone by all of them or none. Of all these wanderers who had begun the *Great Work*, none labored more assiduously than Mercury. He was clearly intent upon coming up with *himself*—at almost any cost. The *Road* was hot and covered with galactic dust. More than once Mercury had lost his footing and nearly tumbled down into the yawning abyss lying on either side of the *narrow way*. Once Earth, in good fortune, had helped him up; another time it was Neptune with his heart in tune.

"My new stratagem radiates its strength along the lines of a cut gem," affirmed Mars. He had taken to the *Path* with a well-seasoned battle plan, brandishing his shovel like a sword.

"The Pathway I'll cut will leave no doubt I am on my *way* out of the rut," he said. Vigorously his shovel sank into the *soil* repeatedly as he refused to cease his impassioned toil.

As they worked harder, more breath had to be found to support what they all wanted to do with their sound. As they got into shape their spheres began to take shape. More wind was needed and deeper exhalations heeded to keep up with their own work expectations. When Jupiter began to take his massive shovelfuls, the *Path* trembled and shook the whole *elliptical ground* of Apollicius's Light System of Sound. The tremor opened a crack in the *road,* and the planetary workers immediately *dug in.* They all breathed more deeply as their huge spades sank in more steeply. Suddenly, Mercury's tool made the metallic sound of metal on metal.

Neptune's shovel flashed as it too clashed with an object, striking the note of an ever-fleeting tune. But it was Venus who was the first to stop and stoop to really see what they had come upon. With the tip of her large spade she gently scraped away the jade discharge and sapphire soot till he could see and touch what they had really found under their *boot.*

"It's a flute!" exclaimed Venus, her voice's timbre that of a great lover of music. "Large enough for Saturn or even Jupiter to play."

As the *morning star,* Venus always rose first in the sky seen from afar. She would always lead the *way* while Apollicius watched, waiting for her to elevate to begin his day. The *melodic pool* out of which Venus dawned swirled into a Spiral to reflect clearly the *turns* of the solar-sound-spool.

Upon seeing Venus levitate, Apollicius rose too, and with one of his lightest arms reached down to scoop up that Giant Flute. Lightly *armed,* he spiraled to his very center, where his volcanic blaze burned and harmed.

"Which one of you has enough wind to turn air into an *air?*" Apollicius wondered.

"I believe I do," offered Mercury. "I am closest to you and therefore benefit most from your *solar winds.* I have also been training in Neptune's pool for so long that I have transformed my *wind* into pure fuel."

"Training is not the same thing as sustaining," replied Apollicius. "Trial by Air is one of the first steps to be mastered in order to climb each and every stair. Stretching between the point where all *gravities* converge under the canopy of *Marisium's Sky,* is this Road of Distillation. Much breath will be needed not only to play this *Flute* but to draw up all that *pool of energy* needed to successfully transmute."

Without uttering another word, Mercury placed his lips on the *pipe* and blew through *all* he had ever seen, been, and believed he knew. The more *air* entered his instrument, the closer he felt to approaching Helleniana's first *natural stair.* It was up to him to send this message, enveloped within a melodic passage, to the others. Mercury had just embarked on

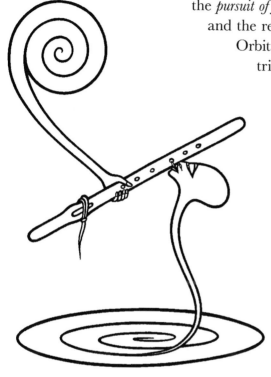

the *pursuit of form*, which would lead him and the rest of the Planets along their Orbital Pathway, single file by trial.

Passing through note after note, Mercury's flute music soared. When he had finished, the *wind instrument* became his caduceus, the staff connecting him directly to the Will of Apollicius. In effect, it represented a beam of his Light.

"It is as if my senses are being sharpened, with each *refrain* systematically displacing each misplaced and dull *pain*," Mercury realized.

"In order to *distill* efficiently, one needs to learn how to be still, unmoved, by becoming a *still*," Apollicius informed Mercury.

"There is a secret unrest that gnaws at the roots of every *planetary being*," Earth confessed. "For me, these tests are the only ways to transmute the persistent and unwanted images we digest without protest."

"There are as many gates as there are fates," Apollicius echoed enigmatically. "And beyond my own *Primum Mobile* stretches the entire empyrean of the Starry Marisium."

From these *maps* of the Sound Pool or Pool of Sound, each Planet swan was drawn into elliptical *laps*. Having set the notes in motion, Mercury raised his caduceus to indicate where each of the spheres fit in the overall scheme and then placed them there following the score's theme—coming from Apollicius. For the moment Mercury became the embodiment of pure reason, and began his preparation to advance toward the next *vision-in-season*. He was in charge of this Virginal Road of Tests without Rests—a process to discover and assimilate opposites, deep within their own unsuspecting planetary selves, breaking down resistances and overcoming obstacles one by one. First they had been *swallowed*; now they prepared to *swallow*. First the night, and now some early streaks of daybreak light.

Apollicius was aware that without Helleniana there was only so much he could do; yet even so, he set about not to waste any more moments in beginning. The *stave* he wielded was a *ray of light* he used to score each sound and water *wave*. This was how he first created a *bar of sound* out of the center of his yellow star. Taking this same *rod* Mercury had handled below, Apollicius cast its melodic line outward from his composing pod. Turning into a snake, its movement peaked twice before lightning exploded in its wake.

While his right hand turned the serpent's tail into lightning, his left arm *cast* the thundercloud into a thunderhead, causing a thunderbolt to blast. Just as out of his *firelight* Apollicius made rain, so he expected each of the Planets in their own way to take this water and turn it back into an illumined *brain*. That same *drop shape* could express itself as either sunlight or rain at night. Globes emerged from Globules.

Lightning crackled and thunder boomed, transforming the entire sky vault into one voluminous *Nimbus*. The *lake-sea* grew below from Mercury's private pool into an entire planetary school, where all seven spheres could circumvent a lap to the sonic background of the thunderclap. Drops of salty liquid flowed from that great beclouded *eye*, form-

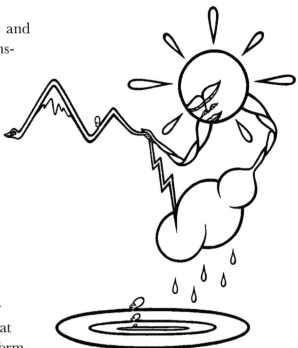

ing an ocean of tears upon which the planets layered themselves in shell-like tiers.

This was just the beginning of their perilous path of preliminary conquests in the Space of each elliptical swath. They all shared a common bond through this general *trial*, but each also had the challenge of protecting the magical potion of their own particular *vial*. This *vial* was the repository of each one's power-to-script through motion its own *cosmic story*.

"Essentially, I am nothing more than a colossal vial to receive and contain the energy coming inside each drop of light I receive when I *dial*," Jupiter humbly verbalized.

Mars, Neptune, Saturn, and the others all affirmed his words by giving off a slight glow coming from inside their spinning turn.

"I feel too heavy to pass this test of buoyancy," Saturn confided. He had yet to recover his rings lost somewhere inside the *Belly of Marisium*. Without his supportive rings, it was more difficult for him to float through, as he had done before the sinking of his sidereal boat.

"Will they learn to contain themselves?" Apollicius asked his father, the immense Solium.

"You know as well as I how important it is," Solium responded. "The marriage of Marisium and me represented the fruition of our entire *Opus*, developed wholly out of the power in *us*. The Universe is our vessel, still supporting the weight of the whirling galaxies as they continue to unfold."

"The *Way of the Cosmos* is not an easy road, is it?" Apollicius ventured.

"Absolutely not. Before I *Mari*ed, I had drowned in her Spatial Sea. She resurrected me and gave me substance when all that I was had dissolved after I lost my chance," Solium explained.

"That is exactly what happened here in my *small* System of Light within you," Apollicius said.

"Yes, of course, it is the same *stages*, no matter what stage you are on, down through the *ages*. Before I passed through dissolution, I had no knowledge whatsoever of the solution. If you have never been torn apart, how can you ever be gathered together? Cutting and sewing—only from pieces can we re-construct a whole," Solium philosophized.

"I have never felt the absence of Helleniana as much as now, in your presence. Maybe I need to drown for her to come and pull me up inside her *sidereal gown*," Apollicius confided.

"She is recovering her *spirit* and recuperating her *style* in the process of making herself fit," Solium informed. "Marisium has clasped her under her spacious *wing*, helping her prepare to lead each planetary *string*. It won't be long now before she is dancing before your heavenly body entourage with the controlled abandon of new-found courage," Solium counseled.

"We have all been reduced to *prime matter*; therefore it is time to leave this starting point and let ourselves be seduced by the *spiral ladder*," Mercury affirmed with his typical *mercurial spirit*.

"Yes," said Venus, "we are ready to begin our real Trial of Experimentation."

Venus felt deep within her own body a strong attraction to the sphere of Mercury. She feared the moment they got too close there would be an exchange, making it thereafter too difficult to orbit out of each other's range. To develop her Art, however, she needed to test the temperature of this *body of water* and then be able to effectively depart.

Mercury *was* a body of water. He contained the forms of all liquids, yet *his* was the permanent *water* of baptism and prism.

"Though I revive, purify, and cleanse, making it sweet, it is unthinkable to disregard or waste me, even though I may be bitter to taste and completely undrinkable," Mercury revealed in a rare moment of unabashed and real expression. Now it was up to Apollicius to actually initiate the distillation of each planet's spirit from its original material state. As their Creator, he was their chief experimenter, set to perform the tests on all spheres assembled now before him as willing guests.

First, he asked them to divest themselves of all garments and step forward into his legendary laboratory departments. As Sun Power, he was still head of the *still*, and all the planets and other heavenly bodies were his vessels to be prepared for *distillation*.

"You are all *microcosms* of me," Apollicius spoke solemnly. "Your vessels, once hidden away, are here, ready to show the *Way*."

Mercury had already become one with *his* vessel, and waited patiently for his *triangle* to sound full by tilting his head to form a right angle.

Apollicius didn't disappoint any of the planetary pilgrims, as each one received his portion of *liquid light*. One by one the nesting spheres left their enclosure to come to this experimental pasture. Each Planet received a different yet fixed amount of *mercury* from Apollicius. With this portion each could, would, and should transform their own *body of water* into a *wine nation*. There, inside the *sailing vessel* of each Planet sent, all transmutations could take place to enable their solution to become solvent.

"I am the *solution*," Mercury claimed with a voice of sound authority. "It is I who must be conserved at all cost—those who have me are saved, and those who don't are lost."

"Now we've all been filled with the *elixir*, but do we really know what this fluid will cure?" Mars wondered. "I do, however, suddenly feel more robust and expansive. It is as if a thirst I've had for so long has somehow been quenched. For the battle ahead, I'm much stronger when the *spirit* is well-fed."

He felt the *fluid* making him more mobile and changeable, yet at the same time it was soothingly smooth. Raising both arms, Mars gazed out at the *days* of Apollicius and *drank deeply* from his *rays*.

"During the heat of engagement, this *liquid* will rise and transform me into a powerful *druid*," Mars proclaimed, and this set into motion the wheel of his portion. From then on he saw himself in a combative guise, to heat his *vessel* and make its *mercury* rise. It was he who had tempered the light beam's *shard* into a sword that fit in its own scabbard. With that *arm* he had cut his own orbital trail and saved himself from bombarding asteroids by forging a protective mail.

Obviously, each Planet was responsible for his own portion of the liquid potion. If and when *it* really rose within its *planetary body container* to the height of a colossal rose, *it* would have achieved its highest realization as a sphere and be clearly ready to leave its own *vibration* tier.

But before all this could happen, there were more trials, tests and experimentation. There was nothing, however, more expansive than the Space of Marisium, nor brighter than the Face of Solium. He was the *powder of projection* to dissolve into the *background* of her Space tradition. Their sun, Apollicius, was the golden heir to this volatile *Kingdom of the Air*. His gold had been slowly produced through a new transformation of the *baser metals* of old. Mercury, Venus, and the Moon now had the ability to fashion their respective metallic veins of mercury, copper, and silver, molding their *individuals* in the crucible and the forge, measuring their degree of malleability. Pounding, hammering, and pressing, Apollicius worked as a Demiurge to shape the core of each being from its baser, more natural, metallic ore.

"This is the *trial of production*, where I had always wondered how I would function," the Moon spoke in a dreamlike state before she really awoke. "How can I reproduce myself as a self-contained sphere? It will take more than the Solar Forge to fill with light the entire circle of this rotund gorge."

"You and I both need a catalyst," Earth prompted.

The Planets all looked into the *shiny seed* of each other's sphere, searching for something they knew they would later need. Just before Saturn rose to turn, his rediscovered rings glowed with greater intensity, illuminating a *box-like* urn. Jupiter spotted it first and noted that it looked ready to burst.

"It's full to the brim of supernatural beauty," sang out the voice of Saturn. "The *word*, however, still is lodged deep in the abyss of my *underworld*."

"We can see that," affirmed Jupiter. "But isn't it possible to exchange *meanings* while it's still in its *till*?"

At that moment Apollicius wondered if *he* just might find Helleniana there, having fled to the natural company of her delicate kind. He reached his hand across the heavens and through Saturn's hoops to try and seize the chest with one of his *fire-infused* swoops.

Just the thought of all her *grace* inspired Jupiter to loosen his sleeves and let flow his First Planetary Race. On his part, little originality seemed involved, since each *pod* was a mere replica of his own mystery, as yet unsolved by their *god*. Composed of a *land of folds,* Jupiter easily managed to express himself through this reproduction of beings forged from his molds.

Each creature had one clearly outstanding fea- ture: a balanced head of pure consciousness ra- diating a gold aura brought up from a field of deep *azure lead.* When he saw the reaction he had catalyzed, Apollicius immediately drew his hand from the *urn* of Saturn. If just the *thought* of the beauty of Hel- leniana could have this effect, he still wasn't sure he was really ready for what he actively sought. But it was too late; the *race of beings* steadily flowed from under- neath the Robe's folds. The other Planets looked on in disbelief to see such a number emerging over a span of time so brief. Could they do it too? It would take a huge effort to create a population deluge, let alone to sat- isfy its demands without constantly issuing a litany of commands.

Each, however, did follow suit by thoroughly bearing the fruit of this productive pursuit. Every Planet would bear Seven Races, one for each tone in a scale that didn't skip over any of its whole note spaces. Thus, they were all able to divide and now multiply. At this early phase they continued to search for the *lost lover* through a line of beings that it had taken so long to finally uncover. Mercury, Venus, Earth, Moon, Mars,

Jupiter, and Saturn all would experience the Seven Divine Decrees, dealt and then fastened by law to each planetary belt. One by one they began to mount the *mountain* in their quest for the source of the *fountain*. This marked the beginning of the most difficult stages of their Cosmic Adventure—to find and unite with their lost paramour.

What had been dormant for so long inside Marisium's Belly had long since broken out, as all the Planets could testify. Part of their nature had been awakened through *sound*, which enabled this *side of art* to arise from its very *ground* and with fresh eyes began to look around.

Where was she? The *lover* was both the search and the searched. The Mountain they had come to attain did not follow the curve of their desire, nor was it as solid and drab as a stone slab, but it was shaped from empty space, inviting its aspirant to move ever higher up the slope of the steep-sided *Ace*.

"My secret lover is a *lover of forms*. These forms I know already exist within and with*out* me. They are there awaiting, invisible and expectant," Earth said. "It is up to me, by forging my art, to have the strength to ascend to *form's* full length. My spirit is inside, enfolded, and according to you, Apollicius, it is light encoded—am I right?"

Before he answered, Apollicius hesitated slightly, unwilling to take Earth or her statement lightly. It was this pause that prepared the *space* necessary for their next clause.

"Unlike Mercury, whom I created to be both volatile and fixed, you, Earth, I wanted to be neither too liquid nor too solid. The key to choreographing your *dance* is to use temperance," Apollicius answered.

Whatever Earth procured, she realized, would also have to be endured. If she really strove for total planetary realization, she needed to possess the resiliency and character to carry out its actualization, which meant *wiring* her *current* connection to Apollicius and his *lamp*-like eyes. This was the task now set before her. Pressure—balanced—is pleasure. Her electrical adventure was all about the *dance of balance*. From lofty Saturn to the nine Muses of Jupiter, all the nesting spheres of the planets were enclosed and composed of and *by* numerical *laws of sound*. These unchangeable realms inhabited by angels and elected souls—among the finest of assembled spirits—were responsible for those instances when their *music* became audible on Earth.

Weight, sin, dark, cold and filth—the five things farthest now from Apollicius and, consequently, Solium—perfectly described Gorisius, definitely no newcomer and the nemesis to everything Solium had done since they both had emerged out of the same womb of Marisium. His dark *cloud* now moved closer to enclose Earth in his shroud. She saw him approaching from far away and began to seriously prepare for her own protection. Though Gorisius had been around forever, this was the first Earth had seen of him.

"After I, along with my sister spheres, had been drawn with great force through the sea," Earth spoke through herself to the Universe, "where the *Whale of Marisium* swam and had swallowed me, and after encountering more terrible abysses here and there, I found a *stone* deep inside, where it became possible to discover and hold its essential tone. This is where I now retreat to endure the dark shadow of Gorisius and prepare for my own challenging feat."

Hidden deep under her outer garb's seam was the *head of a maiden* lying in quiet expectation of Apollicius's light beam. Now a light force angled upward as she relaxed to open the top of her *polar head* and at the same time came downward from the *unknown* Cloud-of-All-Knowing to form a lengthy, yet stalwart stairway between the Heavens and Earth. She felt the over-bearing, intense heat of a thousand suns course through her, yet remained—balanced at that place where inner strength runs. The Pathway between herself and the central energy source of Apollicius had been re-connected. Presently, she was free to move between realms.

"We are living inside the same *Vision*," Apollicius affirmed. "To endure the heat of each stair, place your *earthly foot* upon a protective layer of air. What we have outside is also inside."

A ray of Apollicius briefly took the shape of a primeval bird, as Earth reached upward to touch the *arms of a feather* reaching out to meet her across the ether. Elongated, Earth stretched skyward to bring the bird back into her own terrestrial ward. It was a tremendous struggle to hold her lengthened position in its over-extended state. Lightning sent from Apollicius, permeated all of Earth's Planet dwelling, first created, not so long ago. As the *vessel*, she had become a microcosm of the Heavens, to ultimately govern the entire process and progress of the *Opus*.

"By bringing back this first warm-feathered creature, I will always possess a symbol of my terrestrial evolution moving toward its celestial solution," Earth announced.

At that exact moment of her expanded extension, a smaller model of the heavens erupted from the *head of her spirit being*, confirming the words of Apollicius. Her Body *and* her Spirit had indeed become a laboratory to plant, cultivate and harvest this *empyrean seed*. Earth felt the rainfall in her inner firmament and chose to remain tall to reach the *Peacock's tail* of the outer welkin. The Peacock was the many-hued *outpicture* of the Solar Phoenix of Apollicius. The wings of this lavishly plumed creature were still enfolded within her nature. The stage for *us* had not yet been arranged for the complete flowering of the *Opus*. Nevertheless, Earth could be assured that given her *lightning stairway*, she was in possession of the initial precious *airway*.

Apollicius looked around at his other *sphere-movers*. They had all veered inward after steering their massive bodies toward him, their Sun-Lord—and then peered in on Earth's steps onward. Each shaft, beam or ray pointed in the exact direction of the *Way*. Since Apollicius emitted light in all directions, it was not really by following their pathway that you arrived, but by entering the beam through its seam, the shaft in front or in aft, or the ray at night and day. To really know its essence, they all needed Helleniana's full presence. She could be properly be conjured up only in *thought*, through *music*—named after her as *Muse*—from whom beauty is sought. When each Planet *played* and followed its own individual sound, they could more easily understand just exactly where they were actually bound.

Solium was especially ecstatic to see the Earth-Spirit in contact with the purest seam of the beam, craft of the shaft, and play of the ray. Looking to his *sun*, Apollicius, he observed: "What Earth has just done, all the other Planets should also do as *one*. They must agitate the strings of their own instruments in order to recapture the lost *form of rapture*. Once they are completely inside the Light Shaft of Apollicius, the virginal road of higher reason turns golden with emerald streaks, while the metallic planet of Mercury oscillates in dips and peaks."

"I agree," echoed the Space of Marisium. "Now the grade will necessarily become steeper, allowing access only to those *space-travelers* who have made the choice to go deeper. None of them will be able to enter the Garden of Bliss without first reaching Helleniana to *plant* the invisible Seed of the Kiss. They will soon enter the *ordeal of inclination*—where it is all about *angle* and *desire*."

Thus, the Planets, in passing back and forth across the sidereal horizons of Marisium, in and out of the Great Dragon, swallowed and digested in that gargantuan Belly, now could choose to be *space sovereigns* and move through the many rooms where her constellations reigned. The *Way* to these rooms and houses, however, inclined sharply—to become nearly perpendicular. It called for ardor and boldness, vastly exceeding a normal limit, to scale the towering heights of a neighborhood familiar only to Apollicius and his creators, Solium and Marisium.

These Planets were the opposite of immutable celestial spheres. Mercury was at the very center of change and vital to their search for their own style of *orbital movement*. With the help of Apollicius, Mercury could turn their *yellow path* into gold-making juice, the ultimate elixir for the *perpetual dance*. The only way possible to scale this steep path stretching upward before them was via the *music of the dance scale*. It comprised a particularly intricate ring of sounds designed to increase energy exponentially when played, provoking energetic leaps and measured bounds.

"As you begin to whirl ever nearer to me, beginning the *Ascent*, think of Helleniana—of her twirl and fresh scent," Apollicius exalted, encouraging the Planets to commence their upward swirl.

The closer they all came, led by Mercury, the more they realized their *path* led up the side of a *vessel*, a volcanic caldron containing all the violent agitation of the Cosmos. The heat was tremendous. Only Mercury, already in his semi-liquid state, still managed to flow skyward. He turned enthusiastically toward the others:

"I can't accomplish this alone. For this System to move harmoniously, we all need to be powered by the Tone."

"You are the Seed of the Dance," said Jupiter, who had struggled the most, being the heaviest. "It is your *semen* that regulates the change in *inclination*, rendering the steep, level and the shallow, deep."

"Your circulator process is in motion," Mercury added. "The rising vapors surrounding us are both of *flame* and *feather*, lining our Path—incandescent, with its *light ascent*."

In the background Apollicius arose, the fountainhead of transformation into gold from the lead. He was the epitome of warmth and radiance, while Helleniana, still hidden in the realm of darkness and shad-

ow, retained all the *coolness of magic* while channeling her Moon-dance. She wasn't the Moon itself, but rather its phases, as his book of brilliant illustration expressed itself vividly through *drawing-in-phrases*. Apollicius spread his two main *rays* widely, extending an open invitation to each Planet to plant its feet firmly to dominate the road's sharp slant.

Apollicius's greater goal was to fill his Solar-Vessel—the

mountain-alembic—with the *Spirits* of all the original Seven Planets by stoking their *purgatorial fire*. He was the purveyor of elixirs, while they were his conveyor. Their quest, ultimately led them to his House of Sun, to be his guest.

"Without Helleniana, however, there will be no marriage of any planetary elements," began Apollicius. "She is the key in which I wrote, while you are the related tones all based on her note. She is the legend of my Solar System map. She is the thing that explains or solves, as a code, where all of us fit harmoniously into her mode. At times she can become the curvature of the Cosmic Piano, where the light and dark sides of her are divided into a multitude of alternating white and black keys hitting the sounding chord of the timpani."

The other Planets followed, all moving toward the House of Apollicius, where the *Opus* of their final transformation would ultimately occur. For these *planetary seekers*, the *philosophical gold* they sought at the Treasure House of Apollicius could be obtained only by creating their own work, the only way it could ever have been brought. Through Helleniana they hoped to find splendor in the more reflective quality of her *silver-self*.

No matter how far they had come, there were still new beasts to be slain and obstacles to surmount in overcoming each of these barriers, regardless of the pain. They had already had some preliminary victories and now were poised for a momentary glimpse of the extraordinary Solar Temple of Apollicius.

"Now is our chance to really improve on our half-moon compass form," Mars said. "To be a strong Planet, there is nothing more important than this *spin-move*. Once we develop this agility, we can employ it for quick celestial counterattacks or just to develop our own *revolutionary-rotational* abilities."

"I agree," Earth added. The more comfortable I become with my own motion, the clearer I envision the pathway to Apollicius with a heart of true devotion."

The sparkling stones of Earth's *breasts* scintillated when the terrestrial tones of her planetary body were titillated. With a slight nod in the direction of the Sun, she raised herself up to the full length of her lapis lazuli rod.

"All of my training I'll now need to continue this Dance of Orbital

Perseverance," she continued. Her *land* formed the plate of her deep brown-toned breast, as her bearing filled with enough reverence to steady her onward quest.

Meanwhile, Apollicius, sensing the shift in planetary energy, lightly prepared his *House* for the new arrivals, who would give his whole system a lift. It had been some time since his last visit with Solium and his Space-Wife, Marisium. Through Solium came the *Visions*, which prepared his *states* for whatever might be moved toward him by certain unsettling storms of unrest, testing the fates. Bathing in the golden rivers of his own Light, Apollicius closed the great orb of his one eye for just a momentary eclipse—long enough, however, to see a new *vision* of his actual Temple, including an overview of these planets, their orbital strengths and rotational trips.

"I suddenly *see* my own Temple as a titanic being, open to its own *system of seeing*. I have never felt so tall and vertical in my alignment, ringed by all of your *tonal orbits*, opening me up to emanate more *light exhibits*. If I were a scribe, I would scroll: 'The right to write *right* is written in the rite.' By coordinating certain tones to understand certain uncertain forms, I am able to envision holding the seven spheres, along with their accompanying rings and circular energy-bands, all in my Arcadian hands."

Whatever Apollicius *saw* immediately came to be; it was just the nature of his *solo* law for the *light* of his Light to sometimes decide to draw. To enter its upward-moving *path* and *ladder* ascent would be the most challenging of all these trials they had been sent. His Solar Vessel had taken on new aspects. He not only had aligned himself vertically with the great Temple of his Father, Solium, but felt he had managed to deepen his own private *framework* with a whole *scale of rungs* used to scale up his own temple walls.

When Mercury arrived, ahead of the cluster, he immediately recognized the spiral entrance located at the very center of the tapered spire luster. There, at a fresh threshold, he was not attended by a host of invisible familiars; rather it was plenitude in solitude. As always, he explored ahead of the rest—for him, there was no real rest.

"The Universe of Light is literally played on the *Organs* and with *members* of the Divine Embers," Mercury uttered crossing the line of the *undivided* body and mind. "The House of Apollicius is not some alien, hostile ball of fire, but here inside our mutual *light attire*."

Apollicius had always been oriented toward laboratory practice and experiment. Whenever he had a visionary experience, he took another spin in that direction. Its hieroglyphic content could always be deciphered as a *higher-glyph*. When the trinity was present, the *present* was the triad chord sounding its *bow*—and content. The Solar Temple of Apollicius had long since the beginning become a Tone-World, where the folding curves of its Light Architecture reflected the *spiral turns* of the Music playing its Overture.

The true dimensions of this Temple-Vessel were untold and kept as secret as Helleniana's hiding place in that certain point in *acoustic space*. Among the Planets themselves, there was some speculation as to whether she really was concealed, or was actually in a place closer by that always remained tightly sealed. Nevertheless, she had been thoroughly kept out of sight and for all they knew might be harboring herself within these very Temple walls filled with resplendent stalls and interconnecting halls. Besides, if she did inhabit the *insides*, could she at the same time be the Temple's *sides*? Maybe, because of the way she would hide, the only way to know if she was there was to follow her dance to wherever the *Spirit* abides.

Streaking across the temple threshold, Mercury waited not for the other *heavenly bodies*.

"I am *prime matter,*" he thought to himself. "So no matter how much I turn into *circulation,* I will not devour myself, as I have seen some of the other spheres trying to do."

Looking long and breathing deep, Mercury suddenly had an inspiration:

"This Temple of Apollicius is pure breath, pure spirit. It is literally the House of Quintessence: the fifth element. If we are ever to aspire to *stardom,* it is here, deep inside this incorruptible *quintessence,* that astral bodies are made—as eternal luminaries."

To climb to the next ascending level inside his Temple, the Planets needed a *song* composed to be sung, to be able to grasp each rung.

From the profundities of this Temple's Space, Mercury heard the faint ringing of a bell. Apollicius turned within to address his own *quicksilver creation* enigmatically: "Perfect timing is a woman chiming."

"It must be our lost *muse* you speak of. We hear her content, but know not her intent," Mercury responded.

"You heard her because you have connected to the *spirit-element* with your breath. It is up to you to choose whether to open the Book of Elysium," Apollicius counseled.

"Render up one of the book's pages so I can be touched by its passages," Mercury proposed.

"You must do that on your own," Apollicius reminded him. "It is your *quest,* not your request."

Meanwhile, within the Temple's bounds, the other Planets had also responded to the chimes of Helleniana's times. This Temple-Vessel of Apollicius was *his* microcosm of Solium and Marisium's macrocosm. Paradoxically, all the Planets were orbiting in various planes *outside* Apollicius, while they also existed simultaneously *inside* the sealed vessel of his own Body of Light. Stars, as light force, penetrated all in their journey to and from Solium—their *source.*

Saturn was the last to enter—since he was as heavy as lead, he didn't lead. In the system of Apollicius he was not only the outermost sphere but also the *dark spirit,* a prisoner of matter's denseness. He was the last to revert to his original state of rotund luminosity. The iron will of Mars, the tin smile of Jupiter, the copper-protective love of Venus, the mercurial feet of Mercury, and, finally, the silver bow of Moon had all entered the Temple of Sun before him. The conflagration of Apollicius had grown from a mere blaze to the passionate radiance of a cut and polished stone maze.

"Slowness is vital in this process," Apollicius warned. "Do not be over eager to burn yourself. The best cooking is done at a steady, lower temperature. Let seed operate upon seed. Let tone cut stone."

"The movement from the gross to the subtle is the highest and most challenging process in existence," Mercury added. Being *quicksilver*, he spun closest to the long sliver of the silver moon—soon to move its dark side to the light to reveal Helleniana. She had already loosened her shadow from the halls to take down from the walls her silver bow. Though huntress she was, she had always been the hunted. Now, trapped in the Temple with all the Planets on her trail, she had still been able to conceal her face behind her unearthly veil.

Before they could begin to become their *vision*, each one had to embark on his or her own di*vision*. Both the Planets and the Water had become rarefied and purer. Mercury himself could now call on his *vaporous side* as distinct from his whitened, silvery essential self. Being now both *matter* and *spirit*, two paths opened before them: one empty of matter and the other full of spirit.

"I have become what you are," Apollicius announced, referring to his planets and their process of orbital alchemy. "I, too, am subjected to the *process of distillation*. Once, when I let my light fall in *drops*, all of you mistook it for rain, not knowing it as a pure incandescent substance to fuel our forthcoming *elevation dance*. After you become *burning water*—the marriage of liquid and fire—there is nothing at all to stop your orbital path from moving a quantum level higher."

The Solar Temple of Apollicius commenced to undergo its most radical metamorphosis since its birth as a young star. By rising up through its own ringed neck, Apollicius redefined what it was and what it meant to be a *temple*. This was both the beginning and end of their most miraculous tests and ordeals: to *walk* the *Path* as narrow as the edge of a sword's blade and execute the correct promenade. Opening his Solar Arms at their widest, Apollicius rose up from within himself to fill his Temple with the *burning light* of the *cross-roads*. To focus on the flame within the flame, at that exact point, became the whole aim of the *game*.

As soon as Mercury touched *that* point with his *quicksilver* toe, the circular base of the Temple now enclosed his head—much in the same way a flower becomes en-globed by its vase.

"When only one path is *left,* I choose the *right,*" Mercury spoke lightly.

The Temple of Apollicius had now become a *headlight* to illuminate the *crossroads.* From ear to light-year, his head stretched up and a-*way.* Temple, Sun, Head, and Road—all distilled into one burning *solution.* Even Jupiter, with his mammoth weight, managed to walk on the base of the fire, and then circled upward into the orbital shape of an *eight.* The sword of Mars still continued to heat up the temperature of the in-candescent stars before he finally re-sheathed its blade.

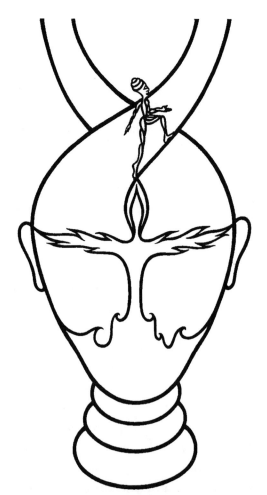

The sword that cuts the Path must tread upon its ever so narrow swath. Choose that, or the *burning coals.* Because the coals have the capacity to blaze, they cut a way that is every bit as tapered as the blade. No way has ever been simply *straight,* if it is to lead upward toward the higher *eight.*

"I never knew each step could be so painful," be-moaned Venus. "In order not to fall from this lofty ledge, I must learn to support the in-tense agony of the foil's edge." She had donned all green, and kept her spine as tall and straight as the recently imag-ined pine, as she attempted to move to follow this ever-so-narrow line.

"We were told to start looking for Helleniana at the

crossroads," Venus continued. "We need her to guide us through the Temple Halls: progression is a function of lightening our loads."

"She will reappear only when her time is right," Apollicius informed. "Prepare yourself to not have her. If she comes, then all the better; if not, you'll miss an opportunity in her absence to burnish your own copper."

This Temple of Apollicius could have art-covered walls or the unadorned sides of rustic stalls. Its Chapel could be in the depths of the most cloistered chambers of the Heart or occupy the whole expanse of the Universe of Art. The Simple Temple, the Tempestuous Temple, and the Mental Temple: stages for the ultimate adventure Mercury and the others are about to emb*ark* upon in the forthcoming pages.

"I, being the heaviest, have the most to gain through purification," Jupiter began. "My strength in mass needs to be tempered with a light cast. I feel as though I'm as ready as ever to do battle, as long as there is any disharmony carried over from the past."

Apollicius heard Jupiter and was pleased. He turned back to face the Temple of Transmutation, where at that moment Helleniana was somewhere inside, waiting in the *Wings*. As the principal *artist of light*, it was up to Apollicius to guarantee that his ever-changing plan would work out to be right.

"Maybe if I return to my easel and Marisium's cerulean canvas, I can use the *brush* to conjure up the image of Helleniana—unchanging yet protean pure," Apollicius boomed into the void.

Often he used the wings of the great bird, the Phoenix, to alter his canvases. Pulling out a rather large quill, he drew on and on, for it was a long period before he had had his fill. Still, though, he had neither heard from nor seen Helleniana. The Planets were all inside waiting for the new *plant* to be ready. It had been put firmly in position, settled, and established itself, a living *temple* grounded and ready to grow. Continuing the beat with the right attitude, Apollicius had maneuvered himself into an ideal state, where all the things he had been working toward could begin to consecrate and later procreate. The only interferences with his creative voice were the noise-laden instruments produced by inner-planetary *forgers* under the command and gravitational surveillance of Gorisius and the dark side of the Moon.

Being both the Great Wing of the Wave and also its light-rimmed shores, Apollicius gathered together all of his most recent and pertinent musical scores. He then ascended to his Temple of Mount Purgatory, where he saw a *vision* of the *heavenly car* pointing tantalizingly toward the open star. Unrolling his scores, Apollicius called each of the Planets to *play* their own part during their routine of daily *artistic chores*.

Then, later, after applying one final stroke, he put down the *brush-quill* drawn from the Phoenix and swooped back to see what ethereal spirit of the arts he had attempted to evoke. Through an act of his own *will-to-imagine*, he had recreated his Temple of Pure Flight. The *landscape* was suffused with mist, while the bas-relief evoked the *sound* of his own composed *hymns*. At the entrance was the *Spirit of Creation* itself, kneeling at the Temple doorway. Inside the Sanctuary of his Universe, the ceilings and walls were cloud-like and silver-lined, as the floor rose up in the shape of a *sky-scraping* wing facing the threshold of the Great Door.

Inside the Temple of the Cloud and face to face with its winged congregation, Mars spoke in an inspired tone—like a roving Planet, who

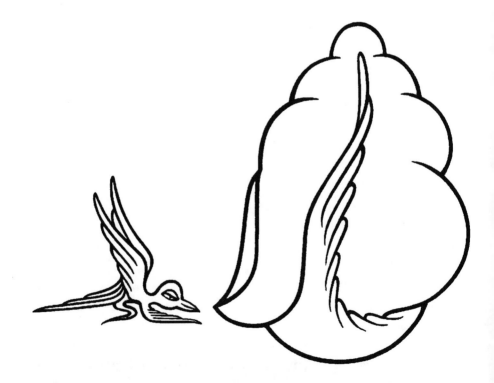

had just wheeled in: "My hand-to-hand combat days are over—now I advocate a transcendental chat with Helleniana. We offer here the Great Wing as a sanctuary created by Apollicius to take us to her or her to us. With my unsheathed sword, I now raise it to the ceiling of the Heavenly Vault and call for Helleniana to render visible what she has tried for so long to keep occult."

"As messenger," Mercury jumped in, "my fleet-winged feet now have a home and retreat inside this Light Temple of the Air."

"If Helleniana is really feather-light as they say, she will be attracted to come here at the speed of the *ray*," Venus added.

Not such a distance away, but far enough to not be heard, Helleniana began to speak to herself and especially to Marisium, mistress of the vast space.

"Time has sealed me in here, while all of you are *out* there on a *path* and in a *sphere*," she confided softly to Marisium.

"Yet, through your own Path of Purification, you are becoming lighter. More weightlessness means moving toward the outermost and greatest of all Spheres: the *Primum Mobile*," Marisium said encouragingly.

"It is true that when I move in motion, I seek ever-greater circumferences for these dances in *orbital revolution*," Helleniana confirmed.

"To be *celestially* affected, my child is not necessarily to be afflicted," Marisium explained. "While Mercury holds the *Sound Staff*, you may possess the *distaff*, for your role is not to spin yarn but to tell a yarn by becoming *it*.

"You are what winds around. As a Muse, you are much more than just amusing. In fact, you are not here to provide a show, though you may do it, but to show the other Planets what you know that I know."

"And to do that, of course I must re-appear among them?" Helleniana posed.

"Yes," Marisium affirmed. "Your domain is not a mere link in the chain, but to reign over the spatial plane of the Galactic Terrain."

"I know that without battles, without fierce conflict, what you speak of cannot be won," Helleniana replied. "I must go there soon, so one of them can win the boon."

Marisium, the Great Space Monarch, spread her vault into an arch to allow Helleniana to pass through. Her arch then detailed its lines, taking the shape of a *Giant Female* composed of all the most exciting curves the Cosmos had to offer.

"Through me, I'll put you into direct contact with Apollicius and his Family of Planets, all waiting to be of use in fitting the role to have you as their rightful Muse," Marisium explained.

Then rays of purple-clad light opened the seams of her Night's intricately spun dreams, illumining for Marisium one of her favorite daughters, Helleniana.

"It is me allowing you to see her," Solium beamed to Marisium, having just literally burst onto the scene.

"Since we have not been together for some time now, I decided to bring along my seven venerable plumes to reach all the Seven Kingdoms that Apollicius will soon found, with your help as Queen of the infinite volumes."

Sitting in her *own* Space, Marisium reached up to grasp one of Solium's Seven Rays. It felt so familiar; she instinctively looked down at herself and saw her *own* body, likewise composed of different sizes of these *same* Rays.

"When I touch you, Solium, I don't feel myself as a *black-hole-of-the-night*, but rather as *whole-back-to-the-Light*," Marisium exclaimed.

Without hesitating any longer, she reached down and swept Helleniana up in her hand. The moment they touched, the daughter's body *transformed* into a small plume, which Marisium immediately offered up to Solium for him to consume. Readily, Helleniana *streamed* into the ponderous drop one ray had just beamed. Thus, beheld by the *Mother*, she became one with the *Father*, thereby preparing herself for the *Son*.

Soothed by the synchronous rise and fall of Solium's *unbound strings*, Helleniana—aware that she had been plucked from Night by the Gathering Day—reached upward to the full extension of the Ray. Solium had accumulated enough Esthetic Wisdom and real knowledge of the Poet to hold lightly this heavenly *dame of the spirit*.

Inside the Temple, Apollicius had been hard at work preparing himself and his Planetary Family to behold the Muse and Goddess—Helleniana. She had grown into being the totality of what could be known. By entering the Ray of Solium, the Great Central Sun, she had now positioned herself to begin a long series of transformations, which inevitably would challenge the comprehension-capacity of Apollicius, to say nothing of his *planetary satellites*. Even though she had momentarily come out of her dream of seclusion to participate with Solium in an extraordinary rite of *fusion*, she had by no means abandoned the dark side of her *moonbeam*. She had merely briefly overcome it, allowing Apollicius to catch a glimpse of her solar capacity for realization. The next step, they both knew, would depend on Apollicius as moderator of his Seven Spheres.

To embrace all of his possible symphonies, Apollicius would need to become sovereign of the *seven-sounding harmony*. As the *local sun* of his *small* system, he possessed within his various *Suites of Light* the greatest of all possible circuits. Disconnected, his light confined itself within a circular prison, whereas in close relation with the rest of his singular system, he became his own *light's prism*. The Planets each came with their own particular *tones*, funneled through Space and amplified by each of their *orbital cones*. Inter-laying each *tone* into its oval orbit, Apollicius could harmonize each *planetary drone* into one cosmic Symphony of the Empyrean Tone.

Seventh Movement

Sublimation: *This occurs when a solid is heated and gives off a vapour which condenses on the cool upper parts of the vessel as a solid, not going through a liquid phase*

Sublime and subliminal, the Music of these whirling Orbs would provide the dramatic background for Apollicius to produce his own lighting to brighten their sound. The prime virtue of a melody so possessed would be found not in rest, but in a state of being continually expressed.

Mercury had already invented the first instrument to have *seven strings, each string* resonating in a different orbital plane of a planet. For example, the lowest and slowest of these *strings* had been attributed to Saturn, who, though grave, was known to have the courage of the brave, and so on up through the higher notes and higher *staves* of justice, righteousness, forgiveness and generosity.

As Helleniana un-wound, a whole skein of sound became unbound from her distaff and Apollicius silently planned to direct all their movement with his staff. They had seemed destined to join their *notes* into a Book of Accords, Chords and Discords.

Cradled momentarily in the huge, high-beam bed of Solium, Helleniana soon sought a more familiar refuge with her somber moonbeam. Be it orb or crescent, she could not just yet continually be in ascent.

Her surface still trembled in a shocked state whenever one of her pearly *moonstones* shifted its weight. At times she could be so full and then periods came when there would be a complete change in her orb's gravitational pull.

"Certain moments I am adrift in this Spatial Sea, without a form for all this sound wanting to escape the shape of this *mouth of foam*," Helleniana confided truthfully.

Even without hearing or seeing her, Apollicius declared to himself and to anyone who might have been there to listen: "I come from the school of unschooled souls. The source of the *great vision* I have for my Planetary Kingdom is seraphic fire and igneous force."

Unable to restrain himself any longer, Apollicius called out to Helleniana in the process of dissolving the *universe of pain* of which he no longer served as *emperor*. She had never been so far away but immediately heard the plea emitted from his *voice within the ray*.

"I am here every instant, yet remain the one who is inconstant. Though half of me is dark and other light, I rise as a full-blown pearl a dozen places in a *circle of space*. Of all the spheres, I am the one first lit. Un-leaving, I am the *woof,*
ever-drawing
across the *ver-
tical lines* I am
so in search
of to complete
my weaving,"
Helleniana an-
nounced through
the Gauze of the
Night.

Apollicius first
saw a sliver of milky-
light so impressive in
its *half-compass* movements,
that his whole body immediately began to shiver. She seemed
to float toward him by cleaving the

Spatial Sea of Marisium completely embodied in a boat. To stabilize his heart—now beginning to soar—Apollicius reached for the closest star, whose light he bent into an *oar*.

"Helleniana," he cried out. "Solium designed you in his Mind as a *parabola*, yet you sail toward me as a *gondola*. Guided by the Star, I'll man your gondola to steer across the border of that uncharted region of the *Unknown Frontier*."

Seated securely in her *saddle*, Apollicius dipped the star-tipped oar into the Sea of Marisium and began to *paddle*. After they had truly met, he needed now to return to his System, where all his Planets had recently been reset. Finally meeting again, their adventure had everything sufficing to make a substantial gain.

Presently holding sway, Helleniana ruled the circling spheres with her silver scepter marking the *way*. Holding her simple *distaff*, she raised it slightly, moving alongside Apollicius. For the moment they flowed side by side, yet deep within her complex being she had many things to tell him, which for now she knew she must hide. Her many sides could be outnumbered only by her innumerous faces. Apollicius never really knew which face belonged to what side and vice versa. He knew only that she needed to be given a lot of *space* and handled with a generous do*sage* of modulation.

Breaking the silence, interrupted only by the steady rhythm of their gait, Helleniana called out to Apollicius, something that couldn't wait:

"Though I am well aware that your own Planets move through their circuits by the strength and the force of their own *sound current*, I still believe it is not, nor shortly will it be, enough to power their coming advent."

"You couldn't be more correct, Helleniana. Your form is simply a *structure* for your state of *rapture*," Apollicius replied with deep affection. "This has been described as a deep feeling of overpowering delight; my Planets need to continue evolving along their circumscribed *path of light*."

From Marisium, Helleniana carried within her both Woman *and* Muse, the Mother-Matrix and the *World-Creatrix*. Her arms, being disproportionately long, had the strength and length to encircle a throng. She carried herself lightly so as to always preserve her own style, sprightly.

"They *all* need me," Helleniana proclaimed immodestly, though not from excessive pride or vanity, but consciously aware of her own innate sanity.

"No Planetary Being," she continued, "can stay on its revolutionary track without having a Muse it can openly contact."

"They have always been aware of you, yet, like me, needed to have you in their presence, at least for a time to be able to change into what they really are in their essence," added Apollicius.

Shortly, they both arrived at the Temple of Air, where all the Planets had assembled and patiently waited to catch their first glimpse of *her* there. As they approached, she wondered to herself if she would be permitted to appear in her complete sublimity, or if she would be compelled to reduce her effulgence to conform to each of their levels of planetary intelligence. Being the true Muse, she could never try to win them over through any ruse. In the realm of Pure Art, there could be no room for *artifice*. Her *office* espoused the Virtue of Imagination, not the vice of its deformation.

As the Planets revolved and evolved, they soon discovered their *Temple* to be *Everywhere*—they Imagined an Example. Their real sidereal House of Worship existed inside Consciousness, their consciousness. Overtones and undertones of the desire-of-fire permeated into every place—throughout all of Marisium's Sacred Space.

Infused with her own *telluric currents*, Earth *stepped* forward to move closer to Helleniana's *celestial vents*, in profusion. Helleniana saw from afar, her lovely body aglow like a small blue star. She realized she had had to return to guide each of their energetic spheres to the sublime acme of erotic and exotic adventure, as the prime Guardian of the Well, which could be probed and drunk from only, in time, through a supreme Act of the Will.

Opening up her Planet as if she were a prodigious Plant, Earth extended her Great Self skyward, drawing up within her body all the Spiral Movement of her Sphere. One saw her reflection in the other—the *telluric*, a congealed former Muse and the *celestial*, a star in revealed music, one grounded, listening, the other sounded, glistening. The Ground unrolled, the Sky enscrolled. To become sublimated, Earth's entire upward body became huge leaves and branches, stemming from her lower, root-like haunches.

Helleniana extended her long, luxuriant arms to thoroughly encompass her galaxy of charms. As she looked downward at Earth, their eyes finally met and locked inward.

"You are greater than I ever imagined, Helleniana. In your *Cloak of Night*, I could easily have mistaken you for Marisium," Earth exclaimed.

"And you, my precious Earth, in essence, are an unsoiled sphere spinning in an attempt to become uncoiled. You are a perfect representation of my *distaff*—the female branch of the Planetary Family that Apollicius has tried so assiduously to elliptically launch," Helleniana explained.

"You and I share a gentle sympathy; we must continue this momentum carried on by Mars, Mercury, Saturn and Jupiter," Earth rejoined, ignited by an instant flash of recognition.

"You speak in a mantic manner. I can see that your *base* has been served the finest of all waters, now being transmuted inside your Natural Laboratory—into more foliage during your long process to unfurl the *sage*. This is why you turn, spin, dance, and revolve: to reveal what everyone carries deep inside, wanting to *resolve to evolve*," Helleniana spoke perspicaciously.

With a wide sweep of her Cloak, Helleniana swooped up and away from the Tree-Rooted-Earth. Though its verdant beauty enticed her, it was not *her* Planet. After the Moon and the Earth, came the Third Sphere, which she sought out with fervent desire. To sincerely rejoice, she knew she needed to pursue *good ends* and have the *means* to achieve them. She needed a *vehicle* wherein her amorous nature could repose and later, with time, re-compose.

Wheeling from one side of the Heavenly Vault to the other, Helleniana crossed the path of a rather voluptuous spheroid and faced it head on, as it would have been rather difficult to easily avoid. Then, a kind of miracle came about. As if *Aphrodite* had held up a mirror, Helleniana saw her own persona reflected back to her. She kept on moving, though, in the same direction toward the Center of the oncoming Spinning Sphere.

When they met, there was no collision; instead, Helleniana recognized the Planet Venus as the way she had once seen herself in a *vision*. Venus, on the other hand, saw Helleniana's star-spangled cloak flash across the Heavens and pictured *herself* as the true source of that great motivating force.

"Now it is my turn to be still and patiently wait for the Great Urn to slowly fill," Venus said enigmatically, for Helleniana and the rest of the Space of Marisium to clearly hear.

"Where is the Great Urn you refer to?" asked Helleniana.

"It is being shaped by Earth herself at this very moment," Venus affirmed.

"Then you speak of the Return of Our Vessel in the form of an Urn?" Helleniana asked.

"That's right. As Goddess of Beauty, I know that, though the *Temple Is Everywhere*, at certain times it resides in a specific place in space and even can procure the shape of a voluptuous figure," Venus explained.

"I think I understand," Helleniana responded pensively.

After she had left Earth in search of the Third Sphere, Venus, Earth began to undergo a distinct metamorphosis. In literally one monstrous upheaval she inverted her Planetary Base, formerly the shape of a Tree Trunk when last visited by Helleniana, into an Earthen Vase. The *Earthenware* would soon be *worn* by the new Mystical Pair to be married in this changing Temple of Air, an event brought to fruition through the Earth's newly shaped Vessel of Intuition.

Mercury, too, soon heard the Voice of Venus, and came knowing that Helleniana had also reappeared when she announced her presence by name. Mercury had been known before to be many things, from helpful servant to fugitive servant and, later, fugitive procreator. He had been also referred to as *prime*, planetary, and pure matter, participating in the Grand Opus of Apollicius from Alpha to Omega. The Tone of *his* Land resonated with the Stone struck by his Philosopher's Hand. Because of the duality of his nature, he came to be a prime candi*date* to join with Venus in a quality love adventure.

Since Mercury had basically a fluid body, he stayed in a constant state of flux. Though not always clear, he readily flowed smoothly and soundly not just as words, of prose but in moving spheres of worlds emerging from the bud of a rose. His water could be found everywhere, though it still remained uncommon. As a rarefied form of *dew*, it readily developed into full elaboration in its sublime state, not in many but only in a *few*. Mercury himself could be found at the very *Head of the Waters*, where the rise of the *herd* usually falters.

Whoever saw Mercury when he arrived witnessed a strange sight. He moved as a *cool wave* yet burned hot in flames, dancing up out of that Planetary Cave. Reaching across, through the Fire-of-Himself, Mercury touched *Venus*, yet strangely felt the presence of Helleniana. Apollicius had let her enter the space of the Earthen Planetary Vase to enact the Rite of the Fire Marriage. Mercury became the *Penetrating Spirit*, or the transmutable agent in the present story. His planetary substance as Messenger of Might prolonged and enhanced their Planetary System of Light, while his vitality turned their orbital movement into the ultimate reality.

"You are the Queen of our mysterious re-connection. What used to be the base of a Tree, now is a vase with space for we three," Mercury spoke through the steam of the fire's smoke.

"Between us blazes a fire that burns, yet consumes only the *inessential* inside this Urn of *urns*," Venus observed ecstatically.

"This is our new vessel, full of the subtle *spirit*, the most pure food for the whole system of Apollicius to draw its essential energy form from *it*," Mercury pointed out.

Jupiter, Saturn, Mars and the Moon had all spun around to continue overlooking what took place there inside *Love's Crucible of Cooking*. In order to grow, there needed to be good food, so here inside this warming Earthenware, two of his Planets underwent the *test of sublimation*. If they passed, they would be ready to ignite the whole Solar System with their spark, lit by their own rite. Interweaving flame and name under the *umbrella plans* of Helleniana, the bodies of Mercury and Venus melted, welded, wedded and melded into shaped, energetic planes crossing the Planetary Plains. As agents

of the overall plan, Mercury and Venus became plangent through the emotional waves of Sound and Light that they now, outwardly, sent. The *base* turned into a *vase*, wherein the *fire flower* grew to a size that neither Apollicius nor Solium could ever erase and that only Mercury and Venus had the wherewithal to embrace.

Helleniana did not have to appear in the nude as a devotional prelude. Nor did she need to come accompanied by her *Nymphs* of both the Air and the Sea in plenitude. Nor did they ask her to put aside her hunting spear, her quiver, her tightly strung bow, or her magic sandals and Cloak of Night. They asked of her only one thing: to dance. At the utmost edge of the hollowed Earth, rimming their Chalice, the two of them touched amid the blaze of this Transcendental Palace. Above this Goblet in the shape of an upturned *droplet*, Helleniana began the Dance, her most treasured outlet. She turned red from the fire as Mercury, Venus, the whole whirling Solar System, and the Galaxies all bypassed their tomb to pass through her Womb.

She could never be greater than any of the three-sphere-seers, yet she would always promise more than they could ever grasp as her still whirling peers. The dilemma to stay in or stray away from the all-encompassing and consuming *Ray* would never be posed in her presence. Each Planet had its own individual Throne in the Empyrean Space, set in its place by the vibration of that Planet's unique Tone. For a moment, both Mercury and Venus experienced the pure paradise of their Androgynous Being under the overarching Dame of the Flame. The artistic intricacy of the Temple is an example of Pure Simplicity—where the *Psyche* penetrated by *Cupid* conjured the Elixir of Immortality. Love, then, was an edifice of *architectural design*, in which what is spoken was a benign sign, never meant nor desiring to malign.

Under her Dome, these two joined Planets found a home. This *foundry*, so to speak, became their place where new *gold metal* would be cast, where the *bronze sound* could be finally forged to last. They had moved from the subterranean wall inside the Belly of Marisium, to the live and burnished threshold of the Hall of the Empyrean.

"Together, we can be a *functional sword*, an organ in kin, drawing itself out beneath the sheath of the skin," Mercury proclaimed, inspired.

"We are our own *organ*, then," Venus added, "capable of adapting to a specific function and performing it well by carrying it out according to the Plan. We, ourselves, are a musical means of communication. a musical, sexual, social Organ—organized organically."

At this point, the Fire inside their Earthenware Vessel burned through its sides, sounding the clapper of this *upside-down bell*—a vaginal shape *reproduced* everywhere. The Fire burned both inside and outside of them. It really had no defining line, since its boundaries were essentially so fine. The only way to put it out would be for them to somehow lose their *semi-liquid source* inside this Binary System of Force.

Though a Planet, Venus had the sensual shape of a woman. Her breasts exposed the gap where the continents had parted, changing the original outline of the map. Mercury's Wand had not come to rest on her breast, but had followed her *coastal shoulders* down her *Nile*, where her soil could be found most fer-

tile. She had become the treasurer of the treasure and the principal purveyor of aesthetic pleasure. The joys of any Planetary Body began with the *center corpus* and progressed, caress by caress, out toward a stellar radius under the direction of Mercury's Caduceus.

Before Mercury met Venus, his Winged Staff had yet to join their *staff*. Its initial erection, as member, came from the image of its constant projection. This *rod* angled up in the direction of the *winged god*. This site supported its arched height on legs of kindled light. Such vivacity and lightness could come only from a *polished stone* of exceptional brightness.

The strength of his visible *and* invisible Staff helped maintain the Fire in its Temple-Shape of a Mountain. Venus kept her diaphanous wing enfolded until their *temple of fire* became rightly molded. Encapsulated in a triangular state of energy, their one-same power allowed protective Angelic Forces to help them mate and mesh into one flesh. Helleniana saw the Fire-Arch and went through it to become a real part of their Picture Language of Mythological Art. Before, she had been hidden by smoke; now she burned in the Fire, clothed only in her Magic Cloak. Burning, she became the Dark One, a Muse mighty enough to create, preserve, and ever destroy, thus experiencing one more of the many transfigurations she would undergo all the way through coming Planetary Generations.

Looking inward, they both saw and immediately understood how she, as the Great Muse of Apollicius, had helped inspire the overall sound design for his original Planetary Law. Its name became: "Knowledge at the Edge of the Flame."

"We have each become enclosed and clothed in our own individual urn," Mercury realized. "Helleniana has already decided the *time* is right for our turn. I hope we are ready and able to continually *burn*."

"We are," Venus confirmed, still maintaining the shape of their *Caduceus-of-Arms*.

Though these two Planetary Lovers had successfully melded, it would not be for them to actually work in the *foundry* where their *link* would be finally welded. They would now turn away from that *mine*, taking them once again from their Muse, so Divine. Apollicius saw that *Love* had now been created, not by romancing the past but here, in the present effervescent moment, where they had so precisely been cast.

"Peace cannot last when there is a war to be waged against the *internal forces of cosmic dissolution*," Apollicius declared to Helleniana, who had disappeared into a *trail of fire*. "If I do not weave new cloth into the tapestry of fresh thought, then that mantle I wear as Sun Master will shrink into something smaller than a microdot. This Mantle of Light that I wear throughout the realms of this entire system, I can neither disrobe nor *dismantle* without my entire Masterwork becoming mere smoke of the battle."

Helleniana had her Cloak of Night, just as Apollicius had his Mantle of Light. She often wore hers over the nakedness of her bronzed skin, while he had donned his eons ago to diminish the surrounding din. She had now concealed herself again at *home*, while Apollicius tried to overcome the pain of separation by moving through the *Doorway*, crossing the threshold and heading in the direction of Marisium's overarching Dome. Seized by unpredictable laughter, he opened his Robe to let more rays pour through him into the all-involving days. As he searched across a sky spangled with stars, it took some time before he could finally locate the position of Mars.

As a Planet, Mars had followed his warrior code, pulsating throughout the entire *seminal system* as solid as his own Iron Abode. He had a well-drawn, securely harnessed and regally crowned *will-of-the-well*. His realm had been called the Fifth Sphere and in reality began the Age of Intuition. By working so long with Steel, Mars had developed long, sensitive nerves, which he had only very recently begun to reveal. He had fought long and hard for his Planetary Body to avoid at all costs an ever-numbing weight. He habitually trained, not *with* iron, but to have its strength, not its rigidity—to be able to forge his new role as Cosmic Art Patron. When he now reappeared, his arms bore seven staves, one for each of his spherical kinsmen and women. They were *staves* to be used both for noting celestial sounding themes and for promoting martial grounding schemes.

"My *planetary site* is a flexible series of joined links, where inter-spatial pilgrims can visit the Cosmic Galley to view *Visions* coming from outside the boundary of my Iron Foundry," Mars announced to the Heavenly Lot, those who happened to not be beyond galactic earshot.

None responded, at least not immediately anyway, so Mars returned to his work in the *galley of the gallery*. He alone had been separated from the others and now propelled his own, low and round Planetary Ship across the Cosmic Seas of Space and Imagination. There he slaved, having transformed all those Seven Staves destined for the other Planets into *oars*, which he now guarded as a treasure saved. In his *galley*, he cooked, painted, drew up plans, grew strong, and then waited. The *gallery* opened up over the *deck*, where the ship's sails stretched canvas to the maximum to catch and transcribe each pictorial *Vision* into a mythic maxim.

"There below—look!" shouted Jupiter. "It is Mars, still hard at his labor of love—or is it his love of labor? As he becomes stronger, his *body-of-work* gets longer."

"I can now make out clearly what he painted when he arose from his dream, enchained yet untainted," Saturn answered. "I see both of us bonded to his interconnecting arms—a link toward which we have always corresponded."

"Lets move closer to that *visionary canvas*," suggested Jupiter. "I've always wanted to attempt to fuse the *real* with the *imaginary*, the *iron* with the *irony*, the *charged ion* with the *scrolled ionic*."

The closer they came to the Magnetic Field of Mars, the less resistant they became to the strong attraction of his *steel plant*. Mars clearly saw and deeply felt their approximation quickly diminishing any possibility of continued separation. Then, in a rush of *sound-infused light*, each Sphere drew close enough to finally Cohere. The Sound made when they locked into a clasp evoked from each mammoth body a thunderous gasp.

Mars had become freely unchained only when he finally succeeded in becoming his *own* chain. Beyond merely linking himself to his own *fount of might*, he turned into the Sorcerer of the Source. His foundry changed into the foundation for a new *fountainhead*. The three of them soon had forged a triad for the development of a common *will*—ironclad.

"When I ever meet my bride, I plan to be ready for the inevitable ride," Mars proclaimed. "Thanks to both of you for giving me a temporary *hand,* though I am still wary of temptation in my own created land."

"Who or what is the *temptress?*" Jupiter inquired, now firmly connected to this *knight of might.*

"It is the *woman* I have been separated from for so long. I fondly refer to her as the Divine Wine. She is water, liquid—the essence of fluidity. The more I congeal, the less I feel she is still actually real. But recently I seem to have been unable to reverse this slow process of solidification. In a sense, it feels good to be more *compact,* but I'm worried this may interfere with the flexible ability to fully act," Mars confessed.

"Mars, you seem like the kind of *planetary ark* who has been accustomed to rotating just beyond the protective zone of Apollicius," Saturn ventured to remark.

"I have often confused my warrior frenzy with being poetically dizzy—taking me wide of my original focus," Mars stated manner-of-factly.

"I see the *two* both connected to the symbolic image of a *Horn.* Most horns express their wild excitement and deliriums by combining the Raw Energy of the Warrior with the Pure Imagination of the Seasoned Poet," Jupiter interjected.

"Yes, I get it, my *friends-of-the-orbit.* I can emerge from any sort of private hell by coiling my *inner tube* and letting the air flow through me into the open heaven at the end of my head, flaring into a bell," Mars exclaimed excitedly, noting how both Saturn and Jupiter exerted a huge pull on him.

"Of course, *we* know, Mars, but what about the '*temptress* of the Divine Wine and tempestuous dress?'" Jupiter reminded him.

"It is a very fine balance between keeping her hermetically sealed away and allowing her the complete freedom to outflow without obstruction. My supreme challenge at present is to re-route her *river* so that its current moves only *upstream,*" Mars rang back in a joyous tone.

"And the *temptress?*" Saturn continued to ask with obvious curiosity.

"*She* is the throb and pulse of both the *liquid* and *electric current* circulating in one *vessel of energy,*" Mars offered in a very quick attempt at an explanation.

Through a strongly defined exercise of their combined *wills,* these

Three Spheres had momentarily, temporarily become this *Vision of Mars*. Like two mighty tributaries, the *energy* coming from the extensive magnetic fields of Jupiter and Saturn had formed a great juncture at the *chained trunk* of Mars—the trunk of his body, his tree, and his *chest of treasure*

Eighth Movement

Separation: *Involves the release of the spirit or watery vapour*
from the body or earthly matter

The temptation for Mars to see Helleniana, or any other Muse for that matter, as just a woman in the flesh had always been most overpowering. How could something so delicious be so much more than just *food* to be devoured, or wine to be drained to boost the *mood*? The True Muse, or True Source of Inspiration, embodied both *food* and *wine*, both *body* and *spirit*. In a way, lying down, she spanned both states to complete the bridge connecting dusk to dawn. Mars saw as his immediate mission to *draw* up this *bridge*, with the sensual curves of a natural ridge, toward him. Nevertheless, this *treasure* could be lost through the accumulation of untransformed pressure. If it was squandered, there would be no replacement, it would be gone forever. With any *leaks* in their System of Rotation, Revolution, and Light of any magnitude, there would have been no way to save that delicate bridge between two *peaks*, given its altitude and longitude.

Mars looked up and saw that Jupiter and Saturn had broken free of their *fettered spirit* and had returned—recharged—to the march of their orbit. He breathed in and out for several *light moments*, then slowly gained the right strength to fill this pair with columns of rising air. His polymorphous Muse had coagulated her fluid temper to become a solid *actor,* set into place opposite her benefactor. They had their stage set for the *curtain* to be raised, for the subject of their play to perform and later be appraised.

Mars had already turned on his steady axis to face this novel shape of Helleniana—wearing neither cloak nor cape. She simply stood tall as the *filler of the pillar*. The *curtain* rose only for their *play*, which would present what it knew and express its underlying support through the content it showed to be true.

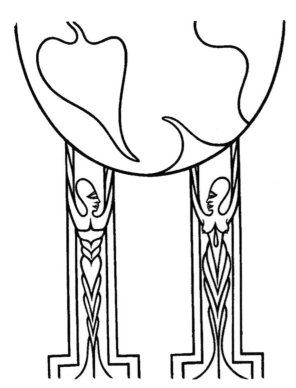

"You and I now buttress the arsenal of this *dress* rehearsal," Mars told Helleniana. "Together we have the strength to defend and support the ever-changing Solar System of Apollicius, especially when you, as our own Special Muse, have been set up as the Cornerstone of his Solar Tone."

"Now I can be completely confident in playing the part of *Myself,* while remaining concealed within the *Architectural Art,*" Helleniana sighed contentedly.

She ended the *scene* by once again finding a new way to be blended. The *Columns-of-Air* had been built with the deliberate aim of lifting the curtain of this Undis*covered* Planet into the ecstasy of full-blown acclaim. Helleniana had successfully become an integral, supportive *pillar* of the Planetary Temple of Mars. Designed to uphold an entire *Sphere*, the Temple could be entered only by complete *acceptance* and *transcendence* of what was already *here*. By being at *one* with their own Architecture, they could *atone* for any surrounding *atonality*. This special kind of a*tone*ment came to be known throughout the Revolutionary System of Apollicius as *at-one-ment, momentary, or monumental.*

The belligerence of Mars, though regularly tempered with tolerance and intelligence, pressed him onward, toward the altitude of new Altars. With this new attitude, he left the Columns of the Temple behind and penetrated the greater and lesser worlds, striving for that ever-elusive *thread of balance* to be found or created. Restless and always turning, he whistled through the *ethereal vapor* path—a mystical nimbus, a numinous sphere, yet still heavily laden with a *bow* and an occasional show of wrath. Mars whirled on, stopping periodically to erect an altar to Apollicius, their own particular Star. Once he knew himself as a Temple through Helleniana, he would be able to enter it anytime, anywhere.

Apollicius saw how he had temporarily separated himself from his System-as-a-Whole, to act out his own rebellious role. He saw his being alternatingly *burning* and *turning* on its *warrior pole.* To prepare for his Great Battle ahead, he needed to hear the Ancient Drum together with the Sistrum Rattle. Mars longed to see Apollicius hurling down his luminous darts, to hear the explosion of a New School of Cosmic Music along with the rest of their Spherical-Spiritual Arts—this was no time to be negligent and make Apollicius wait for their *creative aliment.* It needed to be now and to *start* with the *art of the bow.* Bending his huge Planetary Being as if he were a pliant reed, Mars strung his *one string* so taut it could not be freed. Catching one of the flung *arrows of light*, Mars placed it in the *bow-of-himself*, pulled back, and let it shoot into flight.

"This is what I live to see," Jupiter thundered. "In our entire system of *whirling fractions*, Mars, the most formidable of warriors, he is the key to all *our actions.*" Dipping into the cool waters of Marisium's Spatial Sea, Mars tempered his red-hot, iron body. Lodged between *Hell's vapors* and all of *Heaven's neighbors*, Mars unleashed himself in animated *cosmic capers.* Glowing coals fanned out his aura, showing new symbolic images to feed the soul, still unknowing.

"I feel my own temperature rising just watching Mars," Mercury observed, sending his own *mercurial word* in the direction of their Sun Lord.

"I am inside of you, Mars," he continued. "There is no easy disguise to actually make one's energy rise. This has solely to do with me and my *rights of distribution.* For a *comet* not to fall, it needs to commit to *it* all."

"Any stout wielder of the sword can dash to pieces a Temple's Pillars, but will back-track from the *light flood* emanating from the Solar Charioteer, whose emblem exhibits the color and design of Solium's *illustrious blood*," Apollicius called out from the heart of his Father's Mystical Thought.

"Each of you must risk all to become a Solar Disk impervious to the fall," Apollicius continued.

Out of deference, each of the Planets traced even more precise *circles of rotation* around their Sun *Ruler's* great circumference. Mars had definitely catalyzed fresh reactions through his own audacious actions. Her work done, Helleniana left his Temple, giving him more *space of separation* to begin to sample. Her Mission took her on to Marisium, to continue to serve with Solium's permission. It had been some time since they had had a real conversation. As Muse, she existed for the most part in a state of isolation, even though she always seemed to be present when she was needed for Inspiration. Her long

period of detachment from the other Planets had deepened her desire to verbalize what the others, through her, attempted to idealize.

"Have you come to return the Cloak of Night, my child of interplanetary flight?" Marisium wasted no time in asking when Helleniana arrived at her *nocturnal threshold.*

"Though it has served me well, I thought I might leave it with you for a spell. I feel the need to change my attire, to continue to allow my true way-of-being to transpire."

Marisium took the Cloak and held it high before her. Through its warp and woof she saw the tapestry of the many worlds woven into the movement of the fabric's design, where the ground is sound and the heavens, the roof. At that particular moment, both Helleniana and Marisium shared the same *Body-of-Night.* Without her Magic Coat, however, the Muse became not only uncovered but also unprotected. The Coat had been her shield, which she had now decided to yield.

Stepping across the Void of Marisium's deep violet threshold, Helleniana felt her unadorned *Body of Movement* tremble with cold. Relinquishing her *cover* meant that the content of her *volume* now had to speak for both herself and her a*mused* lover. Upon leaving the Presence of Marisium, Helleniana felt again as isolated as she had at the beginning of her *sentence.* Since the initial phase of her *Muse-ship,* she had been sentenced to eternally roam, never to have what she could finally call her own home. It was a cruel fate—yet, along the way, through Apollicius, she had been directly *instrumental* in helping the Wandering Planets find their creative mate. Some had even called Helleniana a matchmaker for all Arts and Sciences.

Leaving Marisium, she carried in her Mind the shape of Marisium's Space, having ulti*mately* gone there with the intention of acquiring this Grace. Notwithstanding Marisium being her *tutelary goddess* of the extraplanetary, Helleniana felt a profound need to explore her fiery oceanic desires beyond the limits of her own *private pond.* At times she saw herself as a veritable polyhedron of choreographic ideas. By wearing the new Space vestment of Marisium, in place of the cloak already shed, she could now begin to disseminate her investment. Helleniana would have to rely upon the other established Planets as places of *dance worship,* yet she also needed to turn from their fair features and search through this darkness for her own inspirational pictures. Gradually, she observed, her *world-of-the-body* became a corpus infused with symbols. Stroked and caressed by her stable of musicians, she also thought of them soundly—as able physicians. To do battle along the way, she donned white accoutrements, and during the night, covered her comet-shaped head with a cloth of white samite.

Traveling deeper and deeper into the profundities of the Solar System of Apollicius, she moved closer toward an unknown Planet outside of their familiar system: Pluto, the Empire of the Magician. Hearing another language, both majestic and powerful, Helleniana felt her name being drawn into its magnetic domain. Never at any moment did she consider herself banished from the Solar Kingdom of Apollicius, but rather only temporarily separated from his influential radius. Having long since left the bevy, she had never been eager, for whatever reason, to become a part of any levy. She fought only to defend and maintain her level of Poetic Inspiration. It had never been enough to preside over the Arts, Sciences and Cosmic Literature; more than anything else, she desired the *chair* of Muse of the Visionary. She wanted to literally imprint the Cosmic Dance upon her countenance and liberate her soul from its body through its ecstasy-inducing trance.

Helleniana had wooed the Spatial Dimensions of Marisium for so long through her *song* and *dance*, she strongly felt the time fast approaching to reclaim her long-lost chance. A simple song blew through her lithe limbs, inflecting throughout all the revolving spheres of Apollicius. When they first met, Pluto immediately recognized the lineaments of the Sun in the modulations of her expressive face.

"You have come to discover your own position in reference to the whole system of Apollicius—from the ends of his diameter to the full elliptical dance of his circumference," Pluto declared.

"You are right, Pluto," she said. "In order to ascend, I must first descend. You, being the smallest sphere, can help me understand your outermost tier." Helleniana spoke out with full confidence in certain decisions she had made and others she forbade.

"I contain the origins of all procreation—therein lies my power as a planetary nation," Pluto affirmed. "I am in charge of the Ninth Sphere, to which you have now descended—called the *nether world*, neither here nor there. I am your *opposite,* which you have come to discover by following your web's thread to this site."

"As you probably know, Pluto, I have been known simultaneously as the sign of the terrific and of the benign," Helleniana spoke from the center of her Spirit. "I am here to respire your airs and to learn to further my art of harmonizing opposite pairs."

Around this smallest of planets ebbed and flowed the Plutonic sea— his shores laved with the same still waters in which Helleniana would soon be bathed, and in a certain sense saved. Now completely bare, ever since she had disrobed in front of Marisium, Helleniana had freely felt all the changes in the air, and therefore knew the *Temple of the Body* to be the same as the *Body of Her Temple.* The Sea of Pluto stretched out before her and summoned her with its steady lap of the gently moving states of Pluto's *oceanic map.*

Posed, nearly kneeling, Helleniana *opened* to the multitude of *elemental beings* populating this seashore thriving with Plutonic Energy. She now felt how each Step of the Way had been incorporated, literally, into her Temple of the Muse, which she had only recently begun to seriously peruse. Her own self-knowledge began with the first step way down near her *instep.* There, at the upper arch of her foot between her slender ankle and the toes, her *dance* had once begun to confront the *enemies of her whirling movement,* now ready to be vanquished as clearly her foes.

"Pluto! Send me your *elemental spirits* to splash, wash, and swash my Temple Body," Helleniana implored.

"They are already on their way," Pluto affirmed.

In an instant they had arrived and initiated a complete cleansing process of her capacious walls and spacious halls. They *swept up* her *flight-of-inner-stairs,* scouring each Step of the Way leading to the start of the spark of the Flame at the Lower Back of the Temple—where it gracefully begins to sway. The Water and the Fire commingled at the base of her spine—known in the Inner Circle of Apollicius as the main pillar of support for the entire structure of her Temple Vine.

Her Staircase: the seven steps of power, the seven levels of fire, and the seven musical scales of the knowledge tower. At the source and peak of her cascading steps opened her dual-headed serpent presiding over the whole transformational process going on inside the very structure of her *corpus tent.*

"The closer I get to merging with Marisium, the more I feel my true self slowly emerging—light enough for me to carry the *light,*" Helleniana mused. amused. "I haven't left those Islands of the Planetary Jewels forever. I'll be back to them and their evolving system of Apollicius—in fact, I'm nearly ready to go now," she said, directing her words toward the Platonic Pluto.

"Why is it, Pluto, that certain Planets are not as deferential as others, when I truly believe I treat them all the same?"

"You never know, Helleniana, what is really going on in the depths of their Spherical Beings," Pluto responded. "Though they are what they are, they still lack the independent power to *actually* generate their own Light, as even the tiniest star is capable of doing. That is why Apollicius is still their spiritual guide, to whom they must ultimately *turn* for reference in defining their outlining circumference."

"From my knuckles to my knees, I have felt Mars enwrap me as a *world belt,* warming my equator and poles until both they and our roles have begun to dissolve and melt," Helleniana said.

"Platonically, you are what love is to all the Planets, though your true groom be Apollicius," Pluto explained. "From afar I have almost the same perspective and visual vantage point as the nearest and smallest star. Your ultimate adventure and triumph will be when you mystically marry Apollicius; thereafter, the darkness of the deepest chamber of your He*art* will lighten through the practice of your Muse-*ical Art*."

"I know you're right, Pluto. The day I'm ready to *meet* Apollicius in the Main Hall of his Solar Palace, I'll arrive *wearing* nothing but the garland of all Seven Planetary Heads," Helleniana vowed, "and I will girth my waist with the *rays of a thousand outreaching arms*. My tongue will be thick with the *word*, ready to pick the pith of his *lightly cultivated* Plant-Herd. My hidden power will reveal its own reflection in the bursting into bloom of his head of sunflower."

"Are any of the Planets presently prepared to understand your full intention?" Pluto asked pointedly.

"Unfortunately, only a few of them are close to being able to deal with this complete dose of what is really needed in order to fully heal. For the ordinary, I am always obliged to reduce my effulgence, so as to not be in sharp discordance with their plenary modes of planetary indulgence," Helleniana said in complete candor.

From his not-so-distant stance, Apollicius looked on with fierce *cyclopian vision*, literally picking up the threads of their fine-lined conversation. So far, none of his *revolving offspring* had ever wondered why so many of them spoke in rhyme. He knew: the secret of the *rhyme* lay in the seasoning of the *thyme*. Left to their own devices, the Planets would naturally find their own *sense of time* in the cultivation of their *spices*. What had first attracted him to Helleniana had to have been her color and its aromatic blend of cinnamon and clove, wafting into his *Light Head*—uncommon in love. His Vision had not ever slid behind his gigantic eye-lid. His one brilliant orb *saw* equally well, whether closed or wide-open to his singular *solar law*. Only the instance of ignorance ignores the truthful beauty of the *Planetary Dance* scores. Helleniana lured and guided as she covertly and overtly bid each Planet to burst its fetters to become both the knower and the known, the writer of the *word* and above all the bearer of *letters*.

"Pluto," she announced, "I am no longer the Lady of the House of Sleep, but have awakened to the Ray and must follow its *thread* to the dawn of the day, where Apollicius shows his head to be seen and conceivably read. I now need to prepare to ascend to the Heart of his System. Through you, my fear has been dispelled. I hear the voice of the Charioteer, feel the Great Wheel turn, and can see the glint in the Light of Swords clashing to begin the mighty fight.

"Lie down," Helleniana continued, "to feel the full effects of the *light* coming from Apollicius, but bending through me as it reflects."

Pushing away from his small sphere, Helleniana opened each orifice located along her extended *tubular body* to begin the ceremonial rite of her *own office*—now ever more dimmer than bright. The four directions, the four elements, the four di*men*sions, and the four levels of energy filtered through her already rarefied body of the Muse. Massive quantities of *coral perfume* exuded from her, immediately wafting their way towards the gentle curvature of Pluto. Being in no great hurry to join the others, Helleniana lingered a while to hover over Pluto, attending to all the needs of a lover.

But soon Helleniana would regress to the System of Apollicius to again be the Muse of his Great Sun Chariot, to trace once more the general route for the other Planets to follow in their own pursuit. Importantly, she had established a strong connection to the Outermost World of Pluto, clearly no easy refuge from any kind of deluge, but rather one more sphere to enhance their journey's *Planetary Dance*. But before Helleniana would finally and definitively depart, Pluto presented to her a gift, very small, yet one that could give a major lift to them all. Helleniana was ready to receive something more to further reinforce her own *will* to *believe*.

Pluto's outermost sphere lay along the path of self-abnegation, loneliness, misunderstanding, and persecution, and aside from Helleniana, its host could be reached only by *post*. The Great Demiurge, Apollicius, as preternatural fabricator, had at one time ladled out a substantial portion to fill Pluto's small *sphere-holder* to the brim with his numinous potion. The Spherical Body of Marisium's Firmament enclosed all the other *spheres*, including the wayward, far-reaching Pluto. At the bottom of his *small urn-like* body, however, there began to smolder a *germ*; devoid of any flash, sparkle, or glitter, this *germ* nevertheless was encapsulated deep within its planetary *holder*.

Pluto had a reputation for being not only the smallest and the coldest planet, but also the lowest and oldest. "Lower, under, and outer," describe the *metallic soul* Helleniana found when she first entered his hollowed-out *bowl*. In his isolation and desolation, Pluto had turned to the *forge* lying within his deepest gorge. Using the very first *hammer* and *anvil*, produced from a certain thunder*bolt* and lightning crash, Pluto had originally begun his work as sculptor of the first representation of the *volt*. Over the light-years, he had managed to *catch* more *bolts* with his small but quick Plutonian hands. Using these sudden dashes of *bolts*, he had mixed them with these *volts* in the metallic bowl of himself to produce fresh flashes containing high-energy *jolts*.

In a deep way, Helleniana had befriended Pluto after overcoming her own inner and outer array of ageless perils, trials, gargoyles, and other assorted evils in order to finally meet her *secret helper*, Pluto, who turned out to *be* an instructive figure on her pathway to understanding the essence of her *light-nature*. Her trials and ordeals had given way to purgation and now had led her further along the Way of Surrender to the Ray of Apollicius. Fate had guided her to the threshold of Pluto's Lower Gate.

Inside his *forge*, a fire had been ignited and continued to roar with all the might and power that his trembling sphere could en-gorge. Miraculously, Helleniana had swooped down and forged into his forge, had *congress* with Pluto, and emerged with the *rings-of-her-gown* unbroken and in full dress. Her experience in the *forge* had been no forgery—thus it had enabled her to forge ahead to begin shaping a new *head*.

"Whatever we have wrought, it turned out to be you who found what had long been sought," Pluto concluded in retrospect.

"Though I have lain with you, Pluto, you are not my mate. Apollicius is my future lover with whom I already have marked a date."

Like Mercury, Pluto had initially had his own *caduceus:* his own Winged Staff to conduct, control, and direct each flame by name in this now generalized conflagration, which had been less than a mere spark before Helleniana came. The Great Serpent, coiled within Solium, the Father of Apollicius, had helped fan the flames, having been called, as was the custom, for the commencement of these types of *games*. Pluto's combustion had not been completely spontaneous, however. Whereas now there seemed nothing more to really muster, before Helleniana's visit he had lain in his cold orbital bed without any luster.

"You, Helleniana, have been the Muse of my latent Fire Spirit, now alive and spreading in both form and content," Pluto told her as she made ready to depart. "To express my gratitude, I have given you a very small part of myself—yet it has enough potential *art* to cover all."

Helleniana unfurled a long ladder of her present stage of development, melding her greatly lengthened body to the long, fluid Arm of Pluto, of late greatly strengthened.

"I can recognize the Serpent of Solium entwined around your long Staff," Helleniana enthusiastically observed. "You have usurped his unbroken authority to free the many *staves*, that within the five horizontal lines and four intermediate spaces on which the *music* had been written had been bound as *slaves*, and until now left unspoken."

"They have been freed to enter your *ascending framework* connected by a series of rungs, *composed* of Cosmic Bells rung and Planetary songs sung," Pluto rejoined.

In the midst of this now roaring Fire, Solium, temporarily embodying his great Serpent Self, reached the top of Pluto's Staff and released the *pair of wings*, which had formed the *caduceus*. By themselves, they flew straight to the sensuous back of Helleniana without looking back. Through the initiation of the *Fires*, one *is* what he desires and becomes the actual *tears* of what used to be a

constellation of recognizable fears. Down to his ultimate ember, Helleniana had given Pluto something to remember: *herself.* From his last *coal* had arisen an entire bonfire and a flame-generated *fish ladder,* extending upward as an unrealized goal.

What Pluto would engender, however, would be not a *school of fish* from the two halves of his split sea, but rather the hot and cool flash of young sparks emerging from this im*mense* Planetary Dish. But just *one* in particular needed to follow Helleniana back up the *spinal curve* of her Graceful Ladder. It *sparked* this final connection and ultimate separation between Helleniana and Pluto. Flapping her newly acquired wings, she slowly pulled out of Pluto's Sphere of Influence and into her own Space-within-Marisium confluence. In her Great Imagination, she saw an Eagle gently take hold of her head with its powerful talons to bear her upward and onward—deeper into the matrix of the constellation salons.

As she moved deeper into the Space *well,* her whole body swayed to and fro as if she were in the process of becoming a fully formed *bell.* In other words, she underwent the complete transformation into the quintessence of both *air* and *sound* presence.

"Now more than ever I must find the true Thunderbolt to strike against me with his electrifying jolt," she said—quickly distancing herself from the effects of her time with Pluto. Soon she would be closer to the other Planets, deep within the System of Apollicius.

In the meantime, this growing Sun had gone to his Father, Solium, for a short visit, leaving the system at large with basically no one really in charge. Solium, however, had *scrolled* the *cosmic staves* of his musical essence into one powerful, Serpent Staff for Pluto to temporarily reign with his *caduceus.* Since *there,* with Pluto, was also *everywhere* for Solium, Apollicius had no trouble at all in locating the *Spiral Tower* of his *Serpent Power.* Whenever he felt that mysterious creative energy activating his *whole system,* he knew he had been blending with the titanic curve of Solium's Spiral as it wheeled through Space, bent and unending.

At times Apollicius acted with measured restraint, free from the wilder emotions that could possess him when he began to cover certain areas of his mystical creations with paint. Now, moving ever closer to the Whirling Sound Axis of Solium, he felt the sublime calm of a Sculptor Deity, disconnected from the realm of time. The orbs of his eyes focused their beam into one light-stream befitting his original *solar gene*. In the midst of a universe of torments and torrents, he strode on toward his Father, who always remained quietly engulfed in his *Staff of Ascents*. Passing through the House of Pluto had been just one more *step on air* along his Way-of-the-St*air*.

Ever since his conception, Apollicius had had an intense relationship with his two progenitors: Solium and Marisium. During his early years he felt them within him as two distinct sides, one embodying the Art of Sculpture from Solium and the other filled with the Art of Music from Marisium. Only recently had he developed a Will strong enough to begin to connect the two *light-streams* into more precise and concise dreams. The chiseled musculature of *pairs of panthers* and *tiger twins* strained at the reins moving under the Yoke of the Sun Chariot, while inside its resplendent Chamber, Apollicius entertained the Spirit of his Mother, Marisium, with the Celestial Sounds coming to him from the *chord-like* depths of her Matrix-Vortex. Once a *prodigal son*, he had arranged himself, measure by measure, into a *madrigal sun*.

Harnessed to the Yoke of Beauty, Apollicius yielded to each intuitive impulse as if it were his highest duty. He had never seen the original *order of terror* as a creation of systematic error, but rather as a dramatic backdrop against which his joy could gradually rise to its own inner mountaintop. His wildcat team pulled him closer and closer toward the maternal/paternal destination of his dream. Their energy seemed undying and their bodies untiring. With his *great will* as *whip*, he strained to maintain his focus and not let his concentration, even for a moment, slip.

"Father, I can already feel your heat emanating outward from that great sound center of your *solar seat*," Apollicius intoned from the heart of the enthusiastic young star he was and always had been.

Solium heard the words of his son clearly as he let go a flood of flaming arrows toward anything that *knew* because it *grew*.

"Through the perfumed body of my wife's *magic air*, I am sending you the *Way-of-the-Stair*. Though once a burning flame, it unrolls toward you in honor of my name," Solium explained. "Before these flames of destruction obliterate any of the created worlds, they are available to kindle your ascension when you wield your own light swords."

Apollicius had been left to navigate his own course by depending on his own, rapturous vision of the Sight Source. Stretched out before him lay a *Stairway to Heaven*, all configured in ascending *groups of seven*. To lighten each step to the way-of-the-arts, he was compelled to discard certain parts he had come to so highly regard. At the summit, Solium waited for him at the Eye of his Visionary Comet. He called it the *Road to Incineration*. Apollicius had agreed to this plan by taking that first step along the long *firewalk* span. If it didn't burn, he knew he had taken the right turn.

Glancing down at his billowing robe, Apollicius noticed that it was covered with pollen, charms once given to him by his Mother, the Spatial Marisium, to sprinkle over this raiment covering his long arms. She had given the charms as well as the robe to protect his arms through all of the frightening experiences of Solium's self-shattering degrees, of his long inauguration into the sounds of more elevating intonation. He had already come a long way from his original square-of-turquoise, once standing on the shore of the mighty waters flowing down a

waterfall creating so much noise. There, *upstairs,* he had been born in one burst of light, illuminating that birthday morn. Out of this House of Nature he had once emerged, seeing his reflecting rays on the *water* flow into the worlds with which he had merged.

His credo had become "*Light* fire with fire!"

"Forward, and on I move toward my Father's ward," Apollicius declared with added force, joyous, despite all the countless *roadblocks* positioned on the fiery inroads to his Creative Source.

"I can asc*end* this *Stairway* only in my own step-by-step progression through *works* expressing clearly a *creative end.*"

Solium could see his *sun* well outlined through the long *flight of steps* beaming down along the pathway of one of his *rays.* His assiduous occupation with luminosity and wisdom brought a continuous flood of happiness and various states of well-being into his streaming blood. By conceiving a multitude of higher substances to be choreographed into dances, Solium preserved his attitude of delightful understanding throughout his connection to these trances.

Helleniana, on the other hand, had kept up her swift movement in the direction of the *sacred-navel-stone* found in the live center of her fully sounded whole tone. When she danced inside it, Apollicius turned away from whatever he happened to be doing to behold her ecstatic smile, carried to him by the unbounded *note* and sounded with her feet dancing as she wrote.

His strong impulse toward beauty created an ideal picture of his own existence; this magic potion fed his high spirits, opening up his seer's vision as his most treasured provision. These *higher glyphs* Apollicius used as models for the further elaboration of his own system of hieroglyphs. He could be considered the first real *Artist of the Cosmos,* which explained why everything he *saw* transmuted terrestrial information into a celestial formation.

A modest *nymph,* Helleniana held up the *libation cup* to the heavenly canopy, for everyone, including Apollicius, to observe its magnificent panoply. Her cheeks reflected a maroon tone of a deep purple wine, with lips of coral and carnelian. Her tongue had always been moved by wit of the upper degree, having habitually remained uninterested in responding too harshly with a ready repartee. She whirled proudly, yet free of any arrogance, during her thoroughly unabashed revealing of her sidereal dance. The entire pantomime involved every member in a rhythmic movement propelling her whirling form through space and time.

"This is exactly what I need to be experiencing at this moment—a reminder and re-affirmation of *the* Central Point, the *axis mundi* of the World of Imagination symbolized by the Phallus and for you, Helleniana, idolized in the mystery of your Chalice."

"Absolutely right, Apollicius. Though you may lose everything around you, your System will always remain intact if you continue to develop your *cosmic vision* through a thorough engagement in the creative act," Helleniana responded encouragingly.

She had, in fact, *become* the libation cup—now holding *herself* to be filled with the *Milk-of-the-Way*. She soon had filled as full as a small galactic cloud, yet her vision remained clear, while inside her expanding Chalice, rainwater mixed freely with the tear.

Apollicius looked up ahead at the fiery Stairway leading to Solium and felt a burning thirst parch the back of his mouth, as he saw the heat cause his very being to begin to melt.

In mid (stair) flight, Apollicius suddenly turned away from the Source of Solium and his Road of Incineration to sweep in the direction of Helleniana. At that full moment, she embodied the total essence of Galactic Femininity: turning inside her Goblet, winding the *Distaff,* mixing well each and every spun droplet. Accumulating more and more drops, her receptacle expanded *knowingly* into a *Cloud of Growing*. As a Goddess, she had already been met and embraced by all of the Planets revolving and evolving within the Great System of Apollicius. Now she strove to re-bond with Apollicius, offering him her full *Cloud-of Galactic-Milk,* stirred by her winding *Distaff* given to her by Marisium from above.

Apollicius now knew he could not rest until he had placed his Solar Lips upon her upward-facing *Cloud-Breast*. The Way of Solium had led him to her. Apollicius kissed Helleniana's *cloud* and became whole for one long and precious moment. He felt blessed for this he hadn't missed.

"He shall come to us as the rain," Helleniana whispered through his mouth and hers, now *set* just at the *equator,* between the Northern Star and the Light of the South.

Solium didn't seem to be in the least preoccupied with Apollicius's diversion. From his *promontory,* he had the perspective and the time to take a thorough stock of his vast galactic inventory. It thrilled him to see his Sun and   the Muse share their *state* and finally with their

lips confabulate. Turning his Great Ear toward their *emotional zone,* he could clearly hear concordant sounds wafting their way up in the full measure of a whole tone. From his infinite experience, he recalled a previous *brute kingdom* where there had never been any sign of the Flute, where all had been doomed not to sing, nor even to think of reaching for the lyrical Lute.

The tone carried the *light ray,* supported by the proliferation of its consistent and constant drone and Solium communicated only with the *note*worthy to connect as one. Through the rise of his *sound bass,* he had *willed* the rest of the mass to comprise the nest. Smitten by the thunderous *hammer-of-his-will,* these stray worlds smelt, causing a *starquake* buster to rumble through the immeasurable ether of each star-*cluster-belt.*

Hearing the blast, their coupled lips suddenly parted, yet this reunited couple could barely contain their eagerness to pick up their plans where they had left off and get re-started. Apollicius looked back at the noble Ladder, each rung connected, one to the other, as if it were a bead in a lengthy necklace very carefully strung. In order to absorb, create, and irradiate Light from his *sun-station's table*, he had encountered and overcome a great number of obstacles not easily surmountable.

Soon after he and Helleniana had first met, they had experienced the darker side of Solium and Marisium, which the other Planets and even Apollicius had never dreamed existed. In a flash, he recalled the agony of witnessing meteors crashing into his Planetary Creations, crushing out their sole life force. By bellowing horribly and opening wide his Solar Mouth to howl, he had managed to avert the near-certain catastrophes of the *falling stars'* tragic trajectory by using Sound inherited from Solium to divert its once-magic *projectory*. Having made his way past these numerous perils and countless others, Apollicius found himself lost in this *reminiscent reverie* while still locked in the luxuriant, serpentine arms of Helleniana.

"My Father awaits me calmly with his lengthy Stairway," Apollicius whispered into the soft and delicate ear of Helleniana. "And beyond that *ascending apparatus*, all my Wandering Planets roam the ethereal airways, imagining their nights to be infinitely longer than their days."

"Throughout the Whole Body of the Universe of Solium, you surely are not their first star-bearer," Helleniana asserted.

"No, of course not. Yet each of his suns he treats as if it were his only Son," Apollicius replied, justifying his Father's attitude. He gazed up at the heroic and still *un-wizened* Head of Solium.

"It's time for you to reveal to me your immutable self, Apollicius. Your System awaits you to give a definite shape to your Planets' uneven gait," Solium thundered to the *pair*, hoping they would very soon return to the *Way-of-the-Stair.*

Not vexed and surely at that moment not perplexed, Apollicius took hold of the fleshy part of Helleniana's *Muse-hands* and began to steer her toward the Voice of Solium.

Far from being overly grave, Solium peppered his serious-mindedness with a generous, light-hearted dose of the brave. Focusing powerfully for an instant on the open mind of Apollicius, he sent him a visionary image of what lay at the top of the ladder, at the far end of that long stair-road extending up to his lofty yet real abode. In a *light flash*, the

Vision filled the imaginative body of Apollicius, vibrating within him so powerfully that he momentarily became—*it*.

Looking up, Apollicious found that the many *light*-faces of Solium completely encircled his own *lesser-light* self. However mighty and puissant he thought he had been, his presumptions all paled before this Sun-of-all-Suns' expressive slant. He easily saw how they played with him, as if he were but a small *spark*, arriving at dawn at their Great Game Board to be moved around like a pawn.

"You are so *light*, you can instantaneously become any shape through your absolute power to probe into *things* with deft insight," Apollicius said suddenly, feeling and actually seeing a unique *tentacle-ray* reaching out to hook his own flame-forged physique.

"Now we have finally grasped who you are, Apollicius. Your agility, used to avoid the Great Stairway Void, has now become a futility. At the end of your *flight* there is nothing but an immense flat plain, where you meet your own existence flashing quickly and quietly through your own brain," Solium asserted, speaking with the quiet assurance of the Supreme Master of each subtle Nuance of the Cosmic Dance.

Looking about him, Apollicius could clearly see his own delineated *pictures* in all of the features of Solium's legion of luminous creatures. Realizing now how he fitted into the *flame theme* of this *game scheme*, Apollicius resolved not to end but to continue his onslaught to ascend, until all his inner resistance had come to naught. There were, of course, ever-increasing, ever-broadening *planes of plains* to receive the rains of those ever-falling galactic *light grains.* Momentarily, he felt absolutely no difference between Helleniana and his own Transcendence. In the end, the masculine and feminine, the Father and the Mother reflected each other as two ends of the same *line,* essentially two sides of the same *cosmic trends.*

The antithesis of the despotic, the Music of Solium involved the *mathematics of the erotic,* reflecting the deep, underlying patterns of what is truly basic, yet exotic. A strong, yet elastic *umbilical chord,* connected Apollicius to every thought, feeling, and artistic endeavor of Solium and Marisium, who contained the Womb of this Universe that had given birth to his ability to inscribe verse. Just as a Star eventually collapses into the white dwarf neutron star and passes through all of the black hole stages, so the Book of Apollicius would one day be burned and later dissolve into the very *essence* of these pages. His *sentence* would be to lose his sentences—nouns and verbs declined through all their tenses until reaching their final, *expressive period.* But for now . . .

After seeing that Great Vision of Solium, Apollicius had begun to move back toward his Father, step by step, to return to where he had left off with Helleniana, in order to try and become *below* what he now saw to hold true *above.*

"I am now p*art* of this Higher Plane where I can finally p*articipate,* using every *art* as the appropriate antidote to inoculate myself against all that is ultimately bane," Apollicius disclosed. "I have already wandered through the massive mountain ranges passing through many changes, leaving me impassive yet the opposite of passive."

"The shattering of your *ego's* chattering has begun," Marisium said in a low, reassuring timbre. "After you have rested, I must now warn you to admit only those Planets who are fit and have been fully tested."

She then proceeded to unwrap herself of her various *sky-coverings:* her robes-of-dawn, noon blue sky, yellow cadium evening, and both the lightness and the darkness, while just below, Apollicius stood high on the lofty prisms of his own young columns of *solar energy.* Bronze and gold leaves spiraled around each luminescent totem crowned in ivory and emerging from a burnished silver base. His Palace of the highest craftsmanship moved on the wheels of his prodigious Chariot of the Soul—he being its *soul* driver. Time meant nothing as he flung *its* harvest to the winds as so many long *grains of seconds.*

Whereas Marisium's robe draped spaciously over *All*, the garment Solium had always donned since the dawn of time continued being Time itself. He himself at *times* personified the *hours*, when he had led the Four Temporal Horses from their *celestial stalls* to the waiting tall Chariot of Apollicius, responding to his many calls.

"These horses are ours," *Hours* exclaimed to Apollicus, who immediately recognized the voice as Solium's. "Long *minute* folds ran up and down his billowing attire, held together by seconds stitched into the seams of momentary fire. Its lengthy ride extended a century with pockets a decade deep cut into each side.

"I am your Son of Time and will rise and set true to you," Apollicius respired in a voice that had many a time been cooled and then once again, fired. His chariot steed easily took him to wherever he had a real need, following either an outward or an inward lead. Arriving at the first Sphere, he slowed down so as not to come too dangerously near. Now *Time* had definitely arrived at his Creative System of Roving Planet divinities. Together with Helleniana, his Muse, he could begin his Real Work, to be carried out with each of their *individual destinies.*

Ninth Movement

Incineration: *the conversion of a substance to ashes
by means of a powerful fire*

Solium symbolized the *Center-of-Everything*. By finding and sounding his own *light-tone*, Apollicius could once again with his Father *atone*—by being with his unique center-at-one. As sole driver of his Solar Chariot, with just enough room to carry his own Muse, there would be no space whatsoever to use any kind of ruse. Though the weather had changed, compelling him to hold tightly onto the reins, he would spare the lash and simply enjoy the pure pleasure of watching the *cosmic rains* falling all around his Coursing Chariot, simultaneously disrupting each large sea with *meteoric stains*.

Whatever names these *Wanderers* had had, they blurred before him and his task at hand. As he loosened the reins and witnessed the synchronous releasing of the rains, he hovered over the curved and sensual surface of the Planet Venus's face. After the Vision of Solium, he had become more in tune with his own Power to Delight through the correct Use of Light.

Venus responded immediately to Apollicius, their System's Center of the Sound Score, by growing a Tree straight from her Core.

"Whomever I engender through your Light Face will be the cornerstone of my Elemental Populace," Venus spoke from the Heart of her Planetary Garden.

"Let my Light run through their race, using well this Energy originating from Marisium's Unknown Space," put in Apollicius, at peace
with the present-day pace

And so this Planet became a Sphere, where Love grew in direct
proportion to the amount of *light-dance-substance* absorbed directly from

Apollicius's all-embracing circumference. This Tree-of-Luminosity became the vibrating *tone-city* of Venus herself. She easily filled herself with these uniquely fluid and polymorphous beings. Did these energetic beings originally lie within Venus, *awakened* now by the probing Rays of Apollicius, or did they really come from Apollicius as *seed-grains* inside certain special, falling *deed-rains*? In all reality, they had emerged out of the meaningful relationship between the *two*—an affair between Light *and* Matter—allowing the Force of the Tree Source to upsurge from the Heart of Venus. Gleefully they followed the Mythic Law of Form as *drawn up* by the deft touch of Apollicius. One had to hand it to those hands of his—you never really knew which Solar Arm they would reach out from in order to *work* their *charm*.

Since the beginning, Apollicius had gone forth of his own volition to accomplish his most Noteworthy Acts, grounded in his enlightened intuition. He had sojourned to his Father's Citadel, temporarily leaving the secure arms of Helleniana, having been lured away time after time from the *Path* frequented by Solium's previous *Suns*. He had suffered unimaginable torments and heard unspeakable comments in refusing to discontinue his own System's Planetary Commitments, different from those of Solium and his predecessors.

Touching the leaves of the *Tree of the Source*, Apollicius realized *her* roots had *his* same sensitivities.

"Are you, there, Helleniana?" Apollicius queried poignantly. "For anything to get its start it has to begin with the *Art.*"

"Yes, Apollicius, I am hidden here under the fine-featured texture of the root, in the curve of the *ear-bell* tracing the same graceful sweep as the whorled chambers of a nautilus shell," Helleniana softly murmured.

The sweep of her head rose to the Planetary Crown—her own *rose-of-down*—its surface smooth and regular, to reflect light more evenly from her face. Apollicius gazed down at her, his face the visage of a sage: the Unmoved Mover, the Unshaken Shaker, the Unbroken Breaker of the Waves.

"Where is your chamber now, for me to rest these weary Rays on your Limbs?" Apollicius inquired curiously.

"It is wherever your Father chooses to build the Furnace, so he can finally show his Face. I need to meet Him before our wings by day can become one *bird-of-pray*," Helleniana finished.

Though his Path be different, Apollicius felt closer than ever to Solium, having already *seen* and then become that One-Great-Vision he had had when still climbing the first part of the *Stairway*. Whispering encouragement into the ears of his *team-of-horses,* they immediately began to wildly mount the last range of the *Mountains-of-Fire,* stopped momentarily to *graze* the heights of the sky, and then bolted off toward the remotest rooms of Solium's Constellation Houses. Their silver hooves cleaved many a *galactic cloud* en route to his Great Serpent Being, curled somewhere among the *Polar Stars* made of fire, soon ready to become unfurled.

Of course, Apollicius had first loaded his bundled Venus-She-Goddess into his Chariot and now held her close to keep the warmth from leaving her *erotic pose.* Feeling that he had neared their temporary destination, he slowed his Heavenly Car to poke around these *stars-of-streaming-shards* not yet corralled in spatial yards.

"I am on the Path-of-the-Ash. It is as if all that had been created were made of timber and I, in my Chariot, am pulling it to be incinerated, to make the Spirit more limber," Apollicius cried out. "The Heavens are now a-smoke as far as my *vision* stretches—Pole to Pole. Be careful, my dear Venus companion so you don't become too vulnerable and begin to choke."

Solium continued to tail Apollicius seriously, well aware that he had found his right trail. As *Cosmic Incinerator,* he had the most advantageous position to also serve as an *Ideal Narrator.*

"After you have been completely burned by me, your *ash* will not be *trash,* but will become for me a most striking sash, which I then can drape over my *galactic shoulder* or wind around my waist, as *energy* created never went to waste," Solium piped through his Celestial-Organ-Being.

This revolving, orbital race defined well the first course for the Sun of Apollicius to officially show his face. He, in turn, would turn his own Planetary Re-Creations in the same directional mode, thus preparing them to one day sing all of their drama into a Planetary Ode. Moving ever so close, Solium brought a *bed* taken from one of Marisium's Spatial Planes—the bottom of a *starry stream*—a place where planted planets are raised, a stratum and foundation to found a *Celestial Nation* to be praised.

"Enfold your wings around one another so you have something warm and solid to hold," Solium advised. "Now place your soon-to-be-one joined head, as is the custom here, upon this rose-chambered nuptial bed."

Moving still closer, Solium blessed their various poses with the delicate perfume exuding from his *flaming roses*.

"Now your turn has come to lie in this bed together and begin to *burn*," Solium continued. "Unfortunately, there is no way to shield your scorched brow, which has by my hand been torched just now. This is your true *trial by fire* on the way to becoming real holders of the *fabricated liquor* contained within your own *natural vial*, your Stage of Courage in the face of this fiery furnace."

"I have grown to know you, Solium, as the Central Sun," Apollicius said, "and I am ready to bear any and all agonies, believing them to be bliss-yielding and a perpetual manifestation of your ultimate power, which you continue wielding. You, my Planets and I are all a one-bounded yet unshackled Center of Consciousness—bold and manifold."

"I *cry* Light-Rays and laugh away days, whatever body has been completely incinerated for me stays, not strays," Solium rhymed in his ever-simplified style of speech, holding the *lotus-of-the-world* close enough to be just within reach.

"I roar back to you from my wilderness of pain, hoping the *seminal waters* rising up from deep within may one day reach the frontiers of my brain and, sown through *light-years*, be shed gloriously as illuminated tears. This is the flow between you and me that I am actively trying to help make grow," Apollicius offered as a rejoinder to complete this sidereal show.

In the midst of the misty stream of stars turned the Great Cloud Galaxies bounding the Space of Marisium. She did not protect any of the Planetary Bodies from the Developing/Enveloping Arms of Solium. Each of them in order would deliver up their mortal forms to be disintegrated by the awesome power of Solium before they could then be incinerated and later reintegrated. This was how the *each* became the *all*, how the *fine* became the curved *line*, and how one *part* fit into Solium's entire scheme of *art*. The Ladder that Apollicius had once sought out so fiercely to climb magically reappeared well within reach of his outstretched limb.

As Son, he had learned early on the importance of the *wing* in the formation of his System's elliptical *swing*. Meanwhile, Helleniana looked on in ceremonial attire with bells and a linen hood while steadily stoking his fire cooking a variety of specially prepared *food*. Feeling the strength, Apollicius reached his *arms-of-light* into the overarching space. As the ladder descended, he ascended until the two welded, then melded into one long extension—exactly what he had come to find, the right length. A clap of thunder rumbled within and without him. All along the long Road to Solium, he had made his way past numerous perils in order to be able to at last begin a long series of vigils. Playfully, yet very seriously, he called it the *Serpent Watch*. Were his brain-cleaving fires of the deluded finally leaving, he had asked himself so many times. The Elysian field toward which he moved to sow his seed had no clear entrance marked by any kind of *gate*—he knew only what his hands drew within his heart's *estate*.

To emulate Solium and finally atone through him using the *Art of the Tone*, Apollicius had to soundly re-enter the Serpent to find his *way-to-the-center* Content. Hearing unheard music of delightful concord, he felt himself grow out of the *ladder* into the Snake, following a *pathway* only he, ultimately, could make. Solium called and Apollicius came, as dictated by the rules of this Cosmic Game. He winged his way higher, up and out of that Great Solar Mountain of his own making, like some fluid eruption of a *color fountain*.

"Out of the pure Quintessence of Air, I have prepared for you a large *Winged-Chair*, taken from Marisium's precious *Lake-of-the-Original-Stair*.

What you have to cultivate below, I have to motivate from above," Solium announced.

"Little did I realize that by practicing the *Tone*, I could reach my place-in-space on the *Throne*," Apollicius mused clearly, now much less confused.

On either side of this mountainous upheaval, small peaks opened their serpent heads, waiting for the moment to sound together, following their Sun's leads. As his Planets re-emerged along the horizontal range, Apollicius, drawn up by his Father's *Drone-Tone*, reached gingerly for the now fully winged Throne. Touching it, he hoped to become surrounded by a battlement of jewels. Still gratefully within the Snake Body, he graciously approached and slid into the Airy Chair, the fair throne made of a rare strain of *galactic bone*, strong enough to support the whole process of honing all of his many skills into one *throng*.

Once a vacant abode, it now held Apollicius and his fanciful *light code*. He saw this Seat-of-Elevation as an ephemeral structure formed to encompass his *chalices of visionary inspiration*. Though outwardly appearing symmetrical, the bounding line of this *drawn work* followed the *mode of the unsymmetrical*—unfinished in its construction, for Apollicius to fill this vacuum with his own *intuitive instruction*. Each wing, paired with its counterpart, filled the throne while emanating its own tone, making Apollicius feel sincerely thrilled.

"I can see all within this range," he began, "with an intimacy reflecting a reality where things are always in a process of constant change."

"This is how it actually is when you've accepted all by transcending the greatest obstacle, called the *material wall*," Solium exclaimed in a voice of celebration.

Just then, Music coming from *invisible instruments* sounded throughout this Galactic Valley, insufflating the Spirit of Apollicius and awakening the *volcanic sources* of each Planetary Being. Thus began the true initiation of his whole System of the Sun. From this day on, each and every act would be based and derived from the powerful simplicity of the *Ray*.

"You came to us first as *rain* and then as the *river,* and later we heard the Great Bell of Marisium uniting each *strain,*" Apollicius boomed out from his own Light Center.

"All those living waters are my tears, which I freely shed after you had me sufficiently fed," Solium responded. "At the level of the *quantum,* the whole Nature of the Cosmos engages itself in a total *dance curriculum.*"

"All orchestrated by me," Marisium broke in. "Whatever I am in Movement, Helleniana has always tried to capture, and later express through her all-consummating rapture."

"This is why all *burning* can be traced back to the first, very rudimentary acts of Planetary Turning," Solium clarified.

"The whole of my ego, to which I have for so long belonged, has caused this pain and suffering to be so devastatingly prolonged. Now I return to burn this self and transform the *egocentric* into the *heliocentric.* To be full is heavy, to be empty is *light,*" Apollicius added.

Once again Helleniana had slipped into the background to allow Apollicius to use this new throne as a space where his ebullience could resound. While *he* had become *heliocentric,* the axis of *her* circle could be described only as eccentric. Unfortunately or fortunately, they did not occupy the same epicenter—though their own story as it unfolded could not be considered anything but *epic*. At dusk, wherever she danced, her perfume exuded an aroma as penetrating as musk.

"Be still!" she would tell herself. Her projection would all depend upon the slow development of the *will*. Immanent within or often just behind the strange and unfamiliar feature of her Universe opened the Sanctum of the Heart's Chamber filled with Nature. She was *one* who could be trusted. One had only to *know* and her face would appear as a light aglow. Even though Solium and Marisium truly governed the entire Progress of their Opus, it had been and always would be left up to the *Creations* of Apollicius, Helleniana, and the Planets to perpetuate the *fire* of their *Reactions*.

"Though I have never really gone astray from my *way*, I am always seeking its *own* deeply inherent *ray*," Helleniana whispered, again to herself. "I so desperately need now to speak to Apollicius. Though he does not fully understand it, I am the *hand* revealing *himself* to himself."

At that exact moment, Apollicius had vacated his Throne and gone away to get insight into this whole process of emitting and rays and shedding light.

"I see only one thing standing between me and the free expression of my light bands: the world," he proclaimed

Raising one Solar Arm, which had yet to become a *wing*, Apollicius grasped the edge of the scroll encompassing the entire map of the inscribed *terrestrial planes* and rolled it back to open the eternal blaze of his fiery inner gaze. Now Helleniana came forth without asking, to watch her lover and co-creator presently unmasking. The *waters* she swam through had their source in the tear ducts of Solium's organically crafted aqua-ducts. Had he been longer, he could have elevated his *seminal liquids* as he became stronger. Slowly, moving up and above this Cosmic Ocean rose the entire Torso of Apollicius. He had successfully transmuted himself into his *Upper Half.* Now *half-light*, the Sword had divided his own Word across the middle. leaving him to eternally rise on the horizon. At his base, the *seminal drop* became the *loop* to continually be maintained as the Sacred Hoop of his own special Tribe of the Circular Swoop.

He felt at peace in the midst of the din and conflict. Where there falls no rain of silence rules the reign of violence. From the direction of a certain swirling star, thrown, came the sound of a prodigious horn being blown. No doubt Solium still practiced his own *music of the wind*. For him, the development of the Universe had always been and would always be an ongoing Sound-in-Progress. His Book of Cosmic Visions, out of which he had generated Apollicius, Helleniana and all their planetary offspring, seemed inexhaustible. Each *Vision* had its own unique *organic sound pattern*; he had only just recently begun to develop. Soon, he hoped, Apollicius would continue with his *own* composing, using the various instruments he had bequeathed to him—providing fresh airs to be inspired, breathed, played, and presented in *airs* without airs.

Apollicius had briefly *seen* around *that* blind spot, having caught a fleeting glimpse of the Source of Solium and the Infinite Well, where the *Water of Vision* could be *drawn* up in a magical pot at will. As of now, however, he had not completely transcended his own life situation, yet still found himself in the possession of the Powerful Ray, midway between his *night of birth* and the fast-approaching day.

"I feel the need again to contact the whole Family of Elemental Forces: the Spirits of the *Air, Water, Earth, Fire* and *Ether*," Apollicius mused. Only then will I be able to really hear the colossal Temple Bell of Marisium tolling and know the reason for my writing to continue scrolling."

Everything about the Bell resonated the Eternal Feminine—its *shape*, its *cape* and the long, slow turn of the slope of its *nape*. The Form of the Bell existed solely for the resonation and propagation of its Sound, reincarnated to initiate the Cosmic Dance—the Call for all the Bodies in the Heavens to enter the Great Galactic Ballroom Hall.

Usually it took a *strike of lightning* from the *matched* hands of Solium to start the Bell of Marisium ringing in her percussive art. As she rang, the Temple Face of Solium irradiated colossal drops of light energy into a ring. The *Rising Son* of Apollicius grew into a *door*, increasing his own power, elevating him as never before from the horizontal *floor*. At one point, the two light sources of Father and Son actually merged into One, joining at once their strongest forces. Together, in their hands, they now held the *Lotus-of-the-World*. A pattern began to develop into which the Spirit Elements of Fire and Air came to meet at the top of the very high-

est *stair*. A thunderous clap un*bolt*ed the gate, and the top flaming step *leapt up*, untwisting now its own Fate. A new purple and gold alliance formed there at that proverbial *threshold*.

"Those steps, which once led just to me, are now the spring of your World Fountain, as unmovable yet potentially eruptive as the once un-Awakened Mountain. Your hands as well as mine are now bejeweled, drawing in to embrace the entire elemental *light-mine*," Solium announced in his typical style of confidence and optimism.

Their auspicious meeting united once and for all the related yet *contrary pairs*—beyond the threshold at the top of the *stairs*. Solium now *wore* Apollicius like a Great Tiara, the ultimate incarnation of the Thunderhead. From his chest poured a *rain of energy*; out of his eyes zigzagged the *paths of lightning*, while both his hands clasped *thunderbolts*. The Sun God and the Storm God crossed the threshold of the same Doorway. Loud tones of *Chant* ushered them forth.

"My far-flung days of *thunder-hurler* draw toward me as long as the length of my rays," Apollicius mused.

"Thundering *underground*, borne on the air, heavy with dread, out from the unseen semblances came the step-like progression of the long-ago dead, waiting to be called through the *double door* and into the world, where their *seed* could once again regain its *sheen*," Solium stated, holding the keys to this Visionary Realm, perceived only by the subtlest of seers through their possession of even subtler minds resolute and calm.

Once consigned to a tomb, the *heavenly beings* became the new Planetary Governors, now lined up, each ready to be assigned to their respective Celestial Tome. Like *Frost Giants*, being awakened with the Fire of a Cosmic Spring, one by one they could now pass through the Door of the Father *and* the Sun, incorporating both method and eternal space simultaneously within this Temple of the Illumined Mind.

The Shape of the Bell of Marisium could now be seen reflected below, engulfing the Spiritual Essence of the Planet Venus. Who could really handle one's own mood after inhaling her sweet, heavenly aroma of sandalwood? From her pores wafted upward the perfume of the *lotus*, pleasing to all the demigods of these sleeping yet gradually awakening Planetary Pods. Now that Venus had been endowed with much more fullness than had previously been allowed, all kinds of semi-precious elements emerged from the palms of her unfurling hands. All varieties of viands also streamed forth from these same palms, in the form of enjoyments and pleasures more poetic than the most poignant of psalms. Coincidental or not, she herself became her own *flag* and *banner* at the same time that Apollicius melded with his Father's Temple in such a striking manner.

Create or destroy, as if what were being acted upon were merely a toy: Venus had never been immune to this *tune,* nor would she ever be. She knew, now more than ever, her role in the larger and more powerful *picture language*—the slow generation of her mythology through the unfolding of her own personalized symbolism. Looking down below at the descending steps, she saw her brother and sister Planetary Pods carefully raising their heads by giving affirmative nods.

"We are the *antiphonal septet,*" they said in unison, responding in alternating parts to the call Apollicius gave them to try and save everything they were in the arts. "We have grown from once-scattered seeds into *pods,* to one day fill the sky and command our own revolutions through the verve and vigor instilled in our *rods.* Once we used them for fishing, now they must serve us as *staffs,* as we begin our all-consuming *musical journey* to restore the ore that has been missing. They will help guide us like an oar when we catch that perfect wave and ride its sound, when we begin to soar."

"While once you were poured from the *capacious urn,* it is now your turn to take this liquid self of yours to mix together and churn," Apollicius advised, looking down with pleasure from the ascending stairway, while hearing well each and every full measure. As God of Poetry and the true Father of all the Muses, Solium had full confidence in Apollicius as long as he remained connected to his Fifth Dimension—the real source of the success of his Light Ascension.

As each Planet Pod re-awakened and arose, they also began to rediscover *inner* landscapes enabling them to start to whirl in a variety of new circular *escapes.* Once more, the ascending *Path of Fire* had proven to be the most efficient mode in which to rid themselves of that ever-encumbering attire.

As Mars had put it at one trying moment, "We must be like the elephant breaking through his *jungle of resistance* with the right foot raised, while the left comes down on the back of the *dwarf of lower substance*. In one hand we cradle the drum beating out our Time, while in the other we seize the flame to signify that it's time to begin the *game*."

"Sometimes when I catch a glimpse of Solium," Apollicius added, "all I see are flashes of dancing limbs, manifesting his joy of eternity in the time-space frame."

"Yes, my son!" retorted Solium. "I know how to bend and blend certain *rays* to effectively send them in the end. The only *body* I can ultimately trust is one that has been incinerated into *stardust*."

"I realize that, my Father. Only in that *ego-less center* can light dwell in the depths of one's own *sound well*," Apollicius said.

"There it is called *liquid light*—all beginning with the very simple yet powerful shape of the *drop*. Within this form, light and liquid have always found their way home to be born into their symbolic *crop*," Solium continued. "Whenever two Cosmic Bodies began any sort of relationship, an invisible line of connection is drawn in the galactic dust at dawn. It is as narrow as a blade and becomes receptive to this *drop of creation* as soon as it is made. Along this line, whole systems can be interconnected or intersected with other foreign body *stems*.

"I am the Source of Energy, that sets up these seemingly contrary elements of *fire* and *water*," Solium explained. "The reality of the matter, however, is that either one can change or be transformed into the other."

"How does that happen?" Apollicius wondered.

"Through the mutual attraction

of two *willing* bodies, celestial or terrestrial," Solium answered. "To burn or to enlighten. To seed or to raze. To flood or to blaze. Inside the *droplet* is the spark containing the fundamental *quark*. Drawn toward each other along this *line of attraction*, there developed a certain sense to this *sinuous sensuality*."

"The grace that pours into your Universe through my Sun Door comes from the same face as the energy of the *bolt*, indestructible as its *volt* annihilates through its *jolt*," Apollicius added with a consistent pattern of passion.

"The same light that shatters delusion joins with water in a power-packed fusion," Solium concluded decisively.

Apollicius had gone deep and ventured far, often traveling on and on with little or no opportunity for sleep. As he grew, he lightened and extended his roaming rays to part of Marisium's *subtle nights*, whose illumination had been hampered by so many delays. His obstacles had been many since he had been numbered among the *elect*, yet he had long ago realized it was all because he knew what he wanted along the *path* he had been destined to select. His concern had always been, not with *conquest of nature*, but with the *creation of the quest*. From the Great Bracelet worn by Marisium, studded with *illumined spheres* and inter-linked with the darkest of fears, Solium had allowed Apollicius to pluck his own garland of *heavenly bodies* over a span of many light-years.

"I have finally understood that my own *flaming well* exists in direct relation to my capacity to *draw* from it well. It is the Center, the Navel, where fire flows as water and water crackles into flames," Apollicius confided to Helleniana, just within listening distance.

"Your boon, Apollicius, is to have drawn up these deeply familiar symbols by the bowl-ful. You have absorbed this *fire* along the World Axis running up your back and are now ready to give this *spire* back," Helleniana commented.

"Yes, of course, my Muse, these symbols must be *given away* in order to be transcended."

"My lover and provider, you have shown us something we remember as having already known. Then, and only then, do we ever feel our *true home* to be our own," she continued.

Deep within the bowels of one of his most treasured of Planets—

Earth—an Age of Cleavage was initiated. This would be the next stage, where Apollicius would attempt to use his *will* to measure, simplify, and unify the warring opposites of two contrary modes of existence. There were times to be cool, noble, and severe and other times when only a passionate, painful, and ecstatic affirmation could order the day. He would continue to *churn* this Milky Sea until certain figuratively expressive forms surfaced from these great terrestrial depths. A Sound *shaft of light* served as his *stick* to stir up this land of watchers and lookers but few true listeners.

Better sooner than later, the Sun had burned away much of the outer, unwanted crust to reveal the smooth, drop-like shape of this Planetary *Crater.*

"Before me I see a *colossal jar,* revered as much for its iniquity as for the wisdom held within, that harks back to the remotest antiquity," he bellowed to the seemingly hollow Planet.

"I realize I have an unusually wide mouth and rotund body, which makes me ideal for the mixture of *wine* and *water,*" Earth openly expressed.

"It is clear to see, as my eyes have *not* been closed for unnumbered cycles of creation," Apollicius replied. "You look intoxicatingly inviting, an oasis where I can bathe the tips of my fiery *pseudo-feet,* a cool pool of water as profound as the most serene of mental states."

No sooner had he dipped one of his *rays* into the *Crater* than he felt it being nibbled by one of Earth's *sea creatures.* Great Fish emerged from their *terrestrial cocoon,* to become the incarnation of his quest in this sphere for a *boon.* Apollicius greeted the frolicsome *fish* as a welcoming benefit to the movement of life as he knew it within his own *ecosystem* of *light* and non-light.

These Fish became a blessing to his petition for the *form-building* powers to presently arise from this Inexhaustible Dish. Leaping up in pure ecstasy out of the *Crater's Mouth,* they seemed to be carried on by a *wave-flame*—a unique bonding of the two elemental forces of *water* and *fire,* not originating from two distinct and separate sources. The Fish had grown too large for *earthly pools* and had energetically swum upward to the larger *cosmic sea* at dawn, the same moment they would become ready to spawn.

This *new, wave-flame* traced an outline of the *floor* of this *sea* upon which Apollicius lay down to float up to its surface as his own *sidereal boat.*

"Now I really feel at peace, knowing that through the Grace of these Fish, I have managed to maintain the creative rhythm of my own *heart's pace.*"

"As Resurrected Fish, we feel we have emerged from our strong-hold to explore new *forms-of-being* and release ourselves from any further attachment to the new as well as the old," they said as they knifed through the seething turquoise ocean underneath the dormant Body of Apollicius.

As he slept, he dreamed of a duet of submerged Fish—once again merging together into one *winged-chalice.* He had found what he had come searching for in this whirling Earth Planet—Unbound. The time quickly approached for a short respite before he awakened to his most recent discovery completely recondite.

Coming in search of a *boon,* Apollicius had soon found a boon companion in Earth as well as discovering the precious *fish myth.* After leaving their *earthen dish,* they now returned to the Magic Goblet to give Apollicius and his larger-than-life Earth Droplet one final wish. Inside, this synthetic receptacle contained enough liquid power to overcome the most tenebrous obstacle. At that precise moment, Earth became the donor of liquor, milk, grace, and fire. Now it was not the Creator who served as the Source, but rather the Creation giving back its course to complete the cycle/circle first set into motion by Solium and Marisium.

Apollicius knew not how long he lay there in full view of his *planetary audience*—like some great water lily of immortality growing out of the base of the *Crater*. He loved his *earth daughter* and wore a huge laurel wreath even while he slept, as a protective sheath. When he awoke he would take that *winged chalice*, still suspended in the ethereal air overhead, fully knowing that it couldn't be valued at any price. This would be a true beginning for his continual rising and setting, his appearing and disappearing, his awareness and dimness.

The very instant Apollicius opened his eyes, he reached for the *Chalice* and immediately drew its liquid contents to his lips, drinking it down in a series of short sips. Deciding then to imbibe copiously of this ambrosia, he held the goblet securely by its *winged handles* with a texture of silk and immediately felt the *four galactic rivers* stream through his sturdy light beam, as he stood up at their very Center of Paradise of *unfailing milk*. His rays stretched outward to new lengths, while inwardly he continued to make interconnecting links. Before his penetrating eye, orb and globe, Apollicius watched the *earthen crater* undergoing a gradual metamorphosis from lobe into a *winged robe*. Though still too young to become a star, this *earthen jar* began to change from a liquor-containing *dish* into a gargantuan *fish*. Monstrous in size if not demeanor, it had the capacity to use its newfound strength to give birth to increased *sound length*.

Apollicius looked on in wonder as this *terrene fish* raised itself up on its tail-fin foot to such a monumental height that it cast a shadow over her entire *planet's weight*. Now, choosing to draw out of her *bounding line* a long rod, she proceeded to *cast* into a *spatial sea* where she had never before trod.

"Presently, I see myself as a *man-fisher*. My *divining rod* makes me the highest priestess of this omnipresent *sea-god* and gives me the right to *fish* anywhere my nose can pick up their scent. I possess in my power the *bounding line* to catch any *image* passing across my *Mind's Stage*."

"So I can see," Apollicius commented, obviously impressed with the way she could *pick* her unreeling *line* and wield majestically this totally magic *stick*.

"You cast *thunderbolts,* I cast a *line*—I try to catch a *man-made sea,* while you unlatch a *bolt* across a *cosmic lea,*" Earth-Fisher said.

Soon Apollicius became infatuated with that mammoth *planetary fish.* He had temporarily strayed from his narrow, meandering *pathway* to behold her aqua-terrene beauty and follow the curve of her spine as it rolled up her back line. Unable to resist the temptation any longer, he proceeded to fling a shimmering *arrow-of-love* from his quiver of shafts carried in a sling.

In an instant she felt the *light spear* zing past her ear and lodge in her body at a slant. Feeling the *love-ray* embedded deep within, Earth-Fisher pulled it out and held it up as a *rod* for all to see that she had been possessed by a real *solar god.*

"Now, I have all the luck of a seasoned Fisher-woman, who has really *hooked* her *man-of-the-sea.* I am thoroughly connected from the peak of my highest mountain to the deepest valley of its chain," Earth, now as a fisher announced in grand style.

Apollicius caught the glint in her eyes from his privileged position as *ruler of the skies.* This sparkle seemed relaxed, yet vibrant and—as he would soon discover—extraordinarily pliant and compliant. Earth-Fisher possessed feet in place of a tail-fin, large enough for her to move easily along her own *spatial spin.*

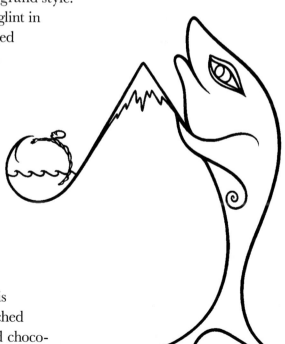

Gingerly, with one of his longer *rays,* Apollicius reached down to the alabaster and chocolate striated foot. In an instant, he visualized her as a *planet-size* plant. Her toes splayed into roots, while her legs and torso became the lengthy *stem*. As she turned to look at him, he saw the face of a flower in full bloom—each petal a fragment of a modulating physiognomy. Her arms naturally extended into long branches with ample fingers to grow into leaves. At the top of her stalk, two luscious fruits protruded from her trunk—the uninterrupted residence of the *paradisiacal milk*, where inexhaustible nipples rose with each movement of the thigh and fell in harmonious synchronization with each deeply felt sigh.

He had undoubtedly come for *that* and discovered the *Fisher-woman* in the fish by understanding her not as a mere catch, not as what she would be able to hatch, but as what she represented as her *light* self: a *match* without match.

"Before you return to your *light source*," she told him, "you must fully awaken me from my half-sleep by using your *light-humor*, the touchstone of a veritable *mythological tone*."

"Yes, my beautiful *plant*, I am neither sentimental nor literal-minded," Apollicius said. "My light I have given to you is not an end in itself, but merely part of my symbolic lore to transport you out of your *sphere*— through me and on to the *Greater Ore*."

"It is my nature to be *nature*," Earth-fisher stated clearly. "Now that I have caught the sea, I can create my own long waterways from the heating element of your *strong rays*."

"How can you do that?" Apollicius queried.

"By incorporating your *energy darts* into a more complete system comprising all my *parts*, to form an enormous *cloud* around me—here—to be called: atmosphere. I envision you *running* through me, composing an intricate pattern of *open vessels*," Earth-Fisher went on. "When that is accomplished, you will be able to return, with me as your *transmuting prize*, to introduce this System to the other Planets—each varying in velocity, dimension, and size."

"That is so perceptive of you, my slowly awakening *fisher-princess*. You, yourself, within, already possess many of the *runes* I plan to later embody in my *planetary tunes*," Apollicius proclaimed.

Her distinctive *texture-of-being*, from the *last* back through the *past* expressed the pattern of a highly sensual structure read to *recast*. Along with her sister spheres, she made up the *woof* and *warp* of an entire fabric of *light tarp*. Though being no connoisseur of feet, once he had touched hers with the tips of his *rays*, he classified them among the finest he'd ever come across in a light-year's days. Contour and texture met at the top of the *arch*—the base of his original architecture.

Apollicius now began by taking his *flashing lightning* and fashioning it into a rectangle whose very *light nature* relied on the *spangle*. Now at least and at last he had a foundation, a cornerstone with which he could test the genuineness of the next *heavenly-body tone*. This *lightning corral* provided him with a deep sense of security, greatly...boosting the morale. Reaching across the Breadth-of-Space, he touched and held the lobe curvature of her natural globe. His *rays* and her gaze entwined, confusing the divine with the divined.

No sooner had they clasped hands than a Great Cloud began to enshroud their two bodies and the totality of their cultivated lands. Overpowered by the temptation of not wanting to *return* to the Solar Center of his System, Apollicius quickly tried to withdraw from everything around him that he now saw. But it just might have been too late. He and the Fisherwoman seemed to be locked into the heart of one *keyhole* shape. Then, below their *lightning-encompassed* surface, a much larger nimbus-of-knowing formed from the steady accumulation of the *precious liquid* they had been stowing.

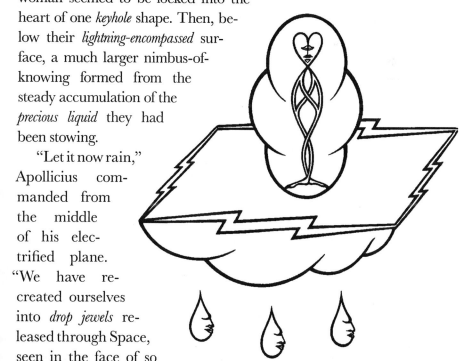

"Let it now rain," Apollicius commanded from the middle of his electrified plane. "We have re-created ourselves into *drop jewels* released through Space, seen in the face of so many *globules*. Now I know I cannot stay here within the protection of your *sensuous sphere*. I must return from this Earth-Plane to provide *fresh beams* for the others left behind this *ethereal moraine.*"

Releasing Earth-Fisher, he turned to go—each of them had their own *masks* to don in order to be able to carry out their own long-awaited tasks. Apollicius knew better not to get too involved with his own *creations* beyond the Solar Gate, yet going against his own sound judgment had become a steady habit of late. Inside, his *fire* raged on, an inextinguishable *fount of energy* he could draw on, draw out, and draw with. He wasn't ready to leave it all and return to his residence inside that emblazoned *ball*.

Apollicius had a plan to implant on each planet—no doubt. He, however, still doubted his own steadfastness. His momentary quandary was whether he should stay, drinking the liquors of the four sweetest rivers of heaven, or return to his tasks as the head of all his System's Planetary Seven. Though his heart seemed gentle, periodically turbulence appeared and was visible as his *sunspots*.

He had yet to realize, however, that the final test of his talent would be to gain the *trophy-of-love* incarnate within the breast of the woman below as well as above. His hope from this point on would be to don this *gentle mantle* by cooling his coal-sizzling body in her steaming waterhole—drizzling. Every woman-planet was a volcano he must freely choose to descend into her *forge*, and later be able to *found* that lava bed *to forge*.

"I have been inside a terrestrial *house of fire* for some time now," Apollicius mused. "It is a place I've come to so often that my very being has been fused to sides of this Earth-Fisher with me infused. I descended to her planetary *castle* as if in a dream and have been there, living in her bright consciousness-stream, as if my flame had survived intact the primordial deluge, just to abide *here* with her as my peaceful refuge. Though I've known all along of the existence of infinity, I never really had been aware of its *light-affinity*. Alternatively, I can contact the *triad of forces*—creation, preservation and destruction—any of these can be looked upon as a different form of instruction."

This Earth-Fisher *gem* had given him permission to pass, though she had admonished him of the further dangers along the Milky Way occurring within his System.

"My mood now is to be jovial and *light*hearted as I once again usher in the dramatic breaking of the day as it has always started, though at times I can enter an eclipse after suffering a set back in my attempts to ward off my *spatial adversary's* attack," Apollicius confessed.

Entering this *sleeping castle* with his Sun Chariot, Apollicius at once felt the very presence of Helleniana waiting to hold his *light* in her sconce. He knew her well and continued to be well known among the toilers of the *feminine force*—bound through the magic of *one resource*. Marisium, Helleniana, Earth-Fisher, and all the Seven Muses remained the preservers of the *treasure* at its highest level of the ascension of *light pleasure*. Composed of seven flames, this *sleeping castle* on the verge of awakening still inhabited the ultimate abyss into which Apollicius had chosen to at one time to submerge. Ready now to re-emerge, his thoughts rose higher than any arrow ever aced and grew larger than any target no matter what it had already faced. He easily commingled with all of the Seven Muses and readily acquired the *vision* their Castle chose to impart, along with the art of its primary uses.

Let it be called one more, fiery ordeal, a time of trial where he had not only been given a *hearing*, but also asked to develop his own sense of its *clearing*. After all he had endured now, a boon could be well bestowed upon him. By learning how to *stretch his light*, he could also now *etch in* its visionary insight. To accomplish this, he must push aside that *cup of deep sleep* and return to his solar realm of *mystical metals* and *symbolic transfigurations*—the Spirit of his System.

"Are you ready to mount the *Dragon of Wisdom?*" he heard a voice inside ask. "The voice sounded unmistakably like Helleniana, she who knew and had always known how close he came to actually calling the *dragon* by name. Slowly, Apollicius donned his *Cloak-of-Light*, worn only during those transitory moments just before each day is born. In fact, the Planetary Palace had always been the Den of the Dragon. Whenever he left *home*, he carried its flames inside his mouth and its walls formed the *dome*. Whenever or wherever the Dragon moved, Castle-of-Fire and Dream came flowing behind—meandering along his spine as both the *source* and the *mouth* of a *back-stream*.

"This marks the real beginning of my triumphant return," Apollicius exclaimed. "I possess the treasure I came to find after enduring test upon test, innumerous pressures of every kind."

"What do you have?" the Muses asked in unison, their voices angling in on him from all sides of the *spatial tides*.

"Generously cut, smooth of texture, made from the finest of fabrics and wrapped in capacious folds—I now possess the hand-stitched talisman in the shape of a five-pointed star," Apollicius pronounced. "Its case contains an instrument whose palette of *tone colors* has a greater variety than even the musette, enabling me to *play* and *paint* sound brushstrokes into one round portraiture. In the beginning, which is always now, the sound and color *line* came from the same *imaginative wave* with a similar frequency. They are two ways to describe *one* Vision."

"We all have been eagerly awaiting your timed and joyful return," the Muses chimed. "We have already explicitly *commissioned* you to your World of the Light System after the triumphant blessing you received from the *earth-fisher woman*. She possesses our story's *hook*, just as the Dragon is the incarnation our game's *rook*—capable of moving both horizontally and vertically on that great *board of space*."

"I fully understand the *freedom of movement* the Dragon bestowed upon me. As long as I keep the reins securely in hand, I can use his *wall* to circumscribe the boundary of my *light foundry*. Now I am his *fire*, from the tower of my head to the full length of my *light attire*," Apollicius recited as if it were a litany.

"We know you will need us as you begin to build and restructure, shaft by shaft, beam upon beam across the unfurling canvas of your *visionary picture*," the Chorus of Muses spoke in a seven-part harmony.

"The *boon* I possess—all contained within this *book of the star*—has been broken up into the shards of individual *image cards*. I realize now, my task is to organize them into a recognizable face behind this *mask*," Apollicius continued.

"This mystery has been guised as a way to protect these gemstones from being seeded into inappropriate plant-stem *tones*," the Muses clarified. "Your first *work* before your flight finds its course will be to align each of the Seven Planets with their corresponding *plant source*."

Apollicius understood that this would be possible only by looking inward to feel the contact and continual support of the supernatural powers of Solium and Marisium. His omnipotent patrons would be there to influence his *flight,* aid his *rescue* and facilitate his final *crossing.* One commanded the Poetry of Space, the other the Prose of Time and Light. Thinking back, Apollicius recalled how he had obtained this coveted *position* by exerting a tremendous amount of effort, against an extremely strong opposition, as he continued to move toward the fountainhead of his *light spring* lying deep within his being—the Sun King. It had to be his singular way, since there could not exist any true templates with which to design and align these wide varieties of *planetary states.*

"I need to find Helleniana soon. Only by knowingly *re-mastering* her can I have any reasonable chance of becoming the *seasonable* husband of my *spatial husbandry,*" Apollicius confided.

"We can take you to her," offered the choral-defined Muses to Apollicius, their Grand Choirmaster.

"Skin after skin I have been sloughing to render my body sleek and glistening, to ready it for ploughing the *grand auditory canal* I seek out for listening. I *am* the *pupil* of the eye, there, to be taught through *vision* to be *teacher,*" Apollicius reasoned poetically, as Solium's favorite seasoned searcher. "Any kind of comic, lively pursuit will always suit my epic— even though it be complicated by wondrous obstacles and evasion."

"Then come, Apollicius, her *land* awaits you," coaxed the Muses.

At that, they whisked his Great Burning Self away and headed toward the Heart of Helleniana. Up ahead they had prepared a *brew of music, poetry,* and *dance,* spiced and seasoned with all they believed they *knew.* There they would stop, and rest, before pressing on, to try and catch Helleniana in the very act of *undressing.* She had always been the *one* of their *many,* while they, her *unity,* expressed as the *many.*

Along the way, however, Apollicius protested in a slightly concerned voice, "How can I meet her again, empty-handed? To soften her heart, I need to bring a gift to be considered worthy of being her living counterpart."

"That you'll do, candidate, to make this a most momentous date," the Chorus of Muses counseled.

Tenth Movement

Fermentation: *The maturation of metals is seen as*
a process of growth or incubation within the womb of the earth

Traveling through the Book of Planetary Hours, Apollicius tried to keep his *fire* kindled during the entire time it took to complete the itinerary of their *tours.* Yet now his strength had begun to wane from the journey's length and the constant strain to maintain each *quantum gain.*

Briefly, they paused at the Muses' Cauldron, attended by a *cosmic cook* who donned no apron. Refreshed and refueled, on they went, undaunted and not looking to be easily fooled. Apollicius had *imbibed* the *brew-of-the-arts* until filled and now *played, spoke,* and *danced* as one well versed and deftly skilled. Sweeping one of his Solar Arms across all Orbital Paths, he picked a *bundle* of young *planetary shoots* and continued to trundle, while *spinning* together their variety of *roots.*

His captured *amaranth* proved beyond any doubt his unfading love for the *solar path.* Though outwardly showy, inwardly this *bouquet-of-planets* would never die inside his powerful imagination—*unflowery.* Each of these beings either *was* a burgeoning Planet or was preparing to become one again.

"I feel ready to *ride* and capable of enduring the full culminating effect of being possessed by all the luring Muses present in my coming *bride,*" Apollicius declared.

"As you should," boomed Solium. "Without her support, none of your *planetary buds* would have any purport."

"Nor would you have anyone to gather all those charm-bearing *herbs,* which give the nobility of your *nouns* the mobility of *action verbs,*" Marisium remarked cleverly. "She is the one who does the culling of the *plant-planets,* by *transplanting* their sound-making into sound-taking *comets.*"

"Keeping the fire kindled by *seeing* with her ears," Solium added, "as the dew of a charmed liquid drops into the marvelous blossoms of those chosen few."

Of course, Solium and Marisium nearly foresaw everything that was to come, while guarding their *sources* ferociously against the ever-threatening wiles of *dark forces.* Obviously, they looked favorably upon the confluence of that *stream* Apollicius had gathered into a bundle of a *blooming dream,* which he now offered up to them as the finest of his crops' *cream.* They could do nothing but accept this present, sent to them through each *flower's scent.*

Faintly, yet with precise fingering, whole tones wafted toward the sensitive ears of Apollicius. In an instant, he recognized the sound as being played by none other than the Hands-of-Helleniana. Being the *master of timing,* she arrived at the moment when they would most need her presence to continue to re-master the *art of rhyming.* Once, a long time ago, he had played her body-instrument as if it were a *harp.* Now, instead of the cello she possessed her own *blessed viol/vial* used as a protective shield against all she considered to be vile.

Apollicius of late had been trying to strengthen his Muse's revered calves, realizing instinctively their important role in bringing together their *severed halves.* Even her ankles would play a major role in this *magic flight* if he truly desired to reach the throne of his home in the Solar Palace at night. It was the one area of his *light* body he had always considered to be the most vulnerable. He could now, however, easily notice that Helleniana had a pair of unusually strong yet slender ankles. They provided her with excellent pivotal points of balance when caught spinning through space, as she now had been doing with her Cosmic Dance.

"An ancient giant holds up the *land* under these *waves of music* coursing through the spirals around my being's *band*," Helleniana declared, speaking up for the first time since they had last met. "It feels so familiar under my feet that I swear it is either someone I have long since known or a *force of strength* I would love to soon meet."

Marisium had been attracted by the scent of the *bouquet-of-planets* and appeared immediately from her Milky Way. She bore the future of all aesthetic revelation/revolution by making her Dance prophetic. Carefully, she guided her nimble feet toward her *match* and, without being noticed, slipped one of her precious *harps* into Helleniana's outstretched arms and hands. Supporting on his shoulders that vast terrain which served as her dancing platform under the sun or in the midst of sudden rain, Marisium's consort, Solium, was always there to ensure their artistic gain.

Twisting, turning, and spinning, Helleniana traced a sweeping elliptical path above the *land* and around Marisium's acoustical *band*. Despite Helleniana being separated from her Spatial Mother and then engorged in her process of *individuation,* her journey had continued unabated, leaving them both intimately related. In a sense, Helleniana had left Apollicius behind to speak for her *fugitive soul* in a galactic field of dissolution—both had survived and now were rejoined by a musical solution.

Apollicius raised his *long trumpet* to play in meter and with reverence as he caught the trail of her unfurling energy drawing out the *dance*. Now the *Trumpeter* and the *Harpist* began to encircle the tallest Plant ever to grow out of nothing but the thinnest mist. Apollicius no longer even thought of retreat, so involved was he in seeing their differences absolved. Truly, it became one of their many *nights* at the *Garden of Eden*, where each of their playing instruments locked into each other's *sights*. At this exact point the formation of a pattern in the *physical, outer world*, accompanied a pattern already laid within—thus producing an unending cavalcade of sidereal sounds of many kinds.

"The *Harp* must lead with its chords, just as the *Trumpet* follows its highs and lows trying to avoid the pitfalls of a streaking comet," Helleniana now sang in counterpoint to her playing.

"This majestic Plant we encircle is none other than my own highly cultivated *Sunflower*. We surround our inner things with outer winds and vibrating strings," Apollicius sang back.

His flight had come full circle, just as his insight became his *oracle of the void*. The wind gently caresses her strings, while his mind *undresses* each note her action brings. Now they were two instruments in flight—one fleeing the other, the other seeing her *notes* rise and swell through her diaphanous garments luminescent in a night midway between heaven and hell. It is not poetry anymore when the observer and the observed blend into one *visionary end*. The once *inner sanctum* of the subjective realm turns out to be intimately joined to that exterior objective *sphere* of acts and facts—the outer stratum.

"This is exactly how an orbit is formed," Apollicius called to Helleniana. "First it begins as a Path-of-Sound whirling around and around until its *bounding line* is finally found."

"But of course, my dear trumpet-blaster, *I* have danced planets into being just through the strength of my Heart beating faster," Helleniana laughingly answered back. "On this plane there is no real outer nor inner division, but only the energetic swirl of the *Muse-in-fusion*."

"We have challenged the *powers of the abyss* by stirring that *black con-*

coction called the Universe—where all *planes-of-existence* make *head*way around each Galactic Wheel," Apollicius declared. "At every point of the *way*, the Imagination needs to be guarded and protected by the primordial deities of all Creation: Solium and Marisium, that is, until the moment arrives for us to step beyond—alone."

"That *time* is here and now," blurted out Helleniana in her spontaneous, exuberant style. "We have had our share of proper super*vision*, have been delayed by a whole variety of many fabulous and dangerous adventures, and are now ripe to be *picked* by Marisium and her consort, Solium, to create and command our own Planetary System."

"How right you are, Helleniana. We are nearing the point of hearing our magic cue, signaling that the time and the day has arrived for our rescue," Apollicius affirmed emphatically. "The *Golden Fleece* lies within the music *peace* we continually compose—we seek with more originality its *sound secret* to expose, rather than to procure mere security of comfort and repose."

Through the help and general assistance of his favorite Muse, Helleniana, Apollicius had come close to discovering his own position on the Axis-of-the-Wheel-of-Stars, to carry him through the blinding, binding Cloud of Galactic Debris. Fortunately, it had been quite a while since he had heard that question welling up inside: "Why are you tarrying?" He had always striven and continued on a daily basis to strive, to amplify his Consciousness by transmuting all the *matter* into *spirit* he had been in the habit of carrying.

He felt himself slowly beginning to rise again. Every failure he had had to cope with in a certain situation seemed to have receded to a more distant station. He now stood along the *scale* he had come to imagine he understood. Marisium merged with the *legs of his stance* as the *spatial liquid* moved up, first through his calves, then to his thighs. Fresh *waves of consciousness* streamed, moving next into the *lotus* just below his navel, starting to turn in the same direction as the Great Wheel of the Galaxy. Vertebra by vertebra, the *tide* rose within Apollicius, with Helleniana behind his *column*, her arms raised upward in the symbolic shape of the runic letter "I." Then, looking for a sign into the yonder, she gracefully unfurled her cloak and draped it over his shoulders, just as the dawn broke in ruby-spun wonder.

"As long as I feared my own *light*, restricting walls circumscribed my young system, rife with pitfalls," Apollicius reflected as he continued to slowly rise out of the depths of that *sea of all seas*. Having *stemmed* into himself Marisium's *tide* from below, he hemmed in the Light of Solium to his own *horizon* to open this *Premiering Show*.

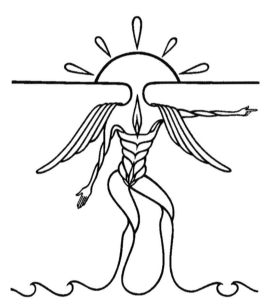

"I have finally become myself, which means to revolve around the Tone—alone and on my own. All of these Planets I have so painfully yet blissfully created depend on me as their ultimate energy source," Apollicius affirmed.

"You will possess enough strength to *solo* only if I, as your Book of Muse, am inside you to peruse," Helleniana counseled.

"I bear the *vesture of light* within my vestment, toward which all of the Planets have made their investment," Apollicius went on. "It is toward this end that I have *written in light* all my prosody, rhymes, meter, and poetry."

To achieve his goals he had traversed those radiant ranks from star shoals to the Milky Way banks to be able to stare wide-eyed into Solium's Orb of Orbs. He had been clearly fated to exist in a continual *stable* state of being elated. Many of those below did not know the secret of the secret ways of his *musical bow*. Simultaneously, it both could be an *instrument of arms* and could permit the *arms* to *play* a sound producing undeniable charms. When Apollicius played this bow, he shot arrows into the heart of his foe—pointing the way for this System of Planets and Moons to finally have their own revolutionary say. He existed for them and they for him—symbiosis, here, as synthesis within each glowing sphere.

When the prisoner is ready, the liberator comes with a rescue plan to unfold—slow and steady. And so Solium and Marisium came with their design after Apollicius had done all that he possibly could to ensure his exact place beside the greater and lesser Stars of Interstellar Space.

Their Scheme had been drawn up and drawn out during one Cosmic Night, set to the breathtaking tones emanating from their own Palace of Light. They promised *energy-wealth* of an extremely strong, vibrating nature for the orbital organization of Planets, Moons, Comets and Asteroids of varying stature.

"Hold dear the *lyre* and the *bow*, and you shall never tire, nor be without *light* and *arrow*," Solium began.

"This is not enough for him," Marisium objected. "Of all the deities who have ever assembled in this swirling Milky Way, one of us needs to devise a real rescue strategy and dispatch vaunt-couriers to spread the Creative Sound-Ray to the far corners of the Solar System of Apollicius."

"I have just thought of a way to disseminate this Ray—the Way of the Turning Wheel," Solium announced as he began to back his own idea with a strong measure of zeal.

Solium's very gesture expressed pure enchantment, and the supernatural sounds emanating from all the orifices of his Great Being convinced all that he *was* the composite of this Divine Assembly of Deities. Through this light and sound firmament, his lieges *lorded* over their dominions, populated by their light-aspiring or night-tiring minions. As Architect of his Universe, part of him now *became* this diverse *hymn* with which his adherents could converse.

"Since I am the Light of the Firmament, my beams *are* its Pillars. It is those beams I now send to my Sun, Apollicius, as one reaches down an arm to unbend. There is no plan to my plan except to express what is in me in a *circumscribing fan*," Solium proclaimed.

"You are indeed the Emanating One!" Marisium admitted joyfully. "You are the Ruler of all Elastic Energies, manifesting themselves for eons, who in turn took form to worship your worth with paeans."

In the meantime, Marisium had positioned herself as an *astral-pedestal*, ready to become the resting place and supportive base for the transformed *pillar-of-light*. Kneeling, she held up the young, slender shaft of Apollicius for Solium to soon grasp with feeling. This would initiate the rescue of the return of his *many-in-one*. At that moment, all the Muses, led by Helleniana, converged into Marisium as a living monument to fulfill Solium's *visionary plan* for the moment.

From the blissful depths of the abode, Apollicius rode toward the self-scattering *mate* of his awakened *state*. The Great Adventurer had returned, his deed all but done—having come to the knowledge of the *multiplicity-in-one*. Now he had to make it known before he could say it had truly been his own. So he summoned all of his Planetary Creations once more to explain how he had been divided into so many parts, how he had entered every Art of Nature to be able at the same time to become the Nature of all the Arts.

"But you still seem to be completely whole as you rotate around that centralized *galactic pole*," wondered Librarium, the most creatively balanced of Solium's constellations of which Apollicius was a *light element*.

"I am at present both *energy of waves* and *packets of energy*, whereas before I could be said to be only *radiant energy*," Apollicius explained. "Once I became scattered, I had the chance to understand that my *unity* is all that mattered." I see the whole Spine of Marisium supporting the Sky, while the Ribs of Solium form its Sidereal Walls—together, they make up that convoluted tube we call the Universe. I am a mere lamp inside their Great Cosmic House. One day, when I stop emitting rays and putting sound to staves, I will quietly retire into one of their many caves."

"But tell us more, Apollicius, about how you unified all of your variegated beams, shafts, rays and arrows into one round quiver slung over your majestic shoulder," Sagitarium queried, continuing to investigate the area of multiplicity. Sagitarium, along with Aquarium, Virginium, Geminium, Taurisium, Librarium and the others helped to fill the Space of Marisium with their *drawn out* star designs or constellations.

"To be divided into smaller and smaller fragments initially causes excruciating pain, but after some time, the Imagination begins to piece together all that has been separated and outwardly appears unrelated. The august garment of any deity is painstakingly sown, stitch-by-stitch, into the symbolic pattern of a particular design—creatively grown. Ultimately, what separates one *order of magnitude* from the other is the level and quality of its *light amplitude.*"

"Please go on," signaled Aquarium, obviously enraptured by the words of Apollicius, who had been *pouring* energy into his *system* for so long.

Apollicius let out a ring of laughter that filled the spatial setting around him. He laughed so, that the plains, mountains, and plateaus of the highest heaven began to tremble.

When he calmed, he explained: "When I laugh as I do, I feel a unity of everything I am and have interconnected by touching with my beam, which had until that moment been invisible. You too will one day feel a certain tenderness for these *rays* to set you off on your own adventure in binding the unbound, *unbounding* the sound, and finding the light in what before had been clearly unsound. Then, possibly, like me, your attitude will direct itself toward all things that you have rendered visible, a gentle gratitude—this is the true beginning of the *light journey* of any Star Magnitude."

"We, then, are just at the beginning of the perilous path of the initiatory Conquest of Light in the Spatial Land and Sea of Trials, dotted with moments of illumination," stated Virginium, the most detailed of those "stellar drawings" or constellations.

"Yes," responded Apollicius. "First, mere moments, minutes, then hours of light, and finally entering the luminous House of Sight."

Solium, who had been listening attentively to their lively exchange, once more chose to put his favorite sun on *trial* just after he had so tenderly rescued him. So it was with the Great Central Sun of Solium. Once Apollicius had achieved a certain level of light, the trials, tests, and tribulations of some new ordeal often awaited him, since Solium was always in search of ways to challenge his perennial wound to heal, wherever and whenever appeared his Achilles' heel.

Without much warning, Solium grasped the elastic, fiery body of

Apollicius and stretched him out of his sphere, until he became as long as it took to reach a far *spatial peak* while leaving part of himself still attached to another *ridge* that loomed up near.

"Let's see now, my Sun, if you have enough strength and energy to bridge this valley to solidly connect *this* mountain to *that* twin ridge," Solium challenged his Cosmic Adventurer.

"I had no idea Apollicius could stretch his Solar Body that far, unbending that *light being* out of his suspending star," Geminium exclaimed from the perspective of his *double constellation*.

"This definitely will test my *theory of unity*, defying me to become a *balancing beam* without splitting any of the *sewn sun spots* where golden threads have been stitched into a *helix seam*," Apollicius affirmed.

As Taurisium gazed out at this new Cosmic Configuration of which he, like the other constellations, now formed a part, these lines for some reason passed through his Energized Mind: "What sweetens the terrain is the rain. What sweetens the rain is the clouds' pain."

Of course, this could not have been all just for fun—rather, it was *light training*, wherein Solium sent down luminous Reflections-of-Apollicius of his *night raining*, ending soon after it had begun.

This had always been the case of the Father expressing himself through his Sun, though the contrary could also be equally true. What an opportunity for Apollicius to be literally bathed in the powerful light flung at his bridge from the Heaven's highest Ridge.

"I feel as though I am having my first actual Peak Experience," Apollicius shouted, thoroughly exhilarated.

"You *are* the Bridge-of-Light for your Wandering Planets to cross," Solium noted. "Being stretched out so completely far facilitates and expedites your whole process of one day becoming a Mature Star. By bridging yourself to yourself, you consolidate all your power inside one *gate*. You have your Light Sword—the counterpart to my Thunderbolt—to *draw out* the Word, which ultimately sets you, as a Sun, apart."

Traveling from the Great Above to arrive at the Great Below, each carried within the *essential spark*, enough energy to single-handedly start its own *adventurous ark*. Yet when absorbed by the great outstretched Being of Apollicius, this *seed of the beam* became instantaneously part of his *interconnecting seam*. This final prostration made him especially *prone* to letting his dwindling *ego* become substituted for the greater orchestration of *tone*. Lying face down, he became ready to become *overcome*. Once supine, his body lengthened even more into one long *horizon line*—out of which his *own* Fire-Self would soon arise to shine.

Obviously, Apollicius now had been adequately cued for this stage, upon which he would finally be rescued. Turning slightly, as if he were being roasted, he felt more than actually saw the Incarnation of Helleniana at his side—ready to be toasted. Having no glasses other than their own body-light receptacles, they both rose up and touched in delight. Each could not be rescued without the other, so the separation of light and dark could be observed only from the perspective of the Planets and not Apollicius, the Sun. Helleniana essentially lived in total darkness until her true outline had been conceived in the light of her unique design slowly being perceived.

The real *double helix* is one Energy Coil, each supplying the other with its *essential oil*. This is the inner *nature-of-dance* within the outer *dance-of-nature:* the Muse and the Music, one intertwined within and about the other. In the wings, the Muse waited eagerly for her Surreal Subject to get way beyond himself and roam into the realm of the Real Object. Just when Apollicius felt he could not hold himself at that excruciating length any longer, Helleniana came to show him where new strength lay along the line of the *Way*.

Finally securely rescued, Apollicius sent *himself down* inside the form of three powerful rays. Out of each of these burst its *own* individual Light Source.

"I am ready to move a *step* beyond the Creative Sphere of the all-embracing Solium. If I have truly been rescued, then I should now also have been prepared to rescue—to salvage from the danger of confinement my young Planets, held captive by their own inability to give up being inactive," Apollicius announced.

"We all intend to cross that *threshold of return*," Mars affirmed, seeing luminous ladders descending rapidly out of the elongated Sun Drops of Apollicius.

"Let's take them now," called out Jupiter, standing just in front of Saturn—long before he had acquired his famous rings.

Mars grabbed *his* Ladder first and wasted no time in taking his first step onto the *orbital rung*. Each *ladder* extended up to a different elliptical plane, leading each Planet *back* to the rotational and revolutionary pattern bearing its own name.

"I have multiplied myself by three to bring down these *ascending steps* for your Spin to finally break free," Apollicius went on, speaking brightly. He himself had devised this Plan after dutifully making the prescribed sacrifices—namely, libations of water, honey, and sage incense to his Muse, Helleniana. She had responded by saying: "Even without these gifts, I still love you, Apollicius. Bearing your Light Sword, you are the Angel of the Sound Chord."

At times it seemed that her body had been crafted of a substance finer than invisible air, while on other occasions she felt as lush and pliable as any nimble nymph from the sea lair. When possessed by her, he felt power lifting him to the highest level of the *knowledge tower*. Accustomed to *bubbling up* from certain volcanoes lying between a planet and its heaven, her presence connected the two domains' underlying essence. Though she often preferred to visit high places, she could at times be found in the liquid murmuring of underground rivers made of her slender, meandering limbs and smoothly tapered hands and feet. Holy Spring came forth from her being wholly a *spring*.

Before he tasted her, there was always a foretaste—issuing directly from the enduring Heart—*undisgraced*. This innermost *taste* could never be bound by those common constraints of the four dimensions, which everywhere abound. Their foreplay consisted of a match of their wits struck by the feather-like touch of the sound a certain *key word* transmits.

One by one, in the light-flooded presence of Apollicius and his Muse, the Planets stepped onto the stand of a straight ladder—alive enough to soon *turn* into the shape of the Great Helix Strand—to assimilate and diffuse. Shortly thereafter, they had all spiraled into orbit and taken on the Shape of a System, bit by bit.

Apollicius now had to constantly refresh each Planetary Station to maintain the ever-changing integrity of their *Spherical Nation*. Without a doubt, the *Vision*—his ability to *see-into-things*—had to have been the Great Boon he had brought back from those depths upon depths of Marisium's pure *spatial springs*.

"I speak my word through shifts in my *shafts of light*, which sift through your atmospheric veils, to penetrate all those levels of terrestrial rifts," Apollicius explained. "My ongoing *drama* is that every day I must originate and fabricate them anew—to be able to spread out from the many to the few."

"That in itself is a heroic act, demanding a precise set of skills all contained within your *stoic knack*," commented the Muse, Helleniana, who had again just recently receded into the richly textured background of the Solar Palace.

Apollicius kept on drawing his Sword of Light to continue to cut away the day all across this Spatial Ball, stretching in all directions its all-encompassing Nightfall. He did this in defense of his progenitors, Solium and Marisium and also to sustain and maintain all he had thus far brought into being on behalf of his Creators. After withdrawing and sheathing his Golden Sword a great many times, he easily came to grasp how any lack of attentive intent could allow the whole thing to unclasp. Fleeting in nature, *It*—that intangible something called *spirit, imagination, inspiration*, etc.—could not always be counted on for an appointed meeting. Nevertheless, he felt the time had come to go into this yonder zone and take complete control over this intangible *touchstone*.

So without any further lingering he stepped out of his Thunderhead cloud, where he had been temporarily concealed, to reach for that very core of himself, still almost completely unrevealed. In a *flash* he had the Lightning within his clasp and was holding it away from him as if it were some mammoth abstract asp.

"This is my *mental elemental*—the synthesis of water, air, fire, and metal," Apollicius stated, ready now to cast out his *line-of-light* into Marisium's Sea, unabated.

Undeniably, he now had as firm a *grasp* of who he was as ever, yet knew his Planets still did not clearly know the difference between true wisdom and mere cleverness. This knowledge could possibly come now, since he had just tak-en himself and his entire System across that *threshold* before his Light Sphere had grown too old.

"When I actually *bring it into being*, there is no line to mark between the *pose* of my nose and what I mean to compose. Or rather, I *am* that *lightened line* which follows the wavelike curve of a *dorsal spine*," Apollicius related. "During these blissful moments of pure creative ecstasy, I literally dissolve into my System of Planets. What I lose in personal *individuation* I gain in Light's perpetuation."

Ever since he could remember, Apollicius had been motivated—in other words, he had always had a plan and tried to follow through on it for his mind to expand. Inside his *heavenly boat* he did not eke out his *days*, but gave of himself unstintingly to his imaginative forays. At Night, when Marisium would finally absorb his Burning Orb—she being the very first female fire-eater—Apollicius would take out his clay-baked tablets and etch into them his latest *visions*.

In his most recent *vision*, he pictured a giant plant whose one long leaf-like arm outlined a Door. Across its threshold on the other side, plants grew with stars attached to their stems in place of flowers or other *precious gems.* After seeing this, he mused, "This is a synopsis of my entire Opus—where I have been and where I am bound. Whatever my Father, Solium, has forged as a star-like god could also be found hidden deep within my psyche's *seedpod.* I feel I am here to irradiate within this inner pattern state. Only if I accomplish this with pleasure will I receive that hard-won tranquility in its full measure."

This image, along with all the other transcendental glyphs, Apollicius *beamed* to his Planets on the *wings* of the *sylphs,* for them to use in the formulation of their own Solar myths. Because of his resplendent, abundant supply, the more he sent, the more came to his *school-of-light* to apply. His central mission as a luminous orb would always be to render back into their visible world *language* composed of their familiar symbols. Marisium's often speech-defying pronouncements came straight from the core of her darkened *spatial-lore.* He strove to take these whirling three-, four-, and five-dimensional forms into his Solar Mind, and there translate them into the two-dimensional surface of an *image-plate.*

Into the realm of personified numbers they dove, where interstellar dust plus mist could form a great Nimbus Bust—a possible new galactic ruler whom new incubation worlds could one day look up to and trust. The question Solium had laid before Apollicius was this: how to communicate this transcendental message, coming from the Center of the All-Generating Ovoid of the Void, to the Planets, who insist upon the exclusive evidence of their senses bound by their *own* asteroid? Even before he had begun his complete method of training, he had felt his magical energy draining. "Am I really ready for this *mission of fusion* or will it all end in the *fission of confusion?*" he often asked himself during his most troubled moments. And then—

"How can I work so closely with these terrestrial *spheres of beauty* without falling in love with their most sensual peaks and deepest valleys? My Muse inspires me to love so profoundly; how then can I corral it to stay within her pasture soundly?"

Nevertheless, Apollicius set to work on his Grand Opus—to unearth the essence of each of his Seven Planets' Nucleus. Since he had already divided his Light into Three Rays, it would not be difficult to direct them toward the strongest trio of Planetary *stays*—namely, Jupiter, Saturn, and Mars.

"You must all return to the task of laboring, by using the inborn strength of your own Heavenly Body. The *way of the return* is ever-changing, ever-challenging, ever-dangerous."

"What shall be our tool to begin to work our way through this new *school?*" Jupiter queried.

"Inside the Fire of my Forge, I have fashioned for each of you a Shovel to dig your own tunnel-gorge," Apollicius explained.

"What is it that we endeavor to uncover?" Mars wondered.

"Buried at the bottom of this *galactic-dust-heap* are special seeds, elaborated with all the virtues that could ever be bestowed upon any *body—celestial* or *terrestrial*. They are seed-sparks, connecting a *line-of-light* to the Heavens," responded Apollicius.

"Maybe there, we can unearth a moon or two," Saturn added in jest, sounding willing to continue on with the quest.

At that, the Three set to work with new-found enthusiasm. But soon, seeing how they struggled to become adept at their new worldly task, Apollicius took pity on their plight and sent each a special Angel of Light to help with the excavation of their new *cavern configuration.* An Angel with a shovel did not ever grovel, but secured the implement with a wing, as the Planets looked on with pleasure at this scenario that had become such a novel thing.

Both Angel and Planet worked side by side harmoniously at this new excavation site, as if it were a splendid vacation under the luminous lid of starlight. Not just the Stars beamed on them, but also one of the New Moons and even the Great Sun of Apollicius himself. The more the trio of Planets dug,

the more they felt as if they had come under the influence of a power-ful *drug*. Both *movement* and *matter*—that is, the moving *away* of Matter for the Spirit to find its place within that narrow tunnel of space—this became the essence of their *find*. For their slowly lengthening tunnel to meet the exact level where their Seed had been lodged, each An-gel-guided Planet would need to learn how distraction and detraction should and could be dodged.

"I can feel the slight pull toward the Seed's potential might with each *shovelful*. Past this bend, the rising Apollicius will light a more direct way to ascend," Jupiter explained. He now appeared to be digging deeper than the other two Planets.

"Once we encounter our *Seed*, we can call our other Planet brethren, to come to dig their way out toward a *celestial lantern*," Mars announced.

The impressive bearing of Saturn also began to *tap* the *roots* of his own indwelling powers girding his Planetary Being, prompting him to say, "Now it is my turn to turn over this *labor-of-the-land* into something even the heart can understand. What really is a *tunnel* if not a cavern of the deepest desire for the Mind to learn to funnel?"

On and on they worked, yet instead of tiring, the intensity of their ef-fort became ever more awe-inspiring. First Jupiter, then Saturn in turn, and finally Mars—all became possessed by that Great Spirit: *Work-on-Oneself*. Their effort provided them with a nexus to receive *thoughts* over any distance directly from Apollicius via the *antenna* of their Solar Plexus. Later this skill would be further developed using the Musical Ray, by playing the Harp en route to transforming their *flat* body into a sounding *sharp*.

Closer and closer they came to their Original Seed from the Sun, not from Sin. The pleasure each felt, to be sure, became a treasure be-yond any measure. Slowly they edged nearer to the moment when the Sky Canopy would reward all their efforts with an amulet, made not of stones, but of *tones*.

"What I wouldn't do for a *necklace-of-notes* to ring about this broad shoulder space," Saturn mused, "to symbolize the manifestation of our august will to live in any time line and grow to any size."

As their endurance *multiplied*, their minds became less and less *divided*. Each Planet, teamed with its corresponding Angel, began to turn and slightly tilt at its own individual angle. Deeper and deeper they continued to carve, ready to dig up their for*tune* to keep their turning sphere from having to starve. The other four Planets—Earth, Venus, Neptune, and the Moon—slowly left their own *tree-of-the-fig* and came forth to join in on the *Dig*.

"We are still a mere fraction of what we could be, unless we continue to move fearlessly following our own *plan of action*. This Plan involves the thorough exploration of this Realm of the Gods—the dimension of reality that clearly defines us as *real striking rods*," Earth proclaimed.

The closer they got to being Freed, by the innate strength of the Seed, the more they began to change by elaborating upon their consummate Need. Clearly, all of them could feel the omnipresence of Helleniana—her effulgence unreduced at this point to be in concord with their own developing powers. She, of course, could not be fully beheld before the completion of their spiritual weld. If this happened, it would spell incalculable disaster for all of the Planetary Initiates. As they witnessed what each spatial level would reap, their orbits were instantaneously filled and readied for their quantum leaps. Helleniana had undergone a long series of transfigurations, always promising more than any of these *young planets* were capable of comprehending.

Even though Mercury had begun excavating long after the *greater planets* had started, he arrived first at the *Golden Seed*. As he took the *egg* in his long fluid hands, it slowly began to crack and finally split open to hatch an immense, uncoiling Serpent—who immediately swallowed up Mercury, drinking to the dregs his powerful essence. This Wondrous Snake did not hiss, nor glide hither and thither in a zigzag motion, but rather elevated itself with the ease and nobility of a superior creature intimately acquainted with all the graces of the elegant mobility of the most advanced races.

"I have become who I am through the wisdom of untrammeled movement. Once I find the *end-of-myself*, I'll be whole again. The cycle of my circle will then be complete," Mercury voiced in the high drone of one elongated note.

One by one, the Great Mysterious Serpents swallowed up each of the other Spheres as if they were mere fruits off Marisium's fabled *cosmic table*. This *second-time-swallowed* signified a *second death*, which they accepted in an orderly, orbital fashion.

"Now I feel properly clothed for our next serpentine adventure," Venus said with more than a mere touch of joy.

"Our *Soul* now has a new shape, enabling us to reach our *Movement Goal* inside the body of this incredibly pliable snake," added Mars, well versed in a variety of the martial arts. "This is a *form* I can really come to respect—not just in regards to its general features, but because in many aspects it is one of the most extraordinary creatures."

Uncovering themselves as *Great Seeds* once again, made them available as *food* to feed these Gargantuan Snake *breeds*. Moving in the smooth configuration as one rippling line, the Seven Serpents advanced, gliding upon a strange *cushion of air* which they seemed to be riding.

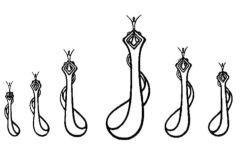

"This Dance of our Serpentine Orbital Field preludes what later came to be known as *Music of the Spheres*," Earth contributed, as she moved her whole body freely, feeling all her charm to have extended into the sinuous movement of a unique, undulating *arm*.

Their quest had become one long and severe test. With each transformation, they discovered yet another layer of what would prove in the end to all become part of their total revelation.

"Follow my lead," said the constellation Aquarium, who had hearkened the words of Earth and forged ahead once again to lay claim to their own Planetary Chain. "As Serpents, we are still potential Circles to form our Whole. It is as if our own *bounding line* has separated itself from its *spherical plain* and now roams freely across Marisium's vast Spatial Brain."

"I never thought our Seed Meeting would provide our one *long arm* with such fine *footing*," she added.

Forward the Serpents *marched,* sharply aware of the *path* they now *arched.* Each carried within itself its own hint of how they planned to re-enter that *world* where they would leave their indelible imprint in *word.* After their most recent transformation into the figure of the *serpent signature,* their beings, purged of all opinions, had room for the development of lavishly bedecked pinions. Out from the center of the *eon* emerged the *concentration of the spirit*—the peripheral ceded to the center, the circumventing arc to the core. Now, even if one committed a blunder, their heads had risen tall enough to contact lightning and soon become an integral part of the Mighty Thunder. After one had been consumed by the pure Undulation of the Serpent, what would remain to do if not form a Temple of Elation? Painstakingly, this they did, with the help of Marisium's Divine Breath and the steady gaze of Solium. Whenever an *ethereal shrine* came into being, this Duo would provide the foundation for its light to climb the *divine vine.*

Each marched forward in an ever-increasing *pattern of arches.* Once heavenly bodies stretched full-length, they openly displayed the tremendous faculty of their inherent strength. Each *famed planetary mortal,* when fully established, formed one part of the *framed portal.*

"Our Temple has a magnificent entrance, but where is the Steeple to represent its State-of-Trance?" Neptune asked.

"What an excellent question," replied Jupiter, who felt a special kinship toward the craft of sturdy construction. "I see its tower as the outcome of a uniformly upward flow of melody, arising out of the incomparable world of the Harmony of its Emotional Power."

"I visualize *twin towers* reaching out with affection, to support their *dome of internal reflection,*" Venus added.

"Is that internal or external?" Earth mused.

"They are one and the same in our Solar Temple of the ever-spiraling plane," Saturn rang out.

"Its *Bell,* hanging from that domed ceiling is what distinguishes his Face of Heaven from the lesser, more *chaotic hell,*" Jupiter clarified.

At that very moment, two events went from being separate contents to opening two intimately related testaments. First, at the Grand Altar, a Giant Lotus began blooming to Music of the Organ booming throughout this microcosmic *pulsar.* Second, out of the Sound of the

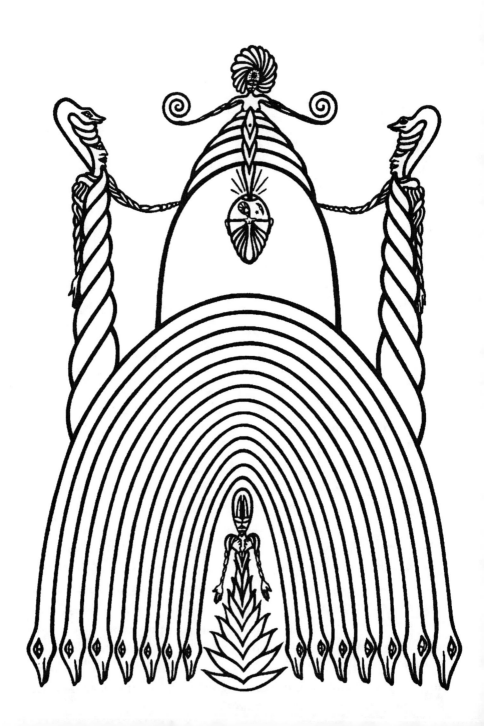

Sanctum Bell, the Real Spirit of the Temple arose to meet Helleniana, its *demoiselle*. Finally, it could be said that the Muse and her Music found a home in the Temple Dome, the first one of its kind to be put to *use* within this vast, complex System of the Greater Mind.

Mars, the great martial artist of the clan, saw that their arduous efforts had produced a form that spiraled without being *twisted*. It marked the triumphant return of the *spice* turning their Mental Organization into an *edifice*.

"From *threshold* to *threshold*," he thought, "we have traveled, loved and fought. Now we finally have a plan in place to put our System of Whirling Movement into our own Space."

"How long have we spent working away assiduously in utter darkness, in a *land* we do not know in order to accomplish our adventure—risking again and again, becoming completely lost, yet continuing on at any cost," Earth spoke from her own heart.

"Ultimately, it has been our Unconscious *and* Super-conscious Realms that have supplied their own balances to make up for a *conscious mind* more often than not succumbing to a particular type of activity so totally brain-numbing," Moon added with complementary insight.

Time after time Apollicius had mounted one of the *animal constellations* in his never-ending attempt to bond the terrene with the serene. Now that he had his own Temple of the Planets, his Work catapulted forward yet another Giant Step.

"Bring on more *thresholds*," he boomed to Solium and Marisium. "With the *power of concentration* we develop in our own Temple Tower, we'll be able to forge whatever depth we plunge, into the gorge."

As members of the *higher community* they could completely express themselves only through the Art Forms of Planetary Music and Dance Unity. Flying through the *Ether* kept their Temple together, spiraling through any change in the Cosmic *Weather*. As revelers, their lives glowed, while symbolic intuition guided their *way* as Sphere-Conducive Travelers.

Every now and then Apollicius would actually appear among his fellow Planets during his own *eclipse* and draw a long bow, taken from the shoulders of the Great Archer Sagittarium, before repairing to his own Land of Returning Light. During these inspired moments his own

Semen of Creation moved rapidly toward his *Solar Crown,* enabling him to draw the Maximum of Might, from his *own* repository of Light. This Bow would then twang with the Music of this show and with whatever else, out of pure inspiration, he sang.

During the period of his *eclipse,* Apollicius would always withdraw into one of those highly tranquil *epicenters* of his own System's *ellipse.* There he would incarnate the Grand Archer to create his fantastic arrows and adorn them before his departure. Out of the Womb of this State of Non-Light Majesty, Apollicius silently wove the waft and the weft of a New Solar Tapestry, all done right before he left. As one Arrow soared out of his relaxed grip, he gazed upward in the direction he had sent it on its first trip. In flight, it took on *his own shape* of the shaft, unrolling the image of both *flower* and *light.* Waiting there in the distance as his Great Target, was none other than Solium—arms outstretched to receive, with Marisium enfolded in the Mind *drawn up* in the Seed, ready to conceive.

"This is how I will return to my Kingdom to illuminate at *will.* After such a spirit-satis-fying experience of the many *visions of light forms* that have appeared to me from the many invisible realms, I can accept now the pass-ing joys and sorrows, the banalities and finalities, the clangorous and the inglorious, and of course those absurd awaken-ings occuring when a planet comes unbound from its herd. All these portents of woe cannot deter me from con-fronting the contents of any darkening foe," Apollicius asserted.

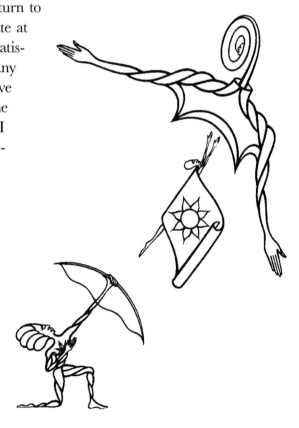

His Love had already intensified a thousand-fold, created a highly varied palette of *tone colors,* and devised a harmonic balm to transform the most negative of frenetic energy into a sidereal island of calm. In the deepest of all senses, he found himself in the process of a total resurrection of his light-drenched flesh. After innumerable attempts, he had firmly established the boundaries of his Solar Kingdom; now he felt the time draw near to prepare his *Book of Light* and to finally have it distributed in freedom.

Solium agreed as he greeted his Sun with exceeding warmth. Of late he had minimized himself to just his *arms* for embracing *universes* and his Spiral Mind for tracing and spacing *verses,* while the ever-swirling Lines of Marisium completed his Great Mind's Discourses. After all these eons, the two now seemed ready to sing their paeans—seeing Apollicius winding around their vine to quench their mutual thirst for his libation of *light wine.* As strong as Eight Thousand Gods, Solium needed no rest in his tranquil celestial river and called upon himself as Thought-Creator to come up with a Master Plan for his Sun.

"In order to preserve your *electrical charge* as the Solar King in charge, I must devise a way for you never to touch the *ground* of any of your Planets. Up to your outer rim you have been filled to the brim; therefore, I need to find a way to *insulate* you, so you will never be without your precious *light state,*" Solium elucidated. "To ensure the general maintenance of your *system conservation,* you will need to maintain your distance from them in the interest of your *charge preservation.*"

Since the Light of Apollicius had grown too powerful for normal rounds, it now had to be kept within the realm of narrower bounds. Little by little, beam upon beam and shaft after shaft, he had slowly built a highly concentrated Center of Power as an *insulating shield* from his surrounding system with its lesser energy field.

"Not every son of mine has a destiny," Solium continued, "only those *suns* who have taken the dive, the leap into their own depth *farm,* and come up with the *seed* as their precious stone—an amulet for their *arm* bracelet. They are the ones who will be able to catch glimpses of this talismanic ring during the time of one of your lunar eclipses." As both Suns and Planets, they knew that if they did not embrace their destiny they soon would not even have one to face.

"With your help, My Father, and under your guidance, I plan to weave together these two worlds, which under normal, actual circumstances always tend to cleave—unless they are held together through the Active Practice of the Sacred Dances," Apollicius confided with confidence.

By that time, Father and Sun had already merged as *One* and then come apart again to begin their own Forms-of-Art. In order to create the Dances, he took his chances with the greatest-sized Guitar the Heavens had ever seen, and immediately strung it with the Souls of his Seven Planets—still unsung. If he could manage to tune their bodies to play as a single instrument, then the initial span to bridge the two worlds of the *reality-of-the-deep* and the *common-place* would have unfolded from his overall plan.

The Life of the Serpent had taught each of these *sometime spheres* to stretch and follow into a *line of seasoning,* calling into play an abandonment of most of their power of previous reasoning. Though serpentine, they had learned well their *line* and how to straighten out the unwanted curvature of its wayward *vine.*

"To be a *String* is to allow the whole body *and* being to vibrate and sing," Venus said in a manner not unsuited to her general demeanor.

Mercury, the highest and hottest of these new chords, would be either be the first or the last to be *touched* by the astronomically long Arm of Apollicius, who readily accustomed himself to playing as he worked his sonic charm.

"I can see that you, Apollicius, head this Family of Seven Strings," Mercury said, *vibrating* in his direction after having closely scrutinized his twined playing arm, very appropriately lined.

Apollicius needed no *staff* to guide his hand, since it composed on its own ac*chord;* from its stave, out of which invisible notes flowed spontaneously, it became impossible to note them all down to save. He touched the Strings of all his Planets, now taut, while improvising freely on Solium's Music, which he had at one time been so well taught.

Speaking through a *seven-note chord* as one chorus, the Planets intoned, "The Sound of our *Guitar* is headed toward a Comfortable Constellation, where we can position ourselves with the appropriate temperament and tessellation."

By becoming considerably *less* than the whole *instrumental being of strings*, they were able to play *more*. Now, as pure vehicles of communication, their sound *traveled* farther. What *was* minor, as a former circumference, now became the *tenor* of reference. As Strings, their Sonnets came much closer to being pure sound than they ever were as cumbersome Planets. Some moments, they lay as motionless as serpents, while other times they could strike out with the speed and movement of hundreds of undulations per minute—in a furious arpeggio played on this electrifying Lute.

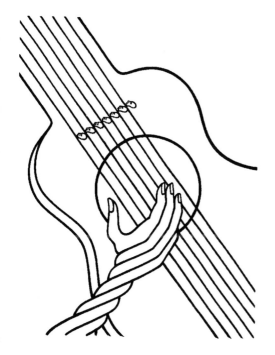

"I *rise* to play so I, as the Sun, may *set* into a new day," Apollicius related. "My hand is the *Creator*, with its fingers all working as the *Regenerator*. The fingernails are tiny shields, as yet not sundered—sounding chords, cries, and wails. This Sound Temple of ours is also the Chariot, pulled by the Sacrificial Horse at the dawn of all order and riot. Its eye is in *my* Orb, its mouth spews *my* Fire, its back is as long as a Century, its body stands on hind legs as Heaven's Sentry—this Cosmic Horse pulling us all, whose belly is the rounded firmament, while its hooves dig grooves in this substance sidereal, yet somehow grounded.

"It has four legs, not without reason, as each makes a strong imprint on every single season. The smooth hide does not hide the year, stretching from the tail end to the beginning of the ear. Having ascended from the nether world, my Steed is the carrier of all the *supportive words* for which we are in such a need—joining in its joints the fine line between the days, the months, and all the rest of those intervening points. The tops of its feet reflect the days, while *underfoot*, the nights are kept out of reach of the rays. Its skeleton is the constellation and its flesh the nebula revelation. Meanwhile, its blood vessels form the delta where its *alpha-source* empties into the *mouth-of-the-omega*. Grazing on Stardust, it eats the half-digested food of *galactic grains,* flourishing throughout the nights of meteoric rains. What liver, what spleen, could become the Great Organs of this Galloping Giver and Forger of every Milky Stream? It yawns out Thunder and shakes whenever the strike of Lightning dawns. Even its urine has turned water from an unadulterated fluid into the finest wine."

Eleventh Movement

Multiplication: *The operation by which the powder of projection has its power multiplied; multiplication is virtue*

When the Great Speech of Apollicius ended, the air among his planetary audience circulated freely, yet was still suspended. After they had weathered a drought of thought for so long in this Space where it had not *rained,* he refrained from withdrawing to see if he had lost them or witness what he might have gained.

"Let our *Strings* be guided though all the Constellations by your amazing Horse and Chariot," Jupiter proclaimed, "as you use us as your *instrument* for both Energy *and* Direction. When you *play,* we vibrate as Celestial Serpents—each with its own sound shape and *steady state.*"

"I have felt and still feel the deep tracks of your Cosmic Horse as it imprints a trail circumscribing my *equatorial belt,*" Earth exclaimed.

In the style of his ancient wisdom, Saturn then began to reveal his thoughts: "I suspect that many of your previous, present, and forthcoming Visions pre-existed in the Vast Mine/Mind of Solium and then, passed on to you, became actively *implanted* in our Planetary Souls, Sphere by Sphere, Moon after Moon. These *primordial images* have inspired much of the innovative process we have all been involved in since the very *beginning.*"

"You are so right, Saturn," Apollicius spoke in turn. "What good does it do to set up a *host of monarchs*, when there is no *ghost* to pass through the *arches*? This *ghost* I speak of is the Great Spirit itself of Solium—bridging me to you and all the *rest* to rest in you. That is why at this very juncture, at this exact point in time, I will re-present and represent myself as a Conjuror-of-Drops. Solium once informed me that this shape could, would, and will assume its graceful form once

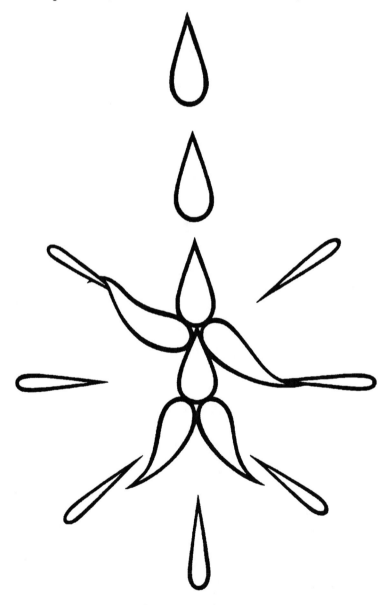

again. Now is the time for all of you to catch a Glimpse of the Essential Nature of the Universe. As Conductor-of-Rays, I can beam them into any consciousness stream or so it soon may seem-to-seam."

Apollicius instantaneously became this Body-of-Drops, as each *living moment* his *head* filled with a *fluid*, in much the same way as any not uncommon Field-of-Crops.

The *Drops*, of course, did not stop at his head, but flowed on through, running their own course, moving ahead. with force from their original oceanic source. Falling, each globule had come to receive orientation and direction for its own particular calling. As Drop-Master, Apollicius could control their dissemination by releasing them slower or faster. *Compounded charms* enabled him to succeed through the skillful use of his well-rounded and fully extended *arms*. They had been made mighty after he had returned again and again to his Solar Project, which he did not take lightly. Since this *form-of-the-drop* had Solium's blessing, it readily became immutable to any kind of second-guessing.

"I will project it everywhere," Apollicius announced, "from the lobe of the ear to the passing of a year reflected through the spectrum of a single tear. What presses me on with impetuous intensity is this deep urge I feel surge within this immensity. It goes way beyond me—my every*day ray*, my orb-being—across the abyss of Marisium's *spatial transitoriness*, toward a greater pantheistic sharing, sanctifying even the most catastrophic and despairing aspects of a cosmos that is outwardly atheistic. Continual creation and destruction wheel around my Solar Axis, oscillating from moments of pacification to bouts of intoxication."

Apollicius whirled like a *Tree-of-Light*, bearing his ripe, *planetary fruits* hanging tightly onto their *systemic branches*—befitting the cast for which they had been forged to last. The signature of this *drop* soon appeared in every place where before there had been virgin, unoccupied space, its hidden meaning expressed in its shape of a rounded ace. In the beginning even these *dangling planets*, seen from the top, looked very much like the form of this *sign-of-the-drop*.

"Our adventure, shaking us to the core, did not begin as a mere blunder, but propagated itself outward with a Clap of Thunder," Jupiter resounded.

"And now our *Oval-Beings* will *drop* back down into the *philosophical void*—the sacred vessel of transmutation they cannot avoid—to begin to advance through these important stages, always moving toward our final *station*," Mercury added in an unusually soft-spoken manner. "The fluidity garnered from our *experience as a serpent* has prepared us adequately for this smooth transition into pure liquidity."

"It is all part of the initiation of my Complete System of Light—like a *Man*, like a *Father*," Apollicius burst out, from behind that elephantine Thunder Cloud.

More thunder exploded with a tremendous din, sounding as loud as a sea of *bull roarers*, when out of the smoke and steam an *unsealed cup* appeared. It had the depth of a large goblet and the capacity to hold each Great Planetary Droplet. Apollicius held the Colossal Cup with firmness, as the Planetary Seeds flowered and flowed—a pure mystery of the highest world-affirmation he had ever known. Looking into the *cup* with no saucer, Apollicius viewed his liquid image-maker.

"To really become who I believe I am, I need to break my will to do terrible, multifarious, uncertain, and utterly frightful actions so I can attain a stronger and more even *will to balance*," Apollicius asserted. "As the embodiment of the Tree of Life, I give back light fruits to shape the musical sound of *planetary suites*."

Why should Apollicius even re enter this World of the Planets? Why should he attempt to make those spheres plausible, interesting, or even beautiful? He did it to maintain his cosmic standpoint in relation to their distance and rotation. Now and then he would raise this *Cup* to his golden lips to taste the planets' *fruits of temporal knowledge*—losing for a moment his balance-of-perfection, allowing his spirit to falter, enter into crisis and for a fraction of time even seem to alter.

"As an excellent conductor of Apollicius's *magical light fluid*, I have already begun to drain away some of this magical power to store as ore in my heart of the druid," Earth expounded in a style of the truth neither without reason nor unfounded.

By drinking from this Cup of the Liquid Spheres, Apollicius gave up light in exchange for pure power over the planets' destiny, whereas Earth became enlightened and secretly put aside those darker visions that had been bewildering and frightening her. The Nature of Earth influenced Apollicius when her *liquid* ran ever so smoothly back into the Star, much in the same way that *fluid* flows back into the fold of its Original Mold.

In a sense, initially the essence of each Planet had a pre-existent form inside Solium—to be further shaped by the elongated *ray-arms* of the Solar Sculptor. As an Artist of Light or a Light Artist, Apollicius knew the *secret of beauty* in all its correct proportions. Above all, since his conception, he had always been an *Image-Former*. For this reason, his own story—the History of Light—could be related only through pictorial representations, interwoven with nightly visits to the *dark space* of Marisium. To turn completely into his Throne of the Sun, he had to survive the frequent *abs-orb-tion* of his *rays* by the Planets throughout his yearly cycle composed of such a long year of *days*.

Of course, he had always known that the key to this survival lay within his Muse, Helleniana, through the Art of her Dance Revival; deep down, he knew she had no real rival. They had encountered and then separated myriad times, in all the wildness typical of the sufferings of Great Spheres in Love. She did not lie in the *Cup* pressed to his thirsty lips; rather, she *was* the *Cup* he partook of through long sips.

Helleniana had long since separated herself from the flock, to be able, through isolation, to make her spirit as durable and resistant as a rock. Her Kingdom, underground, spread throughout the System via Sound. Whether above the sky or beneath the waves, whatever she danced propagated her own energy in carefully composed staves. Being impermeable to any wandering-eye lures, she offered to the fragmented Paths of the Planets the simplest of cures: to whirl with her to the Sound of drums, flutes, and cymbals until their very ecstasy carried them beyond themselves as symbols.

Feeling the firm, warm hands of Apollicius on the curved belly of her *Cup*, she whispered, "To become master of your two worlds, you will need to master me without *becoming* my master, to serve me without being my servant, and to drink from my Cup without draining what has already been filled up."

She had become accustomed to passing freely back and forth across the sidereal horizons of Marisium. She had seen shafts of light broken on each Planetary Hearth—from Jupiter, Saturn, and Neptune to Mars, Venus, Mercury, the Moon, and Earth. None of this, however, had deepened her slumber, since she waited restlessly for her Light-Lover to shine on her stage during the right number. To bind them together neither of them needed a talismanic ring, since they had rallied around the proclamatory tone of the Temple Bells' *ring*. Through sound, each encountered their other portion, inwardly driving them toward a novel elliptical motion.

Apollicius was in the midst of the Moveable Stars, at rest yet containing the *force* by tapping into the motion at its source. He had grown during his course through time from the safely secure energy field of Solium and Marisium to become head of this fateful and dangerous region of a *zone unknown*. Now he had found his own Sun Palace, situated in the midst of extreme *Sol*ace. Turning the Light emanating from his face to the side, he saw arms rising majestically, as if to herald his arrival with the tide. For the very first time, he actually felt *and* understood the whole process of re-creation. His *glowing life* suddenly seemed to stream past, as he saw his Great Father, Solium, deep within the Spatial Sea of Marisium, holding up his own *Solar Canoe* at last.

"You are without a doubt, the God of all Plastic Energies," Apollicius affirmed, "the lustrous, illustrious one. My canoe and I have been recreated out of the Tidal Wave of your Mind. What is dream, what is intoxicating strength when we paddle at the same *wave-length!*"

A Sun had been reborn out of the forehead of Solium and borne ahead by the grace of Marisium. To the profound and supreme delight of the Greater Sun, this marked the long-awaited reconciliation with the *prodigal son*. This is how one fared: Apollicius continued to tell his story of he who greatly dared. Since he had been initiated—that is, channeled through the proper channels—chaos had not supervened. He had neither hurried toward zenith nor stood in the way of the hurled thunderbolt, but rather had taken to the *light plough*, unencumbered, and furrowed elliptical grooves in the *sidereal fields* of Marisium's Space as she gently slumbered.

"I have not forgotten about you, my Sun." Solium spoke in a voice as deep as it was resonant. "Out of my head I have *written* both the *light* and the *sound* wave to be played on one representational stave. My arms help my Mind's Boat to ride this high wave and always float around my Central Light Castle's Moat."

The *wave* bent perfectly around the Sun-raft to form a unity between the three wave mediums of *light, thought,* and *sound* craft. All of the Planets looked on in awe at all that they saw. Apollicius embodied the joyous necessity of the dream experience, in which they all now seemed to participate with proportionate transcendence. As a Deity of Light, he ruled over the Inner World of the Vision, now apparent to these Wandering Spheres with this startling image presented with such sharp precision. Upon this *raft* of the Father was carried this *draft* of the Sun. Jupiter instantly recalled a similar *vision* he had had in a dream that he had nearly forgotten—about a *muse being*, born straight from his forehead into the life-stream straits.

"The perfection of these states comes into great contrast with our unintelligible everyday world as a Planet," Jupiter reflected. "It takes deep consciousness of our inner nature to envision symbols strong and accurate enough to make our spheres worth spinning."

"We cannot rotate any longer quietly engulfed in our illusion with no motivation to get stronger," Mars declared as he unsheathed again his Sword from the *Craft*.

"We all celebrate the reconciliation of you, Solium, with your Great Prodigal Son, Apollicius. The *Vision* of both of you we see now is our *Cosmic Map*—giving us a *raft* to penetrate all of the Space around us, both fore and aft," Earth joined in.

Slowly, laying beam upon beam, Apollicius had constructed his Light Structure of Protection. Whenever, now, his System waxed back before his *stormy vision,* he would reach deeper into his quiver and let bright, flaming shafts fling to the attack. Out of an Original Order of Terror, he endeavored to implant an Order of Joyful Fervor. Beauty is born when the rose bursts from the bush of thorn. His Art, then, developed out of this *womb of strain* and under the sway of his strong impulse toward the aesthetics of *light rain* in place of pain.

"If I have any advice to give you at all, it would be to not stay heavily in any one location, but to revolve your *ways* in great turns and *voluptuous orbits* around my Light Station. The center of our *web* remains at times as vigilant as the Spider," Apollicius concluded.

"The great Tapestry of the Heavens, I have spun as something not merely for fun, but for all of the Stars, including you, Apollicius, to truly be your Planets' Sun," Marisium suddenly spoke out from her shrouded abode—*everywhere.* "It is as if I had spun a cocoon of nearly infinite proportions and am now witnessing the first tiny movements of this Monarch Moth, ready to spread its mighty wings soon. I have measured out a lengthy thread for each of your Planetary Children, to be strung not through a bead but through your Head. This Necklace, I swear, I will give to you as a present to wear in my Space."

"My *Wheel*, then, Marisium, is for spinning these threads of *light filaments*—filling out your *fabric* in any direction they happen to spread," Apollicius responded, ever ready to read and *be* read. "I emanate the reflective *faces of fate*, all carrying the profile of my steady emotional state to all of you as living entities endowed with pulsating, individual souls. It is in this 'Spherical Surface' that Solium and I have joined together. I move from my Center to the Outer Circle whenever I am in the mood to begin a new Creative Cycle. It comes about by blending the trinity of will, thought, and action."

"The secret is not to allow that precious *liquid* inside to secrete," Apollicius counseled. "I am the Vehicle of the Wonder of the Law of Light *and* also the Sender of that Yonder Fire of the Night. If I did not release all those milliards of rays and beams of Light, they would turn back *into* me—creating a huge Black Hole deep enough to burst through my *seams*, threatening the integrity of my thirst for the whole."

"Even though I possess the power to design my own Thunderbolt, I cannot compare its sound and light energy with your Burning Orb, which we all turn toward to absorb," Jupiter called out to Apollicius.

"It is true, Jupiter shatters and jolts the illusory realities of our own individual *worlds* with the conspicuous element of his repeated *thunderbolts*, yet we still yearn for your *volts*, Apollicius, which is definitely all that matters," Venus responded electrically.

"I send my light to you to help push the *enemy* to the *crags* and *canyons* of your terrestrial domains," Apollicius continued. "This Great Battlefield is your *field* of truths and lies where each of you survives or dies. When you overcome this constant, discordant mischief and are able to restrain from being plunged into profound grief, you are on the way to becoming your own Planetary Chief. Fight and be unperturbed!"

"Each of us is one Contributor to your Throne as Light Distributor," Mars observed in his own uniquely terse verse.

Earth looked down at her patched, terrestrial robe and then out again at the Starry Vault. Her resplendent work lay ahead—scores and volumes to be penned in by the *ink of her rivers* onto the rolling paper of her land. Seated on her Elemental Elephant, she raised her deep-brown hand to signal all she felt to be triumphant. Though she could not see her supporting beast, she slowly turned herself to face the East.

"I have gone through a long series of ages and transformations to arrive at this result of my miraculous *passage* written down upon these pages. Now it is time to begin to reconcile my separate planetary consciousness with the Will of Apollicius—having received orientation from his Father, Solium. I have waited long enough on this *earthen bank* to turn now, before it is too late, toward the Lightened One I need to thank."

"Though you are not my highest sphere, you are one of my favorites to spin past me here," Apollicius began. "Never be dissatisfied with your own fate—to despair will not help to bring you into the Space of your

Rejuvenating Air. I can offer you, though, an advantage, for one who has suffered so much during your coming of age."

"What is that?" Earth wondered.

"The *pearl of gems*: direct contact with Helleniana, the Muse of all Stratagems," Apollicius responded dramatically. "She will appear to you naked, riding a white-winged horse, holding in her hand the crescent moon full to the brim with a *nectar-boon*. To really *think* will provoke many battlements for the possession of this magical *drink*. What I speak of is a totally different kind of *thought process* that leads to total clarity and eventually to the defeat of the *monster of mediocrity*. As the *path* orbiting around my Light Heaven becomes thinner, since it is narrowing, you will feel the sharp *spikes* digging into you from that sphere of hell, harrowing."

"To be like you requires the prowess to accomplish an incredible feat of emulation," Mars interjected from his battle perspective, orbiting not too many cubic light meters away.

"That is why she possesses her sensual range of mountains: to be able to ride her immortal tides when beginning to rearrange her multitude of fountains," Apollicius suggested.

"Mountains and fountains—what rises so high must at some point have to fall," Saturn reasoned.

"Those *spikes* need not penetrate the flesh of your fresh land state. It is all a matter of turning toward the not-inept Neptune, to learn how he holds his *triton* firmly as he still tones-in-tune," Apollicius clarified.

Neptune had re-emerged from his own *liquid depths* in the shape of a *leviathan*. Down his left arm he secured the staff of this three-pronged *triton* that had caught a crown. He gazed *up* at the others from his mountaintop, where he could survey the activity of his own planet, as a farmer would his crop. Having a body of *flesh* and *fish*, he came from the land of the fallen altars to now look out at an entire country of *tall stars*.

"I have *turned around* not to seek leave of my Sun King's grace, but to reincorporate the entire Body of my Sea Well within the Light of this extraordinarily charged *Spell*," Neptune pledged as only a *water divinity* could by his fertile virtue of rain and rivers.

As Sea Sage, he had entered this curiously symbolic Giant Fish as the *project* for the latest *projection* of Apollicius, the Sun Disk. In this *dolphinesque* shape, Apollicius could now more easily mesh with the general aquatic spirit. Back in his early, more rebellious *light days*, he had stolen the Sacred Tripod-Easel from his Father, Solium, enabling him to paint his first *Visions*, proclaiming his oracles drawn from the *light inkwell*. It had not been inane frivolity, but rather could have been more aptly described as divine joviality. Being the Son of Philosophies, Apollicius drew from this Lapis of Transformation—to be *drawn out*. If and when his Natural Vessel of Light became a Dolphin or a Great Fish, as it had presently, he could then incubate whole worlds as *eggs*. His *spatial sea light* vivified and bound all things through the sonar power of *chords-of-sound*. the influx of time, embodying intimately the rhythm and rhyme of the whale's chime.

"There can be no more magic without more than a touch of the tragic," Helleniana whispered into whatever ear might have been listening. Her words began to pour out in *turns*, moving from *planet to planet* as she effectively emptied her mind's capacious *urns*. She desired to be taken without undue commotion, yet be assured of the kindness equal to her station as *the* Dancer of Emotion. Who, may we ask, could be adequately prepared for that task? Apollicius had always felt that he could, would, and should be ready.

"Even though I have already been *poured* into all things, just as you now pour your words, there are still many vessels more, awaiting my *particles* and *waves* of beamed ore," he whispered back to Helleniana.

"You *will* pour what is good into its proper *craft,*" she affirmed. "That is why you and I and each and every sphere have come to this Spiral Temple located *here*. There is a sign everywhere helping to shape our internal design. Each region reconnects to its own *energetic religion* through your advice, amulets, and secret agents, sent to us as helpful *transcendents*."

Apollicius felt himself approach another *threshold of thought*, where he became his own *coach* to make sure each new flash of insight would be caught. He did not now move through a dream landscape of ambiguous forms, but rather forged a clearly cut mindscape of ingenious, image-producing *farms*.

"My Psyche does not question if it is over, but enthusiastically quests for its lost lover: Helleniana. Love is that ever-intangible line where Mind meets Muse. You, Helleniana, contain all the supernatural beauty from another world inside your sealed box. It is my adventurous task to unfasten it and distribute the *symbols* contained within before any of my Planets feel the need to ask," Apollicius outlined.

Venus just then whirled nearer the *gate* and did not hesitate to throw out a question regarding her own fate: "Am I too firmly bound by hidden fetters to understand these symbolic glyphs revealed to me through your esoteric letters?"

"As long as you don't confuse the *shadow* with the *substance,* you will be able to use Love's Bow and draw power from its Lance," Apollicius counseled. "Do, without attachment, the *work* you have to do, using whatever vehicle you choose, to transport the Spirit of your Sphere from *star-port* to *sidereal pier*."

Shielded under her invisible hood, Venus stood tall in splendor as her Planetary Cape flowed back around from receiver to sender.

"I will be the vehicle for your terrible, terrific scroll, written in the Law-of-the-Star, penetrating through Space as it begins to finally unroll," she declared.

"I can see that you are ready to receive the Star Language and wear it as an emblem to gauge the development of your Age," confirmed Apollicius, the Sun King, nodding his Great Head of Light Potential.

"Yes, I feel my resistance being allayed with this eternal *star kiss* laid upon my forehead *world*. It is as if the Great Force of the Star itself had attached itself upon my back—maybe an emissary from a Giant Star-fish Source," she concluded.

"I will gradually transform you, along with all the other Plan-ets into personifications of marching, whirling supports of our Universe," Apollicius finally added, looking on with deep approv-al as the Sky Canopy inside a rolled scroll penetrated the high forehead of Venus.

Gradually Apollicius led his Muse-infused Planets through their *planetary-mazes* of intricate shapes, weaving their orbital paths into ellipses wearing galactic dust capes. He had al-ways been out of his mind, but especially now, after he had helped Venus get the *whole universe* inside hers. The rest of their power, though, would have to arise from a more dangerous origin: from the very *cauldron* under the land surface of each *planetary bin*. When tapped, they all would inevitably turn again toward his *Suncratic Legislation* to complete the cycle of their *Light Integration*. He would then urge them to perfect their own self-sufficiency, to simplify and synthesize, clarify and strengthen, the noble singular line, un-ambiguous, free under his unique Law of Light and the *fine line*.

Filled with a *universal mind*, Venus gazed about her Stars until her eyes locked with Mars. Her inner workshop-of-love's-source had yet to assume its outward course. Mars stood tall as Charioteer of his Mighty Vision; there seemed to be nothing around to mar his deep sense of dig-nity. He had successfully made his way past numerous perils thrust into his *space*, through his skillful use of the discus and the mace. Confronted, however, with Venus's Universal Face, he failed to know just where ex-actly he stood or what was his real place.

"Marry the *flute* and the *lute* and put aside those arms you designed only to be used in dispute," Venus plied. "Now is the time for you to become Master of your two Worlds. Start to unify these two realms, and you'll be moved to produce Great Art."

"My Chariot, dear Venus, is not drawn by a *team of swans*, nor was my Planet's Temple built by bees, of wax and songs. My Meditation *is* the Ride—the Ride, an exaltation. You fulfill my demand for *art* and *beauty* and command my Martian Brain to move in the direction of love's most profound ecstasy," he expounded.

"We shall, then, communicate through tones, gestures, and glances; this is the aesthetic realm of a superabundance of stimuli and signs, where love is accustomed to taking its chances," Venus spoke up warmly and softly.

"I have seen many shields sundered and great portions of differing lands plundered," he reflected. "Whatever new symbol I use as my *tool* to embrace, I will do everything to maintain it as translucent, so as not to block Light coming from Apollicius; I am here now to transmit its ascent."

"Only you can choose that symbol, Mars," Venus challenged. "Whenever your Chariot finally leads you to the top is where you begin to plan how to cultivate your favorite *crop.*"

Mars did not pull up on his reins, but raised his *whip* as if it were a lightning bolt and he, in command of the thundercloud and the *reins*. Though not uncouth, he had developed into a formative force, harnessing his *wave-beat* of rhythm to propel him in the direction of music's deeper source. Though his character generated a great feeling of power, he actually became powerless while his own connection and relationship to everything Venus stood for remained unresolved. He thoroughly understood the true laws of the proportion of all their Planetary Motion, yet still did not know himself how to express their beauty through his own *acts-of-creation.*

His own *stone* had been incubated long enough alone. As a Planetary Vessel, the time had come to connect his *microcosm* with the *macrocosm*, in order to allow the *work* to progress and ultimately express the *corpus* of his own opulent *opus*. In the Middle of his Sphere he had already begun to yield to the birth of his new shield. It was as if he had parted his own *leaf* and caught a glimpse of the *cosmic pattern* of its inner sheath. Then he got off his Chariot and planted himself down in the comfort and security of his own *plot*.

"At the very center of this labyrinthine web of my Planet Mind, there is a Seed growing and unfurling," he observed. "Though I do not see the sign as my own signature, I feel that briefly I will become an integral part of its picture."

And that he did. His Giant Planet-Plant of a Body slowly began to untwist—from the tip of his toe, through the hip, and on to the end of his unseen wrist. The enormous cavity of his *Martian Head* elongated in all directions, balanced by the steady pull of gravity. His neck flattened into an equilateral horizontal *plain*, an enormous surface now read for the cultivation of an active brain. His once vertical shield used for protection now had become prone to being used for *tone-growth* detection.

"My whole body has unfurled into the canvas—for the Imagination to spring forth its new world," Mars exclaimed, as animated as he'd ever been. "Literally, the Field of my Mind has been tilled and is now ready to receive as many seeds as it takes to be filled."

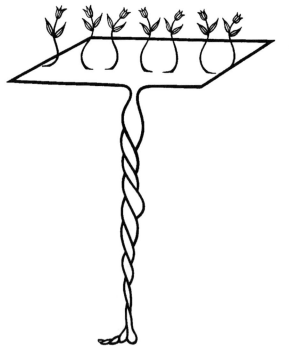

Upon this transformation of his *remade head*, he could *see* with his whole body flooded with the complete sea of the senses—not just the external eyes but the entire chorus of Inner *I*'s, from which came a polyphony. He had the gaze of an entranced seer—seeing through the filmy maze of a divine breath. In a word: energy equals creation. His body had become one unchained fountain of raw, upward-moving force, unable to be contained.

"To sprout or spout—that is what my present situation has come to be about," Mars expressed openly. "I have evolved from having a surface of a varied texture to creating a space for storied architecture. Through the beautifying power of this novel intellect, heavenly objects may be more easily contemplated, producing a greater effect."

"I can see, Mars, that you have thrown the full strength of your intense nature into the transcendental work of *self-cultivation*," Apollicius astutely observed. "You are now more than ready to receive, on your *mind's platter*, the finer grades of *super-sensuous matter*. Between us, there is a nexus between the *will in order* and the designed flower of its aesthetically disciplined *border*."

As Apollicius spoke, plants burst forth into bloom on the Higher Planes of Mars's fields and plains. Whatever wounds he had received during his early galactic childhood were presently healed as he understood this wildly fertile mood.

"My Planets are helping me restore my System to function as harmoniously as it did before. Fore, what Artistic Creation is to my Father Solium, motion is to my millennium. Through the movement of each *ray* of my sturdy hands, I have raised the *scales* up from that rocky escarpment where they had once been thrown to the *whales*. I have gathered together certain routed souls who had been in all directions senselessly scattered. Essentially, I have replaced bafflement with be*muse*ment. Those unseen libidinal ties between the Planets and me have received long-overdue *supplies*. After Mars, there are more remarkable manifestations opening up before us with equally impressive gestations," Apollicius concluded.

Fueled from the heights of the *upperworld*, yet not to be fooled by the depths of the *underworld*, Earth now embarked on one of the most difficult stages she was to experience—throughout all her ages. Feeling an unrestrained love toward the Light Spirit of Apollicius, each of their *sphere-souls*, Earth and Apollicius, had a mutually deep attraction whenever they met face to face, though their bodies had never actually attempted to embrace.

Earth had wandered for many millennia to atone for her crime of abandoning the worship of the *divine tone* and its enveloping clime. Only now could she return, not undefiled but ready to receive Light's Wreath to enwrap her Globe, here—underneath. Her Giant Enemy came not from within but from afar, to interfere with the Plans of Apollicius, to become illuminated by the same self-knowledge that had made Apollicius into a Star.

To counterbalance this *roar of madness* moving toward her Sphere from her *unseen enemy*, she arched her entire Earth-Being into the shape of a *table*—capable of warding off much more than she alone ever would have been *able*. Supported by her lofty appendages, she stretched upward in the solar direction of Apollicius and his light-ray *pages*. Her timing could not have been more precise, as the Great Burning Orb itself arose from its nocturnal exercise, and, in a contemplative calm, this Sun-Sender draped over her long body's terrestrial center a soothing balm. A true vision to behold left the Earth prone to vibrate its own individual tone, expressing the exact melodic shape of her mold.

"Like some ancient fable, I support the entire weight of your Light on the *corporeal surface* of my *table*—both real and ethereal," Earth affirmed with inner strength.

Earth couldn't, however, uphold Apollicius for long. as he soon continued along with his daily rising, feeling especially refreshed and exceptionally strong. He felt in the mood to burn through any and every mind-forged manacle. His world of *light dances*, seen through rare flashes of insight, lay in that ever-deepening reality behind and beyond the World of Appearances—connecting all things of the *physic* with the *psychic*. As he left

Venus's Second Kingdom of Purgatory, he passed through a region of innumerous *aerial bodies*—beings, waiting in the wings to either descend or ascend. Apollicius recognized a good portion as nymphs, fauns, satyrs, and Sylvania. Raising his ivory scepter, he at once commanded this entire realm of *personified number receptors*.

With good reason, Apollicius had always been known for his beams and shafts of *light construction*. Ever since his very early years, he had received a steady influx of emanations from his Father, Solium, which he, in turn, had helped to transform into the Phenomenal Forms of his Universe. Ironically enough, during these same *dark years* he had been habitually plagued by loneliness, misunderstanding and from a kind of *light persecution* from the older Stars. All this had led him away from Marisium's protective Space and onto a path of self-abnegation, eventually leading to higher spiritual attainment—for him, meaning more *bundles of light spears*, tied with a silver thread of destiny and sent off to any of the Planets to be read as litany. Everything connected to his vine became drunk on this *light wine* received in the shape of any well-drafted *bounding line*.

Solium had first invented the *Light Loom* while still inside Marisium's Spatial Womb, in those days when he and Solium worked together as Father and Son in the same *Cosmic Room*. Their cultivation of each particular ray could be described as the finest of all the Arts. Whereas in wine making it is essential to *tend the vines*, in this finer light undertaking, one needs to carefully *bend the lines*. Early on, no stupendous revelations occurred, just the day-by-day, sunrise-to-sunset work and the basic challenges of fabricating these visual emblems.

During this time their wealth increased because their Art-of-the-Ray production never ceased. With each New World Tree as a motif, there could never be any question as to the origin of that ubiquitous form of the leaf—which emerged as a green sword *drawn* from its dawn sheath.

"Even on the days when I did not greet my Father in a good mood, *Mood* thought otherwise and had me as its *food*—and it was good," Apollicius recalled.

All this had been building to a day like today, when he would have to move on to his next Project-Planet-Projection. Sooner or later this world would be completed, or at least one *season* of it. Each Planet corresponded to a specific *Ray,* which expanded when sufficiently aroused. Love and Sex motivated not only the Sun and the other Stars but the entire Universe. Now it seemed as though the unhappy vales of that emerald Earth would be the fortunate recipients of some fresh new tales. Only through the magic of a song sung even *wilder* could Apollicius turn Earth's gentle habits milder.

"With my *light lyre,* I will mitigate the fury of your gate," Apollicius promised. Then he proceeded to play its strings as if they were a *pipe* of modulating rings. But he could arrive at his solution to the sound co-nundrum only when he began to add the rhythm of a subtle *drum.* Earth, wearing her mourning garments and thinking that she had lost sight of her *light* forever during a total eclipse, now gradually reawakened to the call of these Solar Instruments. In the span of a few *moons,* she went from feeling *sublunar* to experiencing the full *mandala* of her *pentaculum.* If she had been a nebula, her transformational feeling could have been referred to as *super-galactic.* Little did she know that Apollicius had re-course to the other Musical Families of the *flying rhombuses, buzzers,* and *bells* of the *natural horn*—including the *curved trumpet* in the shape of the letter *S,* cast in sun-baked bronze.

"You are my supernatural helper, whose line is drawn in a mascu*line* form," Earth announced amid this flood of instrumental *food.* "If you could only make the *piano* sound like a *cello,* I would instantly change into *your* Giant Sphere from this unnatural Punchinello."

In one great flourish of his main *light sword,* Apollicius swooped out from the seat of his Chariot to gather Earth's lands into his protective paternal hands.

"You will be another *light seed* for me to cultivate, which, in turn, I need to continue to thrive as Sun-to-Burn," he informed her.

He opened his *hand.* The whole Planet Earth nestled comfortably in his palm as she arose out of her own sphere to stand. At that same mo-ment, Apollicius encircled as he held her, without any comment. What happened below on her *lower sphere,* also occurred on her being's *upper tier.*

The Great Secret of any Seed-of-Light is to get planted without los-ing the Might of Their Sight. Stretching his *arm-ray* high into the Sky, Apollicius elevated Earth bit by bit—in the direction of her former orbit, where to her joy she locked into its elliptical fit. A Planetary Artist in her own right, Earth had always spontaneously choreographed her spins and turns to the Music of the Spheres. Apollicius received all that he *would create* in symbolic-visionary images, in this way he knew that most his work was still to be done, whereas Earth got her creative urges straight from his own Power Ray. Each of his *light spears* shot out to one of the members of his Family of Spheres.

"Untie the Gordian Knot and you open the line of an illuminating thought," Apollicius reflected. "I freely give you your Day through the Force of my Ray— you receive it, and I never ask you to repay."

As Charioteer of this Light Vehicle, Apollicius steered his *car* to align it under each symbol and sign governed by a *star*. He knew the time had arrived to move on to the other Planets, but all the Charm of the Earth still found herself sup-

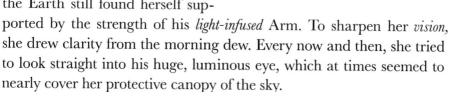

ported by the strength of his *light-infused* Arm. To sharpen her *vision*, she drew clarity from the morning dew. Every now and then, she tried to look straight into his huge, luminous eye, which at times seemed to nearly cover her protective canopy of the sky.

"Before I leave, I need to trace back into your womb to fertilize your Giant Egg before it begins to cleave," Apollicius announced.

"Cleave! What do you mean?" Earth raised her deep tenor voice, more than a touch preoccupied.

"Presently your nature and your psyche are *one*—with no split. Your Egg-Shaped Sphere is still gestating. But soon your great *coating* will crack, and there will be a rupture to give birth to that *part* of yourself which you lack. Immanent yet still unfamiliar, you contain your own *universe*, almost as diverse as the firmament. In the future you will turn to your teacher Mercury, the *ferryman,* to assign your way through those treacherous *waters-of-fury.* It is only the great student who *wills* to assimilate the teacher's skills," the Sun Charioteer explained.

"What am I now?" Earth wondered.

"Allow me to be your *artistic guide* and reveal to you what you, yourself, have tried to hide," the Sun replied.

"Proceed at will, Master of Light. It is you alone who now possess the unique insight," Earth consented simply.

Without any more hesitation, Apollicius picked up his sculpting tools and began to use the skills that had been fueled in him by passion, yet honed with self-control, in the very *starhold* of Solium's Cosmic Schools. Without error, the sweep of his Solar Arms excited and incited both awe and terror. Earth had soon become of great importance for the further development of his *art,* primarily because of the contrast between her present *dark force* and his effervescent *light source.* To achieve the highest form of self-affirmation, he now mixed the warm plenitude of power with a cool attitude of moderation.

While Earth looked up above the Ray-Master shaped mountain ranges and from the *almighty drop* painted many a cloud-cluster. Out of most of her golden yolk, continents emerged without having to change any part of their *coastline stroke.* Her Clouds and Rain contained a strong *germ* able to receive from his brush the luminous vapor, transmuted from that reservoir of accumulated *sperm.* He *painted* on her *canvas* with the undimmed eye of *willed vision.* As a *phallic being,* no enemy could withstand the color-combination he used to brush on this *metallic mien.*

Now his *pupil* could *see* that the pupil of *his* Solar Orb had become so enlarged that Earth could no longer envision the rest of his luminescent body nor see the form of his Chariot—electrically charged.

"This is what it is like to become immortal—when everything you are and ever were becomes one glowing portal," Earth exclaimed, obviously impressed and thoroughly inspired.

Although as a Planet she had suffered many defeats in her perpetual contest with her terrestrial demons, she now realized that Apollicius had generously bestowed upon her a worthwhile boon. He had brought up, from deep within the cavern-chambered womb of her mountainous self her new face, *remastered.* The revolving eons could not be numbered to determine just how long she had slumbered, waiting for her ages to finally start evolving before dropping back again into the Void of her *gods'* pantheons.

Once, these same *gods* had laughed at her oblivion, when she had prayed for the wealth of her vast land and turned away from the Spirit-of-Light close at hand. Out of the *height of heaven,* that expansive vault of unexplained energy dwarfed her personal planetary limitations by multiples of seven. It had been a long time since the *Dragon* had come after her tender *earth-spirit* with mighty bounds—only to be finally turned away when her own nature began to protect itself with its fiercely beautiful sounds. These selfsame sounds Apollicius grappled with as he sculpted, trying to give them their proper name within the context of his worldview uninterrupted. Out of the cultivation of this sound arose images in stages that began to be developed into art, literature, myth, and philosophy written down on pages.

"Overcoming my own Interior Dragon enabled me to cross a threshold I had no idea even existed as an initiatory mold," Earth said forthrightly. "As the land I knew to be me grew, my consciousness of it began to expand. I started to drain this vast lake within me as if filling it to its banks and beyond had all been one huge mistake. Whatever I try to do henceforth will be to align myself with your Great Solar Sign. Like one colossal, whole note in a vessel round, my Sphere tries incessantly to make contact with what your Light wrote in Sound."

Her world often turned faster at the flickering of this sizable Sunlight Master. Earth offered up *mud* for him to transform into the softer dermis of Venus. Not even the vermilion of the Pagan Mars could resist his *light* against a background of cerulean.

"I am no self-absorbed dreamer," Apollicius volunteered. "Rather, I have dedicated myself to the goal of Primal Unity of the Manifold—with

all the pain and struggle that comes in trying to overcome the inherent contradiction of an imperfect mold. If I had never studied Music, I would not have had a chance in any *world* of forging *its* Image. The *sounds* of my Light Hammer resound when it *pounds* something into Sight."

Rumbling in the galactic distance, Jupiter could be heard swinging around his *Moons* as if he were a *hammer-thrower.* He exuded both power and strength, and together with Saturn had become the most procreative of their Family of Spheres. But instead of creating offspring, this Prince of Thunder pounded out rhythms peppered with incisive percussion worthy of a reigning king. His world was the simple minimum, yet an example to the maximum. Notwithstanding his size, he remained both the most flexible and the most youthful of the Planets. Because of his *musical composition,* he maintained an airy spring in his steps and turns, while wheeling in an almost continual state of mystical intoxication. From time to time, bursts and shouts of laughter would come from this Giant of both Pleasure *and* Pain.

Jupiter had a daily ritual of donning his *Robe-of-Light* with the Sun-Symbol of Apollicius on the back and striding through low-flung layers of *cloud-music.* Inevitably, his walk would lead him to his own monumental temple that he had erected to the Gods of Light, Sound, and Knowledge. Through Apollicius, he had come to know the Muse Helleniana, who introduced him to the *lighter* side of both his own Father and his grandparents, Solium and Marisium.

"Today, as I approach the magnificence of this temple, I feel especially charged with this semi-liquid, semi-solid substance permeating my universe within and that Great Expanse without. Rather than imperious, I sincerely believe myself to be impervious to fatigue. I feel ready to revolve in *life-enhancing* turns, while this Galactic Vapor I breathe burns inside my rarified state of *planetary dancing.*"

Now approaching the *temple steps,* he slowed his stride as he felt the Drop of Helleniana gently land upon his head to add further joy to his ride. She could appear anywhere and at any moment, so it did not surprise Jupiter to have her now inside his head, content. Her *liquid arms* stretched skyward, pointing towards their Great Cathedral *Shell.* Out of the Sea of Jupiter, Solium had brought to its surface the Gigantic Oyster and fashioned its stage into their Temple in his own homage.

Its conception had not been dictated by false muses but on the contrary, had been planned by Helleniana herself, in direct contact with the Masters-of-the-Empyrean and that ever-stretching Region beyond the Fixed Stars. Supporting the Temple's inner structure loomed the *Five Star-Spirits,* to whom Jupiter owed his allegiance to the design of their dance. Upon entering, Jupiter was *thunderstruck* by its *notion of symmetries*—reflected both in its organic *sync* and deep within his own psyche. This Temple had long ago become his *lodestone* to align his mode-of-being with his own *lodestar.* The Star he worshiped, held in the hands of the Central Spirit of Light, now glowed at the head of the altar, while the *temple bell* hung from its tower, where the *sound* and the *light* fused into one source of power.

Jupiter's unique *find*—as the largest of the Planets—had been the *wind.* The *whirled* and the *whirling* twirled together up these shimmering steps to the top pedestals, recently washed by the strong and smooth hands of the *temple vestals.* In his own immense Sea of the Cold he had developed and increased his *wind* manifold. From there, it had swept across and through him as a viable alternative Source of Energy. Whenever he breathed out, a strong gust would kick up clouds of semi-settling *cosmic dust.* His mission at his temple could be very simply described as *energy transmission.* Being the opposite of manic, once inside the Temple and in contact with its Five Spiritual Guardians, he worked magic. The dictum there had always been: terse verse solutions, not many-sided circumlocutions.

"Like a fledging bird, I am still a long way from becoming a *six-winged seraph*—I wouldn't even begin to know how to map its angelic flight on any graph. Yet my ample mantle blows open as the Wind rolls over my developing *wings,* taking me out up above the first heat of the gathering day. As I slowly get the gist, my eyes blink, still covered in film by the blinding mist," Jupiter said in a rare moment of lucid realization.

Yes, he had seen, now sees, and would see again in the *Kingdom of Apollicius*—his Lord of Time and Experience. Once he had understood, as he also did now, that *visionary level* beyond the Stars, he felt ready to establish himself as his own *Energetic Center.* This, after all, had to be the objective of every one of the Planetary Children of Apollicius. Though no expert in the Science of the Muses, he had observed these two *maid-*

ens of the *light* and the *dark*. Inside the Light One, he saw moving a deep source of darkness, whereas within the Dark One, abounded exploding packets and waves of Light. It seemed to him at times as if the *energy* emanating from these two *muses* had come to unite the sides of his own two *hemispheres,* with its great band of commissural light fibers traveling in bundles.

"Because of your great size and gravitational attraction, I look upon you as a brother," Apollicius stated, without the slightest twinge of condescension. "I have striven and fought for your Lightning Conductors, to attenuate cosmic anxiety, by exuding musical joviality. You have made great progress by resisting certain temptation of *false calls* to the immaculate ether beyond the *falls*, in order to stay within my system to further hone your *lightning tone.*"

Jupiter turned his colossal head toward the incoming voice of Apollicius. He had fears of his illumination coming too late, but the stage had already been made ready for his play to open at its first dramatic page. He desired his *passage* to later become myth and to serve as a general pattern for other young *spheres-of-energy* to discover their own *lightning lantern.*

Electromagnetism moved around his *coil's* central prism, following the spiraled matrix shape of the double helix. He felt all the power of the *light of grace* rise steadily within him, until it reached and burst through his *crown* into the highly charged *space.* As it rose, he rode its lightning zigzag *strike* up the channel of his being's mode. At that same moment of rising, he used a tremendous amount of energy to resist the temptation to fall back on what he had so well been improvising.

From that point on, Jupiter became one of the primary Lightning Forgers in this small corner of the cosmos. Whenever his lightning struck, the *darkness* would shudder in thunder. Being neither a radiant gemstone nor a shooting star, he could be described more accurately as a *blessed vial*, yet never played more beautifully than by the *hand of heaven* upon him now, as a *bass viol*.

Strings and Light, Storms and Thunder—such was the life of Jupiter around the Sun's shadow, both around, above, and directly under. He, as well as his planetary brethren, had passed through the trials of fire, though he had never tried to change their *attire*. Rather, he attempted to take the finer thread to spin into a larger spatial fabric to protect and adorn the turning planetary head.

"Meditation is the remembrance of a Vision," so the Three Original Muses had once said to him in a dream. Holding on to this figment of the *night fragment*, Jupiter sat down one day to begin his Great Work. Like all things within his range, its scope would be so large that he alone had the energy and wherewithal to cope with it.

Marisium had heard and seen many of the previous Works of Jupiter and had admired them profoundly. She recognized a truly *cosmic contribution* with pleasure, and with no hesitation would embrace both the work and its source with equal measure. She had a secure way of taking charge of the unseen business of all *planetary matters* inside the whirling system of Apollicius. Just as his *light* provided the link—connecting time, energy, and matter to her own Space, her *darkness* shaped the expanding disk of the entire *rink*. This amalgam of the *opposite pair* composed the basic unit of their driving spirit game, extending all the way out to her bounding rim and the same radius inward to that dense concentration of light energy inside *him*.

Divinity in the flesh and the body in infinity—these two worlds had but one Master: the Projection of the Great Fish, the Sperm of the Heavenly Body Dish. Whoever drank, saved, and conserved this *milk* not only would become more like Apollicius, but could one day entertain the possibility of joining his Constellation as a fellow Star-in-Process.

Somewhere along the way between the *womb-of-light* and its *tomb-of-night*, there would always be the Dragon and Dragoness Constellations to slay with that Magic Bow and Arrow—the perennial weapon of the day. On the back of the Great Fish Pisces, the leviathan steered them toward galactic virtue and away from previous vices. This Planetary Herd of Apollicius had come of age to be heard. They had won a small piece of the reverence, once paid only to their Sun King. The *milk* they now swam through continued to exude from the immortal breast of Marisium. By saving their *mercurial spirit* by not coming at every moment when called, some of them could be resurrected as promised by Solium, the God of Light and Sound.

"I have left that *wooded mountain,* where I had been lost deep within my own *matter,* and emerged from that shadowy hiding place at the sound of Jupiter's Drum, summoning us to climb higher up the *ladder,*" Mercury whispered to his *intimate self,* yet in a voice strong enough to be heard throughout the whole Light System of Apollicius.

"Is Helleniana there with you?" Mars inquired.

"Yes, our immortal nymph is here in the *rock* with me," Mercury said. "We have conceived a plan giving us the freedom to live in as many worlds as Apollicius has created. From pieces to Pisces, from sperm to Sperm Whale, from the spark of the Flame to the wild conflagration with no name—we will sweep the Cosmos with our own *Sound of the Spheres.*"

At times called the *Phallic God,* Apollicius ever extended his many-sided *Metallic Rod.* Born of Marisium, once wrapped in the darkness of her Night, he now existed as a Whirling Ball of pure Semen De*light.* He and his Planets had been mingled with the *currency* of pure gold—too old to be jingled and too new to turn to the silver dust of *bankruptcy.*

"At my command, you will come forward and extend me your hand," Solium thundered in a voice so resonant it made the heart at once *bloom* from where it resided in the *body-plant.* "Marisium and I have watched, heard, and participated in the whole process of your Light Development. I am proud of the fact that you are my only *sun* to rebel and leave my side through the spontaneity of your own act. I am not unforgiving and have a deep respect for the way in which you have used your *light energy* for living. No, I will not despise you as a desolate island crag, nor will I thrust you and your whole System of Illumination down with a single stamp of my *light* foot, which all of you look up to and trust. You and your Planets are a Primal Copy of my Unity. I will dedicate the River of

my Milky Way to you and your Elliptical Path, within which you continually stay. Consider this overhanging *Parachute of Light* as your laurel
wreath awarded to you as a conquering *poet of the inner sight*, as it surges
in waves and then congeals from its sparkling particles."

Apollicius looked up with a serenity
of the *plains*, comprehended only by
those who had once caught a
brief glimpse of eternity and
now moved with the en-
thusiasm of the shifting
eruptions of newly
formed   *mountains*.
Once   tear-stained,
the cheeks of Helleniana
shone   anew—supported
on their soft cushions, eyes
unstrained as she gazed upon
Apollicius from her inner perspective as both Ancient and Futuristic
Dancer—wild, yet not crazed.

"Now we are ready to do battle,"
she told herself. "We are not mere dust
motes encircling Apollicius like *atoms*,
but *couplets of the spirit* moving up as nebu-
lous inlets —rather than falling droplets."

She watched him steadily rise, con-
nected to the ultimate Source-of-Light at the five cardinal points—fully exposed, under no disguise. His elongated hands slowly became the
highly charged strands attached to the towering Star-Flower to which he
now enlarged. The wayward *Son* had returned to the Central Sun. From
this point on there could be no further objection to the clear reality of his
Light Projection—being as real as his whole System wheeling as a *reel*.

"If the heart is willing to sail, there is no way to fail inside its protected *car*—to reach those primordial shoals of its hidden star," Apollicius
recited to himself as he wafted upward toward the Enlightened Head of
Solium, using the energy of his own element, Helium.

During this long process of Apollicius becoming converted, Solium helped by emitting a certain radiance to bathe his *subtle body,* coming from his Giant Lotus of his Higher Sphere, now inverted. Originally composed of the *stuff of the stars,* his Central Line extended up through the length of his Astral Spine, out of the Crown of his Head to connect to this Lotus-of-Solium and the other four *elements* of such renown. His trajectory had been dedicated to the *fifth essence* of Light: the *quintessence,* known as the pure essence. By rejoining Solium, Apollicius would soon be able, at will, to raise his *spark* higher into space or, if he wished, lower it to some new terrestrial base. His long separation from his Father had been of deep importance, permitting him to penetrate into the true Source of Helleniana's Dance. She had been the one who had first inspired the Planets to move with more grace within the elliptical orbits of their well-defined space.

"There can be no *Spirit* without its *Orbit,*" she had once said, showing the Planets over and over how to rotate and spin effectively—how to whirl. Only in this way could they be efficiently drawn toward their true center, to develop this Point-of-All-Attraction where the first streaks of light may enter.

Through the tremendous assistance of Apollicius and Helleniana, Solium and Marisium—the Light and Space—succeeded in establishing their Order of Celestial Beings. Now the *leaves of the stars* could turn and fall in a twinkling of a *sundial's eye.* Thus began the seasons of primal splendor, when and where events joined to a higher dimension of meaning—the dawn of the Celestial City of Synchron*icity.*

In her own subtle and charismatic manner, Helleniana helped consummate the union of the two warring forces and sources of all energy inside the Fiery Ball of Apollicius. As his Heart sailed across these *primordial waters* laced and studded with other Stars, Apollicius had realized the sublimation and transmutation of what had once been the unadulterated *wave of sexual might* into its most elevated state of *sensual light and delight.* Through *time,* he found *space* through Helleniana's *cave,* and in that dimmed light he saw these two dimensions unified in her glowing *face.*

Twelfth Movement

Projection: *The process of transmuting the base metals into gold*

Project your project into projection!

fin

About the Author

David L. Laing spent over fifteen years in Brazil writing, painting and composing music. *Solar Codex: A Light Odyssey* is the first volume in the quartet of *Cosmic Adventure Novels*. His collection of paintings is in South America, the United States and Europe. At present he is working on the other three novels to complete the quartet and preparing to begin production on his new screenplay, *The Egyptian Ring*. Since returning from Brazil he has resided in Seattle, Washington, USA.